1996-97 EDITION

easy
CAMPING

in NORTHERN CALIFORNIA

IOO Places Anyone Can Camp This Weekend

TOM STIENSTRA

ISBN 0-935701-63-X

5 1295 >

Foghorn Press
BOOKS BUILDING COMMUNITY™

9 780935 701630

Foghorn Press
555 DeHaro Street, Suite 220
San Francisco, CA 94107
(415) 241-9550

Foghorn Press titles are distributed to the book trade by Publishers Group West, Emeryville, California. To contact your local sales representative, call 1-800-788-3123.

To order individual books, please call Foghorn Press at 1-800-FOGHORN (364-4676).

Publishing Manager—*Rebecca Poole Forée*
Editors—*Ann Marie Brown, Karin Mullen*
Book Design—*Ann Marie Brown*
Layout, Map—*Michele Thomas*
Editorial Assistant—*Aimee Larsen*
Front Cover Photo—*Renee Lynn/Sorenson's Resort*

Library of Congress Cataloging-in-Publication Data
Stienstra, Tom
Easy Camping in Northern California / by Tom Stienstra.
p. cm.
Includes index.
ISBN 0-935701-63-X
1. Camping—California, Northern—Guidebooks.
2. California, Northern—Guidebooks.
I. Title
GV194.C2S85 1995   95-19820 CIP

Printed in the United States of America

1996-97 EDITION

easy
CAMPING
in NORTHERN CALIFORNIA

100 Places Anyone Can Camp This Weekend

TOM STIENSTRA

BOOKS BUILDING COMMUNITY™

INTRODUCTION

Writing this book was the best excuse I could think of to spend the better part of a year adventuring in Northern California, trying to find every vacation cabin and cottage out there, as well as discovering the best easy-to-reach wilderness camps, walk-in sites, and boat-in camps.

I never had as much fun exploring the most beautiful landscape on earth: Yosemite, Tahoe, and Shasta . . . the entire Bay Area, including Point Reyes, Mt. Tamalpais, the Diablo Range, and the Santa Cruz Mountains . . . Mammoth, the Sierra, Plumas Forest, and Lassen . . . Big Sur, the Sonoma, Mendocino, and Humboldt coasts . . . the Redwood Empire, Klamath/Trinity, and way out to Modoc and the South Warners. No other region in America has more quality destinations, more diversity and beauty, and more possibilities for adventure and fun than Northern California.

What's an easy camp?

I discovered the need for "easy camps" after so many people came to me at sports shows, saying things like, "My family won't go tent camping; where is there a great cabin to stay in?" and "We want to go backpacking in the wilderness, but we don't want to hike more than a few miles; where do we go?" This book is designed to answer these and other questions.

An easy camp is one that is reached without a lot of hassle, leaving you with plenty of enthusiasm. An easy camp makes a great home base for adventuring, because all your energy isn't used up getting there and setting up. An easy camp frees you of the need for a lot of equipment and planning. Easy camping is the perfect solution for families, large groups, and people who don't feel like roughing it but want to enjoy the great outdoors.

How were these camps selected?

First, I set out to find every cabin rental available in Northern California. There are write-ups on many of them, with others briefly mentioned at the end of chapters. The standard I looked for was a private unit, usually a cottage or cabin, in a cozy spot that provided privacy. The cabins had to be located close to spectacular outdoor destinations, with plenty of recreation possibilities. For the most part, I tried to find places without telephones or televisions, to keep the trip more like a camping experience. The listings in this book vary widely, so read each one carefully, then choose one that meets your expectations.

I also added an assortment of easy-to-reach backpack camps (accessible via a short hike of a few miles), walk-in camps (a walk of less than one-quarter mile), boat-in camps (accessed by boat only) and overnight horse backpack trips (requiring horse rentals and a pack outfitter). The idea was to find camps that were just one step beyond car camping— camps that would provide wildernesslike experiences without the extensive physical demands usually necessary on that kind of trip.

This book was written as I roamed, much of it on a portable laptop computer. The result is the first comprehensive guide to every cabin I could find out there, 70 write-ups (and 45 additional listings), as well as 30 other "easy camps."

Unless a cabin resort owner absolutely insisted otherwise, I always paid full freight for lodging. Most of the time, I traveled incognito. That provided me complete autonomy, and unless I had to use a resort's office phone line to file a column for the *San Francisco Examiner,* the owners had no idea I was an outdoors writer or that I was reviewing their operations for this book. If I have missed any cabin rentals, feel free to drop me a line at Foghorn Press, and we will try to include it in future printings.

In the process of developing this book the most important thing I discovered was confirmation of the value of the great outdoors, and the happiness that is possible when sharing adventures with the people you care for most. I hope this book will help you in that pursuit.

—*Tom Stienstra*

CONTENTS

Del Norte-Humboldt Redwoods—p. 25

Shasta-Trinity—p. 49

Lassen-Modoc—p. 73

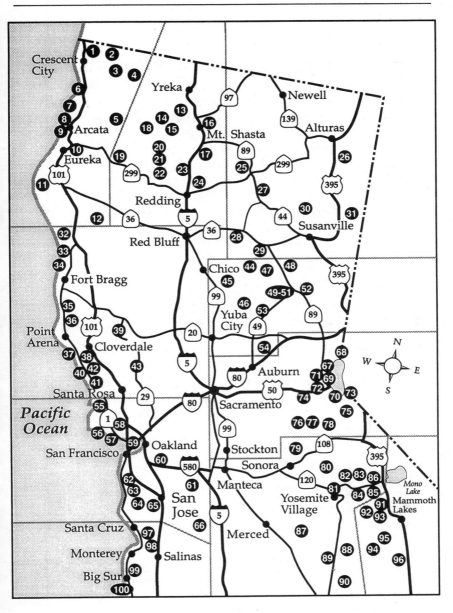

HOW TO USE THIS BOOK

This book is organized geographically, with each camp and cabin numbered from 1 to 100. Use the map on page 9 to locate camps in the areas of Northern California where you want to travel. Then find the camps' stories by using the table of contents or just thumbing through the book. (The camps are arranged in numerical order.)

Or you can simply turn to the chapter covering the region where you'd like to camp and read all of the stories in that chapter.

Each of the camps and cabins in this book is rated on a scale of 1 through 10. Since they have been selected for overall quality, none of the camps received a rating lower than a 6. While the ratings are completely subjective, they provide a marker of the relative beauty of the area, nearby recreation possibilities, and quality of facilities. In other words, the rating is based on the cumulative experience of the camping trip, and not on any one element.

Overall Rating

▲1 ▲2 ▲3 ▲4 ▲5 ▲6 ▲7 ▲8 ▲9 ▲10

Poor .... Fair .... Great

Each hike also has one or a series of graphic icons listed with it, which denote recreational activities and sidetrip possibilities located at or near the cabin or camp. They also denote whether or not a camp has any wheelchair facilities or wheelchair-accessible areas (always phone ahead to be sure that the camp's definition of "wheelchair facilities" matches your particular needs).

Fishing	Boating	Hiking	Wheelchair Access	Swimming	Waterskiing
Rafting/ Canoeing	Historical Site	Horseback Riding	Skiing	Hot Springs	RV

Getting Along

The most important thing about a camping trip is not where you go, how many fish you catch, or how many shots you fire. It often has little to do with how beautiful the view is, how easy the campfire lights, or how sunny the days are.

Oh yeah? Then what is the most important factor? The answer: the people you are with. It is that simple.

Who would you rather camp with? Your enemy at work or your dream mate in a good mood? Heh, heh. You get the idea. A camping trip is a fairly close-knit experience, and you can make lifelong friends or lifelong enemies in the process. That is why your choice of companions is so important. Your own behavior is equally consequential.

Yet most people spend more time putting together their camping gear than they do considering why they enjoy or hate the company of their chosen companions. Here are ten rules of behavior for good camping mates:

1. No whining. Nothing is more irritating than being around a whiner. It goes right to the heart of adventure, since often the only difference between a hardship and an escapade often is simply whether or not an individual has the spirit for it. The people who do can turn a rugged day in the outdoors into a cherished memory. Those who don't can ruin it with their sniveling.

2. Activities must be agreed upon. Always have a meeting of the minds with your companions over the general game plan. Then everybody will possess an equal stake in the outcome of the trip. This is absolutely critical. Otherwise they will feel like merely an addendum to your trip, not an equal participant, and a whiner may be born (see No. 1).

3. Nobody's in charge. It is impossible to be genuine friends if one person is always telling another what to do, especially if the orders involve simple camp tasks. You need to share the space on the same emotional plane, and the only way to do that is to have a semblance of equality, regardless of differences in experience. Just try ordering your mate around at home for a few days. You'll quickly see the results, and they aren't nice.

4. Equal chances at the fun stuff. It's fun to build the fire, fun to get the first cast at the best fishing spot, and fun to hoist the bagged food for a bear-proof food hang. It is not fun to clean the dishes, collect firewood, or cook every night. So obviously, there must be an equal distribution of the fun stuff and the not-fun stuff, and everybody on the trip must get a shot at the good and the bad.

5. No heroes. No awards are bestowed for achievement in the outdoors, yet some guys treat mountain peaks, big fish, and big game as if they are trophies. Actually, nobody cares how wonderful you are, which is always a surprise to trophy chasers. What people care about is the heart of the adventure, the gut-level stuff.

6. Agree on a wake-up time. It is a good idea to agree on a general wake-up time before closing your eyes for the night, and that goes for whether you want to sleep in late or get up at dawn. Then you can proceed on course regardless of what time you crawl out of your sleeping bag in the morning, without the risk of whining (see No. 1).

7. Think of the other guy. Be self-aware instead of self-absorbed. A good test is to count the number of times you say, "What do you think?" A lot of potential problems can be solved quickly by actually listening to the answer.

8. Solo responsibilities. There are a number of essential camp duties on all trips, and while they should be shared equally, most should be completed solo. That means that when it is time for you to cook, you don't have to worry about me changing the recipe on you. And when it is my turn to make the fire, you keep your mitts out of it.

9. Don't let money get in the way. Of course everybody should share equally in trip expenses, such as food and gas, and it should be split up before you head out yonder. Don't let somebody pay extra, because that person likely will try to control the trip. Conversely, don't let somebody weasel out of paying their fair share.

10. Accordance on the food plan. Always have complete agreement on what you plan to eat each day. Don't figure that just because you like Steamboat's Lodge, everybody else will, too, especially youngsters. Always, always, always ask about allergies to foods such as nuts, onions, or cheese, and make sure each person brings their favorite coffee. Some people drink only decaffeinated, while others gag on anything but Burma monkey beans.

Obviously, it is difficult to find companions who will agree on all of these elements. This is why many campers say that the best camping buddy they'll ever have is their mate, someone who knows all about them and likes them anyway.

Outdoors with the Kids

How do you get a child excited about the outdoors? How do you compete with the television and remote control? How do you prove to a kid that success comes from persistence, spirit, and logic, which the outdoors teaches, and not from pushing buttons?

The answer is in the Ten Camping Commandments for Kids. These lessons will get youngsters enthusiastic about the outdoors, and will make sure adults help the process along, not kill it. Some are obvious, some are not, but all are important:

1. Take children to places where there is a guarantee of action. A good example is camping in a park where large numbers of wildlife can be viewed, such as squirrels, chipmunks, deer, and even bears. Other good choices are fishing at a small pond loaded with bluegill, or hunting in a spot where a kid can shoot a .22 at pine cones all day. Boys and girls want action, not solitude.

2. Enthusiasm is contagious. If you aren't excited about an adventure, you can't expect a child to be. Show a genuine zest for life in the outdoors, and point out everything as if it is the first time you have ever seen it.

3. Always be seated when talking to someone small. This allows the adult and the child to be on the same level. That is why fishing in a small boat is perfect for adults and kids. Nothing is worse for youngsters than having a big person look down at them and give them orders. What fun is that?

4. Show a child how to do something, whether it is gathering sticks for a campfire, cleaning a trout, or tying a knot. Never tell—always show. A button usually clicks to "off" when a kid is lectured. But they can learn behavior patterns and outdoor skills by watching adults, even when the adults are not aware they are being watched.

5. Let kids be kids. Let the adventure happen, rather than trying to force it within some preconceived plan. If they get sidetracked watching pollywogs, chasing butterflies, or sneaking up on chipmunks, let them be. A youngster can have more fun turning over rocks and looking at different kinds of bugs that sitting in one spot, waiting for a fish to bite.

6. Expect young peoples' attention spans to be short. Instead of getting frustrated about it, use it to your advantage. How? By bringing along a bag of candy and snacks. When there is a lull in the camp activity, out comes the bag. Don't let them know what goodies await, so each one becomes a surprise.

7. Make absolutely certain the child's sleeping bag is clean, dry, and warm. Nothing is worse than discomfort when trying to sleep, but a refreshing night's sleep makes for a positive attitude the next day. In addition, kids can become quite scared of animals at night. The parent should not wait for any signs of fear, but always play the part of the outdoor guardian, the one who will "take care of everything."

8. Kids quickly relate to outdoor ethics. They will enjoy eating everything they kill, building a safe campfire, and picking up all their litter, and they will develop a sense of pride that goes with it. A good idea

is to bring extra plastic garbage bags to pick up any trash you come across. Kids long remember when they do something right that somebody else has done wrong.

9. If you want youngsters hooked on the outdoors for life, take a close-up photograph of them holding up fish they have caught, blowing on the campfire, or completing other camp tasks. Young children can forget how much fun they had, but they never forget if they have a picture of it.

10. One of the least important words you can ever say to a kid is "I." Keep track of how often you say "Thank you" and "What do you think?" If you don't say these things very often, you'll lose out. Finally, the most important words of all are: "I am proud of you."

Fun and Games

"Now what are we supposed to do?" the young boy asked his dad.

"Yeah, Dad, think of something," said another son.

Well, Dad thought hard. This was one of the first camping trips he'd taken with his sons and one of the first lessons he received was that kids don't appreciate the philosophic release of mountain quiet. They want action, and lots of it. With a glint in his eye, Dad searched around the camp and picked up 15 twigs, breaking them so each was four inches long. He laid them in three rows, three twigs in the first, five in the second, and seven in the third.

"Okay, this game is called 3-5-7," said Dad. "You each take turns picking up sticks. You are allowed to remove all or as few as one twig from a row, but here's the catch: You can only pick from one row per turn. Whoever picks up the last stick is the loser."

I remember this episode well because those two little boys were my brother Bobby, as in Rambobby, and me. And to this day, we still play 3-5-7 on campouts, with the winner getting to watch the loser clean the dishes. What I have learned in the span of time since that original episode is that no matter what your age is, campers need options for camp fun.

Some evenings, after a long hike or ride, you are likely to feel too worn-out to take on a serious romp downstream to fish, or climb up to a ridge for a view. That is especially true if you have been in the outback for a week or more. At that point a lot of campers will spend their time resting and gazing at a map of the area, dreaming of the next day's adventure, or just sitting against a rock, watching the colors of the sky and mountain panorama change minute by minute. But kids raised in the video game era, and a lot of adults, too, want more. After all, the attitude is: "I'm on vacation—I want some fun."

There are several options, like the 3-5-7 twig game, and they should be just as much a part of your pre-trip planning as arranging your gear.

For kids, plan on games, the more physically challenging the competition, the better. One of the best games is to throw a chunk of wood into a lake, then challenge the kids to hit it by throwing rocks. It wreaks havoc on the fishing, but it can keep kids totally absorbed for some time. Target practice with a wrist-rocket slingshot is also an all-consuming activity for kids, firing rocks away at small targets like pinecones set on a log.

You can also set kids off on little missions near camp, like looking for the footprints of wildlife, searching out good places to have a "snipe hunt," picking up twigs to get the evening fire started, or taking the water purifier to a stream to pump some drinking water into a canteen. The latter is an easy, fun, yet important task that will allow kids to feel a sense of equality they often don't get at home.

For adults, the appeal should be more to the intellect. A good example is star and planet identification. A star chart can make it easy to locate and identify many distinctive stars and constellations, such as the Pleiades (the Seven Sisters), Orion, and others from the zodiac, depending on the time of year. And while you are staring into space, you're bound to spot a few shooting stars. With a little research, this can add a unique perspective to your trip. You could point to Polaris, one of the most easily identified of all stars, and note that navigators in the 1400s used it to find their way. Polaris, of course, is the North Star, and is found at the end of the handle of the Little Dipper. Pinpointing Polaris is quite easy. First find the Big Dipper, then locate the outside stars of the ladle. They are called the "Pointer Stars," because they point right at Polaris.

A tree identification book can teach you a few things about your surroundings. It is also a good idea for one member of the party to research the history of the area you have chosen and another to research the geology. With shared knowledge, you end up with a deeper love of wild places.

Another way to add some recreation into your trip is to bring a board game, a number of which have been miniaturized for campers. The most popular are chess, checkers, and cribbage. The latter comes with an equally miniature set of playing cards. And those little cards open a vast set of other possibilities. With kids along, for instance, just take the Queen of Clubs out of the deck and you can play Old Maid.

Bears and You

The first time you come nose-to-nose with a bear, it can make your skin quiver.

Even the sight of mild-mannered black bears, the most common bear in America, can send shock waves through your body. They range from 250 to 400 pounds and have large claws and teeth that are made to scare campers. When they bound, the muscles on their shoulders roll like ocean breakers.

Bears in camping areas are accustomed to sharing the mountains with hikers and campers. They have become specialists in the food-raiding business. As a result, you must be able to make a bear-proof food hang, or be able to scare the fellow off. Many campgrounds provide bear- and raccoon-proof food lockers. You can also stash your food in your vehicle, but that limits the range of your trip.

If you are staying at one of the easy backpack sites listed in this book, there will be no food lockers available. (The exceptions are the High Sierra camps in Yosemite National Park, where rangers have placed high wires for food hangs, the next best thing to food lockers.) Your car will not be there, either. The solution is to make a bear-proof food hang, suspending all of your food wrapped in a plastic garbage bag from a rope in midair, 10 feet from the trunk of a tree and 20 feet off the ground. (Counter-balancing two bags with a rope thrown over a tree limb is very effective, but finding an appropriate limb can be difficult.)

This is accomplished by tying a rock to a rope, then throwing it over a high but sturdy tree limb. Next, tie your food bag to the rope, and hoist it up in the air. When you are satisfied with the position of the food bag, tie off the end of the rope to another tree. In an area frequented by bears, a good food bag is a necessity—nothing else will do.

I've been there. On one trip, my pal Foonsky and my brother Rambob had left to fish, and I was stoking up an evening campfire when I felt the eyes of an intruder on my back. I turned around and this big bear was heading straight for our camp. In the next half hour, I scared the bear off twice, but then he got a whiff of something sweet in my brother's pack.

The bear rolled into camp like a semi truck, grabbed my brother's pack, ripped it open, and plucked out the Tang and the Swiss Miss. The 350-pounder then sat astride a nearby log and lapped at the goodies like a thirsty dog drinking water.

Once a bear gets his mitts on your gear, he considers it his. I took two steps toward the pack and that bear jumped off the log and galloped across the camp right at me. Scientists say a man can't outrun a bear, but they've never seen how fast I can go up a granite block with a bear on my tail.

Shortly thereafter, Foonsky returned to find me perched on top of the rock, and demanded to know how I could let a bear get our Tang. It took all three of us, Foonsky, Rambob, and myself, charging at once and shouting like madmen, to clear the bear out of the camp and send him off over the ridge. We learned never to let food sit unattended.

A Word about Giardia

You have just hiked in to your backwoods spot, you're thirsty and a bit tired, but you smile as you consider the prospects. Everything seems perfect—there's not a stranger in sight, and you have nothing to do but relax with your pals.

You toss down your gear, grab your cup and dip it into the stream, and take a long drink of that ice-cold mountain water. It seems crystal pure and sweeter than anything you've ever tasted. It's not till later that you find out that it can be just like drinking a cup of poison.

Whether you camp in the wilderness or not, if you hike, you're going to get thirsty. And if your canteen runs dry, you'll start eyeing any water source. Stop! Do not pass Go. Do not drink.

By drinking what appears to be pure mountain water without first treating it, you can ingest a microscopic protozoan called *Giardia lamblia*. The pain of the ensuing abdominal cramps can make you feel like your stomach and intestinal tract are in a knot, ready to explode. With that comes long-term diarrhea that is worse than even a bear could imagine.

Doctors call the disease giardiasis, or Giardia for short, but it is difficult to diagnose. One friend of mine who contracted Giardia was told he might have stomach cancer before the proper diagnosis was made.

Drinking directly from a stream or lake does not mean you will get Giardia, but you are taking a giant chance. There is no reason to take such a risk, potentially ruining your trip and enduring weeks of misery.

A lot of people are taking that risk. I made a personal survey of campers in the Yosemite National Park wilderness, and found that roughly only one in 20 were equipped with some kind of water-purification system. The result, according to the Public Health Service, is that an average of 4 percent of all backpackers and campers suffer giardiasis. According to the Parasitic Diseases Division of the Center for Infectious Diseases, the rates range from 1 percent to 20 percent across the country.

But if you get Giardia, you are not going to care about the statistics. "When I got Giardia, I just about wanted to die," said Henry McCarthy, a California camper. "For about 10 days, it was the most terrible thing I have ever experienced. And through the whole thing, I kept thinking, 'I shouldn't have drunk that water, but it seemed all right at the time.'"

That is the mistake most campers make. The stream might be running free, gurgling over boulders in the high country, tumbling into deep, oxygenated pools. It looks pure. Then the next day, the problems suddenly start. Drinking untreated water from mountain streams is a lot like playing Russian roulette. Sooner or later, the gun goes off.

Anyone venturing into the outdoors should be acquainted with the several solutions to the water-purification problem. I have tested them all.

Here are my findings:

• **Katadyn Water Filter:** This is the best system for screening out Giardia, as well as other microscopic bacteria more commonly found in stream and lake water that can cause stomach problems.

To work the filter, place the nozzle in the water, then pump the water directly from a spout at the top of the pump into a canteen. This can require fairly rigorous pumping, especially as the filter becomes plugged. On the average, it takes a few minutes to fill a canteen.

The best advantages are that the device has a highly advanced screening system (a ceramic element), and it can be cleaned repeatedly with a small brush.

The drawbacks are that the filter is expensive, it can easily break when dropped because its body is made of porcelain, and if you pack very light, its weight (about two pounds) may be a factor. But those are good trade-offs when you can drink ice-cold stream water without risk.

• **First-Need or Sweetwater Water Purifiers:** These are the most cost-effective water-purification systems for a variety of reasons.

They are far less expensive than the Katadyn, yet provide much better protection than anything cheaper. They are small and lightweight, so they don't add much weight to your pack. And if you use some care to pump water from sediment-free sources, the purifiers will easily last a week, the length of most outdoor trips.

These devices consist of a plastic pump and a hose that connects to a separate filter canister. They pump faster and with less effort than the Katadyn, mainly because the filter is not as fine-screened.

The big drawback is that if you pump water from a mucky lake, the filter can clog in a few days. Therein lies the weakness. Once plugged up, it is useless and you have to replace it or take your chances.

One trick to extend the filter life is to fill your cook pot with water, let the sediment settle, then pump from there. As an added insurance policy, always have a spare filter canister on hand.

• **Boiling water:** Except for water filtration, this is the only treatment that you can use with complete confidence. According to the federal Parasitic Diseases Division, it takes a few minutes at a rolling boil to be certain you've killed *Giardia lamblia*. At high elevations, boil for three to five minutes. A side benefit is that you'll also kill other dangerous bacteria that live undetected in natural waters.

But to be honest, boiling water is a thorn for most people on back-country trips. For one thing, if you boil water on an open fire, what should taste like crystal-pure mountain water tastes instead like a mouthful of warm ashes. If you don't have a campfire, it wastes stove fuel. And if you are thirsty *now*, forget it. The water takes hours to cool.

The only time boiling always makes sense, however, is when you are preparing dinner. The ash taste will disappear in whatever freeze-dried dinner, soup, or hot drink you make.

• **Water-purification pills:** Pills are the preference for most back-country campers, and this can get them in trouble. At just $3 to $8 per bottle, which can figure up to just a few cents per canteen, they do come cheap. In addition, they kill most of the bacteria, regardless of whether you use iodine crystals or potable aqua iodine tablets.

The problem is they just don't always kill *Giardia lamblia,* and that is the one critter worth worrying about on your trip. That makes water-treatment pills unreliable and dangerous.

Another key element is the time factor. Depending on the water's temperature, organic content, and pH level, these pills can take a long time to do the job. A minimum wait of 20 minutes is advised. Most people don't like waiting that long, especially when they're hot and thirsty after a hike and thinking, "What the heck, the water looks fine."

And then there is the taste. On one trip, my water filter clogged and we had to use the iodine pills instead. It doesn't take long to get tired of the iodine-tinged taste of the water. Mountain water should be one of the greatest tasting beverages of the world, but the iodine kills that.

• **No treatment:** This is your last resort and, using extreme care, can be executed with success. One of my best hiking buddies, Michael Furniss, is a nationally-renowned hydrologist, and on wilderness trips he has showed me the difference between "safe" and "dangerous" water sources.

Long ago, people believed that just finding water running over a rock used to be a guarantee of its purity. Imagine that. What we've learned is that the safe water sources are almost always small creeks or springs located in high, craggy mountain areas. The key is making sure no one has been upstream from where you drink.

Furniss mentioned that another potential problem in bypassing water treatment is that even in settings free of Giardia, you can still ingest other bacteria that can cause stomach problems.

The only sure way to beat the problem is to filter or boil your water before drinking, eating, or brushing your teeth. And the best way to prevent the spread of Giardia is to bury your waste products at least eight inches deep and 100 feet away from natural waters.

CAMPING GEAR CHECKLIST

• Cooking/Campfire Gear
Matches stored in zip-lock bags
Fire-starter cubes or candle
Camp stove
Camp fuel
Pot, pan, cup
Pot grabber
Knife, fork
Dish soap and scrubber
Salt, pepper, spices
Food
Plastic spade

Optional Cooking /Campfire Gear:
Ax or hatchet
Wood or charcoal for barbecue
Ice chest
Spatula
Grill
Tinfoil
Dustpan
Tablecloth
Whisk broom
Clothespins
Can opener

• Camping Clothes
Polypropylene underwear
Cotton shirt
Long-sleeve cotton/wool shirt
Cotton/canvas pants
Vest
Parka
Rain jacket and pants or poncho
Hat
Sunglasses

Optional Clothing:
Shorts
Swimsuit
Gloves
Ski cap
Seam Lock™

• Hiking Gear
Quality hiking boots
Backup lightweight shoes
Polypropylene socks
Thick cotton socks
80% wool socks
Strong boot laces
Insole or foot cushion
Moleskin and medical tape
Gaiters
Water-repellent boot treatment

• Sleeping Gear
Sleeping bag
Insulite™ or Therm-a-Rest™ pad
Ground tarp
Tent

Optional Sleeping Gear:
Air pillow
Mosquito netting
Foam pad for truck bed
Windshield light screen for RV
Catalytic heater

• First Aid
Lip balm
Band-Aids
Sterile gauze pads
Roller gauze
Athletic tape
Moleskin

Thermometer
Aspirin
Ace bandage
Mosquito repellent
After-Bite™ or ammonia
Campho-Phenique™ gel
First-Aid Cream™
Sunscreen
Neosporin™
Caladryl™
Biodegradable soap
Towelettes
Tweezers

Optional First Aid:
Water-purification system
Coins for emergency phone calls
Extra matches
Mirror for signaling

• **Fishing/Recreational Gear**
Fishing rod
Fishing reel with fresh line
Small tackle box with lures,
    splitshot, snap swivels
Pliers
Knife

Optional Recreation Gear:
Stargazing chart
Tree identification handbook
Deck of cards
Backpacking cribbage board
Knapsack for each person

• **Miscellaneous**
Maps
Flashlight
Lantern and fuel
Nylon rope for food hang
Handkerchief
Camera and film

Plastic garbage bags
Toilet paper
Toothbrush and toothpaste
Compass
Watch
Feminine hygiene products

Optional Miscellaneous:
Binoculars
Notebook and pen
Towel

BEST CAMPS LISTS

Can't decide where to go this weekend? Here are my picks for the best easy camps:

5 Best Cabins for Romance:
Howard Creek Ranch Cabins, Mendocino Coast, p. 89
Sardine Lake Cabins, Lakes Basin, Plumas National Forest, p. 128
Serenisea Cottages, Mendocino Coast, p. 98
The Inn at Schoolhouse Creek, Mendocino Coast, p. 95
Any listing in this book with a true love

5 Best Cabins for Hiking:
Big Basin Tent Cabins, Big Basin Redwoods State Park, p. 153
Crystal Crag Lodge Cabins, Lake Mary, p. 217
Elwell Lakes Lodge Cabins, Lakes Basin, Plumas National Forest, p. 123
Kit Carson Lodge Cabins, Eldorado National Forest, p. 175
Tioga Pass Resort Cabins, Tioga Pass, near Yosemite, p. 196

5 Best Cabins for Fishing:
Bucks Lake Cabins, Plumas National Forest, p. 114
Cave Springs/Dunsmuir Cabins, Upper Sacramento River, p. 57
Convict Lake Cabins, Inyo National Forest, p. 219
Lakeview Terrace Cabins, Lewiston Lake, p. 67
Lassen View Resort Cabins, Lake Almanor, p. 81

4 Best Easy Camps for Horseback Riding:
Convict Lake Cabins, Inyo National Forest, p. 219
Red's Meadows Pack Trips, Ansel Adams Wilderness, p. 215
Silver Lake Resort Cabins, June Lake Loop, Inyo National Forest, p. 210
Yosemite Valley Cabins, Yosemite National Park, p. 184

5 Best Cabins for Water Sports:
Bear Cove Cabins, Klamath River, p. 32
Sandy Bar Ranch Cabins, Klamath River, p. 34
Sierra Shangri-La Cabins, Yuba River, Sierra Nevada, p. 130
Steelhead Cabins, Trinity River, p. 61
Tsasdi Resort Cabins, Shasta Lake, p. 69

5 Best Cabins for Winter Skiing:
Cottonwood Lodge Log Cabins, North Tahoe, p. 162
Lakeside Chalets, Carnelian Bay, North Tahoe, p. 164
Meeks Bay Resort, Lake Tahoe's West Shore, p. 165
Richardson's Resort Cabins, South Lake Tahoe, p. 166
Strawberry Cabins, Eldorado National Forest, p. 171

5 Best Easy Backpack Trips in the Wilderness:
Deadfall Lake Backpack Sites, Shasta-Trinity National Forest, p. 51
Glen Aulin High Sierra Camp, Yosemite National Park, p. 188
May Lake High Sierra Camp, Yosemite National Park, p. 186
Toad Lake Backpack Sites, Shasta-Trinity National Forest, p. 53
Winnemucca Lake Backpack Sites, Eldorado National Forest, p. 178

5 Best Easy Backpack Trips at Bay Area Parks:
Henry Coe Backpack Sites, Henry Coe State Park, p. 158
Sunol Backpack Camp, Sunol Regional Wilderness, p. 148
Sunset Backpack Camp, Big Basin Redwoods State Park, p. 151
Trail Camp, Castle Rock State Park, p. 156
Wildcat Backpack Camp, Point Reyes National Seashore, p. 137

5 Best Walk-In Camps:
Angel Island Environmental Sites, Angel Island State Park, p. 143
Mendocino Coast Walk-In Camp, Van Damme State Park, p. 93
Pantoll Walk-In Sites, Mt. Tamalpais State Park, p. 141
Pomo Canyon Walk-In Sites, Sonoma Coast State Beach, p. 105
Surfwood Hike-In Camp, MacKerricher State Park, p. 91

5 Best Boat-In Camps:
Bullards Bar Reservoir Boat-In Sites, Sierra Foothills, p. 118
Lake Oroville Boat-In Sites, Sierra Foothills, p. 116
Lake Sonoma Boat-In Sites, Santa Rosa/Sonoma, p. 99
Stone Lagoon Boat-In Sites, Humboldt Lagoons State Park, p. 38
Trinity Lake Boat-In Sites, Shasta-Trinity National Forest, p. 65

BEATING THE TIME TRAP

If the great outdoors is so great, then why don't people enjoy it more often? The answer is because of the time trap, and I will tell you exactly how to beat it.

For many the biggest problem is finding the time to go, whether it is camping, hiking, fishing, boating, backpacking, biking, or even just for a good drive in the country. The solution, believe it or not, is to treat your fun just like you treat your work.

Consider how you tackle your job: Always on time? Go there every day as you are scheduled? Do whatever it takes to get there and get it done? Right? No foolin' that's right. Now imagine if you took the same approach to the outdoors. Suddenly your life would be a heck of a lot better.

The secret is to schedule all of your outdoor activities. For instance, I go fishing every Thursday evening, hiking every Sunday morning, and on an overnight trip every new moon (when stargazing is best). No matter what, I'm going. Just like work, I've scheduled it. The same approach applies to longer adventures. The only reason I was able to hike from Mt. Whitney to Tahoe was because I planned the trip in advance. The reason I spend 125 to 150 days a year in the field is because I schedule them.

If you get out your calendar and write in the exact dates you are going, then you'll go. If you don't, you won't. Suddenly, with only a minor change in your life plan, you can live the life you've always dreamed about.

See you out there....

—*Tom Stienstra*

Del Norte-Humboldt Redwoods

** For locations of camps, see map on page 9. **

1. CRESCENT CITY REDWOODS KOA CABINS
Crescent City
Off U.S. 101 in Crescent City

The three most important elements in a campground are:
1. Location. 2. Location. 3. Location.

And location is what makes it work for the Crescent City Redwoods KOA. Located five miles north of Crescent City, KOA is far from the urban element. It's just two miles from Redwood National Park and about a 10-minute drive to Jedediah Smith State Park and the Smith River National Recreation Area, where in the winter, you get a chance to land big steelhead.

The campground features nine camping cabins, along with 44 tent spaces and 50 sites for motor homes with full hookups, with most of the cabins and campsites set in redwoods. The nearby proximity of U.S. 101 makes it an easy find, and the little KOA log cabins make for an easy strike. Compared to many other KOAs, this one has fewer amenities—no pool or hot tub—but hey, this is supposed to be camping, right? And with a location like this, you won't want be hanging around all day anyway.

Instead, you will want to see the redwoods. You can do so within minutes by driving a mile south on U.S. 101, then turning east on U.S. 199. This two-laner curves its way through a grove of mammoth redwoods, a classic old-growth forest, with a short, pretty nature walk called the Simpson-Reed Loop at a signed turnout on the north side of the road. My hiking partner and I were a trifle skeptical at first over the prospects of this trail, but we were both surprised at the natural beauty of the forest here, especially a pretty bridged creek, lush undergrowth, and plenty of huge trees, all accessible in a very short walk. In addition, there are several other turnouts along the road where you can park and take photographs of the giant redwoods.

Keep driving, and within a few miles you will pass over the Smith River. Just after crossing the bridge, you can turn left on North Bank Road and head downstream for a river tour, or continue on U.S. 199 for access to the river's more spectacular sections. One mile past the small town of Hiouchi, turn right and you will cross two bridges, before reaching a T in the road. If you turn left (on South Fork Road), you can take a driving tour deep into Six Rivers National Forest, all of it along some of the prettiest and most remote sections of the South Fork Smith. If you turn right, you will pass several homes and then come to the free back entrance to Jedediah Smith State Park, with trailheads to the Stout Tree and later, the Boy Scout Tree Trail, on the right side of the road.

In the winter, the Smith River is well known as the number-one producer of big steelhead in California. Bank-fishing access is good on South Fork Road, and although the fish can be elusive and the weather typically rainy, if you hook up with a wild Smith River steelhead, you will suddenly realize that true greatness is possible on this planet. They are among the fightingest fish in California, and it is an immense challenge to approach, hook, and land one of these big steelhead from the bank.

In Crescent City to the south, there is a full harbor complete with boat launch, charter boats for sportfishing, and, of course, seafood restaurants. In addition, just south of the harbor is an expansive beach that is easily accessed, and where the beachcombing can be excellent during minus low tides.

You see, location really is everything.

Facilities: Crescent City Redwoods KOA has nine cabins, 44 tent spaces, and 50 sites for motor homes with full hookups. Fire grills are provided at most sites. A rest room with showers, a Laundromat, and a small store are available. Pets are allowed.

Reservations, fee: Reservations are advised from June through September. Rates are $36.95 for a one-room cabin, $42.95 for a two-room cabin, and around $20 for tent or motor home sites.

Insider's note: From mid-December through mid-March, prospects for catching giant steelhead can be excellent on the nearby Smith River. Phone Smith River Outfitters at (707) 487-0935.

Who to contact: Phone Crescent City Redwoods KOA at (707) 464-5744, or write to 4241 Highway 101 North, Crescent City, CA 95531.

Directions: From Eureka, take U.S. 101 north to Crescent City. Continue on U.S. 101 five miles north of town. One mile past the junction with U.S. 199, look for the well-signed KOA entrance on the right (east) side of the road.

2. PATRICK CREEK LODGE
Smith River
Off U.S. 199 near Gasquet

The first time I stayed at Patrick Creek Lodge, I arrived thinking in terms of a "fish camp." You know, just a place to throw my clothes, gear, and food while fishing for steelhead on the Smith River. My pal Michael Furniss said he'd discovered a great little place out here where we could stay.

While I may have arrived with that vision, I left with a completely different one. That is because Patrick Creek Lodge is far from a fish camp, although it is situated near the headwaters of the Middle Fork Smith River, where there is excellent bank-fishing access for big steelhead. This place captures the best of California's north woods and water while leaving the worst of the cities far behind. It is pretty, clean, and more of a secret getaway spot than anything else.

For a place you can reach by pavement, it is "way out there"—located near the Oregon border on U.S. 199. It is set near the point where Patrick Creek enters the Smith River, one of the last major free-flowing, undammed streams in America. From Eureka, it takes nearly two hours of driving to get here, so if you add another 300 miles from San Francisco, you can figure on almost a day of saddle time before you can pull up to the hitching post.

Patrick Creek Lodge is well signed off the highway, and if you are hungry or thirsty when you arrive, as I was, your first reward for getting here is an excellent restaurant that has only a medium-sized appetite for your wallet. After my hunger was satisfied, I checked in and drove up to the back of the lodge on a curving, rising gravel road, ending at a cottage set well above the lodge in the forest—quiet and private. In addition to this cabin, the lodge offers 16 rooms in various styles in two buildings.

You want to get away from it all? There are no telephones in the rooms. There are no televisions in the rooms. Pretty soon all you will be able to think about is having fun—exploring, hiking, or fishing—and hey, isn't that the whole idea?

If you are new to the area, the best way to start is by touring the Smith River, first by driving on U.S. 199 along the Smith to Gasquet. Stop here at the Forest Service district office, which doubles as head-quarters for the Smith River National Recreation Area. You can obtain maps, hiking-trail information, and forest-access points. Then continue your driving tour by heading toward Hiouchi, turning south at South Fork Road, crossing the Hiouchi Bridge and South Fork Bridge, then heading left at the Y at South Fork Road and continuing along South Fork for 20 miles into Six Rivers National Forest.

In the process you will get a glimpse of the beautiful Smith River, running free and pure through granite gorges, dropping from rapids into deep pools, both on the Middle Fork along U.S. 199 and the South Fork along South Fork Road. You will also come across numerous turnouts along each of these roads, often just a parking space big enough for a car or two. From these parking spaces, you will discover primitive trails down to the river, including the best bank-fishing spots for steelhead. This is not only the best way to fish—trying a number of spots from these roadside pullouts—but also the best way to see and get close to the river.

Hiking is popular in this area, with about a dozen good trailheads between Jedediah Smith State Park and Six Rivers National Forest. The state park has giant old-growth redwoods and trails with few people.

The closest pretty and easy hike from Patrick Creek Lodge is the Stoney Creek Trail near Gasquet, which traces along the untouched North Fork Smith River to the mouth of Stoney Creek. To reach it, drive to Gasquet, turn north on Middle Fork/ Gasquet Road, drive about 100 feet, turn right on

Big steelhead on the Smith River

North Bank Road, drive one mile, then turn right on Stoney Creek Road and drive a short distance to the trailhead.

After hiking it, we just sat there and watched the water go by, without a care in the world.

Facilities: Patrick Creek Lodge has a two-bedroom cabin and two lodges with 16 rooms of various sizes and furnishings. No telephones or televisions are provided, although they are available at lodge headquarters. A restaurant is on-site.

Reservations, fee: Reservations are advised; the fee is $70 for lodge rooms and $110 per night for the cabin in the summer. Prices are slightly less in the winter.

Who to contact: Phone Patrick Creek Lodge at (707) 457-3323, or write to 13950 Highway 199, Gasquet, CA 95543.

Directions: From Crescent City, drive north on U.S. 101 for five miles, then turn east on U.S. 199 and drive about 25 miles. Patrick Creek Lodge is located on the north side of the road.

3. WILDERNESS FALLS BACKPACK SITES
Siskiyou Wilderness
Off U.S. 199 near Gasquet

If you don't mind trading a hellacious drive for a heavenly hike, then the backpack trip to Wilderness Falls rates as a must-do, must-go, must-see.

But do not underestimate the drive. Long? Why it's like boarding a slow boat to China. From San Francisco, it is nearly a 400-mile drive just to the turnoff on Highway 199 near the Oregon border, and from there, it is another 45 minutes on Forest Service roads to the trailhead, with the last 3 miles rough and tumble.

It is worth it all. What you get is a backpacking trip that follows a gradual descent along a beautiful stream for seven miles to reach Wilderness Falls. Sensational yet pure, this is the prettiest hike-to waterfall in Northern California, and the fact that it is seldom visited adds to its attraction. Wilderness Falls pours over a cliff in a cold, silvery spire of water, first crashing down about 50 feet into a boulder, then thundering across other rocks into a pool about 100 feet across, foaming and surging with white bubbles. Even though you know it is waiting for you, the sight still has the ability to stop you cold, like a glimpse of a true love long lost.

A few good campgrounds are located nearby along Clear Creek, the stream that feeds Wilderness Falls, with the best just upstream and around the bend, on the north side of the river. A wilderness permit is required for hikers who will be camping in the Siskiyou Wilderness. Permits are free and available at the office for the Smith River National Recreation Area along Highway 199 in Gasquet.

Although this is a backpacking trip in the classic sense, meaning you will have to carry a full pack, you can scrimp on some equipment because it is such a short trip. If you get a favorable weather report, for instance, you can leave the tent behind. No reason to bring a lot of camp fuel or food, both of which add a lot of pack weight. So you can camp in paradise without having to carry a ton on the way in, as is necessary on longer backpack trips.

The route in is called the Young's Valley Trail, and the trailhead is located past Sanger Lake at the end of Forest Service Road 18N07. From the trailhead, the hike starts with a two-mile trip with a 600-foot descent from Young's Valley down to Clear Creek to Young's Meadow, set at a 4,500-foot elevation. This is usually the first spot for a hiking break, a place to enjoy the quiet and natural beauty.

From here, it is another five miles to Wilderness Falls. The route follows along Clear Creek, making a gradual descent with the kind of trail gradient that will have you smiling all the way. Because Clear Creek is just on your right, there is never any shortage of drinking water. It is cold, clean, and ample; after pumping with a filter, drink heartily!

Finally, you will come to an obvious camp, drop your packs, then loop around some boulders and see Wilderness Falls. We just sat there and stared in awe for nearly an hour, watching the water go by. Little water ouzels occasionally zipped up and down the stream, attending their nest and maybe wondering what we were doing there.

The hike back is uphill, of course, but most of it along the stream is cake. The last two miles require a 600-foot pull, but hey, by then you will be smelling the hay in the barn, and you'll most likely just walk it out.

All the way back, you'll have visions of the great unknown waterfall you just discovered. It is one of the great secrets of this land, and because the drive there is so long, it will always stay that way.

Facilities: A few primitive campsites are available just upstream of Wilderness Falls. Plan to rely completely on yourself. Pets are permitted but are strongly discouraged.

Reservations, fee: No reservations; no fee. A wilderness permit is required for hikers camping in the Siskiyou Wilderness, and it's available for free at the office for the Smith River National Recreation Area along Highway 199 in Gasquet.

Insider's note: For mountaineers, a cutoff route from this trail leads to Preston Peak, a challenging climb with two problem spots near the peak, but with astounding views.

Who to contact: Phone Smith River National Recreation Area at (707) 457-3131, or write to P.O. Box 228, Gasquet, CA 95543. For a map of the area, send $3 to USDA-Forest Service, 630 Sansome Street, San Francisco, CA 94111 and ask for Klamath National Forest. To obtain a topographic map, send $3.50 to Maps-Western Distribution Center, U.S. Geologic Survey, Box 25286-Federal Center, Denver, CO 80225 and ask for Devil's Punchbowl.

Directions: From Crescent City, drive north on U.S. 101 for five miles, then turn east on U.S. 199 and drive 32 miles (it is advisable to stop in Gasquet for your wilderness permit and for road conditions and wilderness informa-tion). Turn right on Forest Service Road 18N07 and drive approximately five miles. Continue on 18N07 as it veers right and twists its way about 10 miles past Sanger Lake and beyond. The trailhead for the Young's Valley Trail is at the end of the road. The last three miles of road are very rough.

4. BEAR COVE CABINS
Klamath River
Off Highway 96 in Happy Camp

Year in, year out, the Klamath River is the best family rafting river in California, with a good selection of exciting and safe runs, and guaranteed good, warm river flows all through summer. Right in the middle of the best of it are the little-known Bear Cove Cabins, set in the town of Happy Camp in remote northwestern Siskiyou County.

One spring I rafted the entire Klamath River, from its headwaters in Oregon all the way to the Pacific Ocean, but my favorite piece of water was the stretch here, just before and after Happy Camp. This is a lively stretch of water, yet doable for families in rafts or individuals in inflatable kayaks (my personal favorite rivercraft), so you get wild-river fun without risking your neck. In addition, the water is warm, perfect for swimming or falling in "by accident." This is a real joy compared to the ice-shock you get at rivers that receive snowmelt from the Sierra Nevada, such as the South Fork American, Merced, Stanislaus, and Kern. Three major rafting companies run trips here on the Klamath.

Bear Cove Cabins make the trip a success. Tent camping on river trips rarely works well because when rafting, you need to be able to get dry, change clothes, safely stow your extra stuff, and keep sand out of your gear, all of which can be difficult. Bear Cove solves that problem with eight cabins, each of which has a double bed, a television, and a kitchen with a refrigerator and a stove. Highway 96 fronts the property, with the river just on the other side of the road. The cabins are set along a horseshoe-shaped dirt access road. Though the cabins are relatively close to each other, once inside, you can't hear your neighbors.

With your lodging taken care of, you can focus on having fun, and there is plenty to be had on the Klamath River.

Here is a synopsis of the rafting runs directly above and below Happy Camp:

First run: Sarah Totten Campground to Happy Camp: 36 miles. It is Class III for the first 15 miles, then Class I+ until Happy Camp. That means experienced paddlers can put in at Sarah Totten, then challenge Upper Savage and Otter's Play Pen, both rated Class III-. It also means newcomers can put in below the Play Pen, then enjoy easy water all the way home to Happy Camp. There is just enough excitement to get your heart pounding, yet plenty of flat water to allow you to catch your breath or beach the boat and go swimming.

Second run: Happy Camp to Green Riffle: 37.5 miles; Class III; take out above Ishi Pishi Falls. This is an excellent run with a guide in an oared raft, or for experienced hands in kayaks going solo. Highlights include Kanaka Falls (III) and Dragon's Tooth (III+), and a stretch of water with a number of easy rapids interspersed by slicks, making it a kick for all. It is also very pretty, with lots of birdlife and river bends.

The Klamath also has good fishing, but it is not a summer affair. Small steelhead called "half-pounders," which are actually about 12- to 16-inches long, begin arriving in September and provide good fly-fishing in October and early November. The bite is best in the early morning and evening, and guide Roger Raynal out of Orleans often has days with 25 or 30 fish. Fishing here is an excellent way to learn how to fly-fish, with nearly a guarantee of catching as well as fishing. Two superior guides live nearby, Wally Johnson in Seiad Valley and Roger Raynal in Orleans.

Facilities: Bear Cove Cabins has eight cabins. Each has a small kitchen with a refrigerator and stove, along with a double bed with linens and blankets, and a television. A telephone is available in the Bear Cove office.

Reservations, fee: Reservations are advised. The fee is $38 to $49 per night; no minimum stay required.

Insider's note: When you phone Bear Cove Cabins, don't be surprised if all you get is an answering machine.

Who to contact: Phone Bear Cove Cabins at (916) 493-2677, or write to P.O. Box 1350, Happy Camp, CA 96039. For rafting companies, phone Turtle River Rafting, (916) 926-3223; Access to Adventure, (800) KLAMATH or (916) 469-3322; or Living Waters Recreation, (800) 994-RAFT or (916) 926-5446. For fishing guides, phone Wally Johnson in Seiad Valley, (916) 496-3291; or Roger Raynal in Orleans, (916) 469-3492.

Directions: From Redding, drive north on Interstate 5 past the town of Yreka to Highway 96. Take Highway 96 and drive west for 65 miles, passing the town of Seiad Valley, to the town of Happy Camp. Drive to 64715 Highway 96, located on the north side of the road.

If you're coming from Eureka, drive north on U.S. 101 just past Arcata to the junction with Highway 299. Turn east on Highway 299 and drive to Willow Creek. At Willow Creek, turn north on Highway 96 and drive 88 miles, passing the town of Clear Creek, to the town of Happy Camp. Drive to 64715 Highway 96, located on the north side of the road.

5. SANDY BAR RANCH CABINS
Klamath River
Off Highway 96 near Orleans

When a fishing guide chooses to base his career in a particular small town along a river, it's worth looking into. The Klamath River near Orleans could scarcely get a better testimonial than the fact that Roger Raynal, owner of North Rivers Guide Service, decided to settle down here.

That's because Roger catches fish, scads of them in the fall and decent numbers the rest of the year. Along with excellent rafting trips on the Klamath, good summer swimming, and nearby hikes, the fishing makes Orleans a destination trip for vacationers who want to combine outdoor adventures with a stay at the cabins at Sandy Bar Ranch.

These are great little redwood cabins, set in a valley on national forestland about a mile from the town of Orleans. At $48 a night for two, the price is a winner, and each cabin not only has a separate bedroom, but a hideaway bed in the living room. All come with full kitchens, and with a grocery store located about a mile away, cooking can help keep the price of your trip down. A café is located nearby as well.

This is one place where nature has used a broad brush in her artwork, with beauty touching everything. The Klamath tumbles around boulders, into gorges, and then flattens into slicks, all framed by a high canyon and bordered by forest. There is a great abundance of birdlife, wildlife, and if you time it right, fishlife.

The steelhead start arriving in mid-August here and just keep on coming through April, with the peak months being September through November. Salmon roar through in September. In the summer, from April through August, water conditions are perfect for rafting, and in July, the temperatures warm up considerably for swimming. Add it up and put that in your cash register.

Raynal and his customers often have 30-fish days, either fly-fishing or letting Glo Bugs flutter in the river current behind the boat. The most abundant fishery is for "half-pounders," a nickname for juvenile steelhead in the 12- to 16-inch class. When they're moving through, you can catch them like crazy. The action is always best during the morning and evening bites. Raynal's passion is to take his jet boat downstream to Johnson's Bar, then "boondog" (drift) Glo Bugs behind the boat. It's fun, it's easy, and the fish bite.

This is also a prime piece of river for rafting. Aurora River Adventures makes it a specialty. An easy, long run for newcomers is from the mouth of the Salmon River down to near Weitchpec, just below the confluence of the Trinity and Klamath rivers. It's exceptionally pretty country, with emerald-green water, steep canyon walls, and some bubbly rapids and corners (nothing too tough), intermixed with slicks.

If you desire more of a challenge, the Cal Salmon is one of the lesser known but more outstanding rafting rivers in California. The best put-in spot is near the town Forks of the Salmon. From here, the first five miles are Class II+, which makes a good run for newcomers in inflatable kayaks. After that, however, the river really sizzles. The rapids alternate between Class IV and V, and only experienced paddlers who don't mind living on the edge need apply. Highlights include Bloomer Falls (IV), The Maze (IV), Whirling Dervish (IV+), and Last Chance (V). The latter is a mind-bender of a drop that will have your heart leaving your body for what seems like an eternity.

Although the water is cold in early summer, this is the best stream in the Klamath River system for swimming. There are a number of pullouts on the gravel road that runs along the Salmon River canyon from which there are trails that access pools. One of the better spots is near the confluence of Wooley Creek, located at Mile 14 on the access road. Smaller pools are located farther upstream.

Combining the quality of the fishing, rafting, and swimming near here, it could be difficult to ask for more. But more you get, because you end up in a redwood cabin for the night.

Facilities: Sandy Bar Ranch has six redwood cabins that sleep four, each with full kitchens and bathrooms. Bed linens are provided. Pets are permitted. A grocery store and café are located within a mile.

Reservations, fee: Reservations are available. Cabin rates are $48 (two people), $58 (three people), and $68 (four people) per night, with discounts for children. Weekly rates are as low as $300.

Insider's note: Fishing guide Roger Raynal in Orleans can be reached at (916) 469-3492. Aurora River Adventures in Willow Creek can be reached at (800) 562-8475.

Who to contact: Phone Sandy Bar Ranch at (916) 627-3379, or write to P.O. Box 347, Orleans, CA 95556.

Directions: From Eureka, drive north on U.S. 101 just past Arcata to the junction with Highway 299. Turn east on Highway 299 and drive to Willow Creek. At Willow Creek, turn north on Highway 96 and drive 43 miles, passing the town of Weitchpec, to the town of Orleans. In Orleans, turn left at Ishi Pishi Road and drive three-quarters of a mile. Look for Sandy Bar Ranch Cabins on the right side of the road.

6. FLINT RIDGE WALK-IN CAMP
Redwood National Park
Off U.S. 101 near Klamath

Even when the Redwood Empire is completely filled with campers, you can always count on getting a pretty campsite at the Flint Ridge Walk-In Camp. This obscure little spot is reached by about a five-minute walk uphill, is unsigned from U.S. 101, and few people know about it. Tourists from out of state have nary a clue that it's here.

The campsites are set on a high meadow on an ocean bluff, with a cliff dropping off to the ocean on one side and dense forest on the other. So you get both woods and water, along with seclusion—a rare combination. A trail right out of the camp is routed into a redwood forest, as well as a piece of the Pacific Coastal Trail.

Flint Ridge Campground is located just south of the mouth of the Klamath River in Del Norte County. A lot of people miss the turnoff from U.S. 101; heading north, it's the last road that leads off to the west toward the ocean. From here, the road is paved but is a bit bumpy and narrow, without even a divider line. You might say, "Is this the right place?" And chances are, it is.

The road passes two privately operated campgrounds, then rises and curves to the left, with a small dirt parking lot set on the right side of the road, along a beach cliff. You park here, then find the trailhead on the east side of the road, adjacent to the parking area. The trail is uphill, but short enough so you can make as many trips back and forth to your vehicle as you need. This means you can bring just about anything you want, including all the good food and drinks you can imagine.

A secluded coastal tent site on Flint Ridge

The trail is routed to a pretty meadow, with 10 campsites for tenters sprinkled about. Because it is a meadow, you can feel a bit close to others when the campground is full. But guess what? That just about never happens. Plus, people tend to pick spots that are distant from each other. There can be five or six tents here and you will still feel a sense of seclusion from the rest of the world. A bonus is an excellent rest room, rare for a walk-in camp, and piped water is available. No pets are allowed.

Of course, a key factor here is the weather. This bluff gets pounded with rain and wind during storms and enveloped by fog in the summer. The best times to visit are in the fall (warm and clear), the spring (windy and clear), and the winter (clear between storms). Do you detect a pattern here? Right, pick clear weather and you have a beautiful spot.

There are many excellent side trips one could take, with Redwood National Park and Prairie Creek Redwoods State Park to the north offering great hikes and driving tours. But right out of camp is the Flint Ridge Trail, a decent hike that usually has nobody else around. The trail is routed up a moderate grade for two miles, first passing through hardwoods and then entering a redwood forest. It rises up near Flint Ridge amid redwoods, and although the trail then drops down the other side of the slope, you are advised to turn around and return the way you came. Why go down to trail's end when shortly after you just have to turn around and make a steep climb back? Unfortunately, there is no stellar destination at trail's end.

There are better trails in the area, requiring short drives to the trailheads. On the north side of the Klamath, a steep climb on the Requa Trail provides you with a clear-day perch where you can actually see the curvature of the earth on the horizon out to sea. The Skunk Cabbage Trail, located just north of Orick, is like a walk back into prehistoric times. Prairie Creek Redwoods to the nearby south offers many excellent hikes, including Fern Canyon, and the rare chance to see Roosevelt elk grazing in the park's meadows.

The Redwood Empire attracts tourists from all over North America. Only a handful ever end up in a tent at Flint Ridge.

Facilities: There are 10 hike-in tent spaces. Piped water and a developed rest room are available. No pets are permitted.

Reservations, fee: No reservations; no fee.

Who to contact: Phone Redwood National Park at (707) 464-6101, or write to 1111 Second Street, Crescent City, CA 95531.

Directions: From Eureka, drive north on U.S. 101 past Orick and Prairie Creek Redwoods State Park. Just before reaching the Klamath River, noted by the two gold bear statues on each side of the bridge, take the Coastal Drive exit and head west up the hill for 2.5 miles. The road is paved, but narrow and unlined. It passes two private campgrounds, then rises along an ocean cliff, with a dirt parking area on the right side of the road. Park here. The trailhead for the campground is adjacent to the parking area, on the east side of the road.

7. STONE LAGOON BOAT-IN SITES
Humboldt Lagoons State Park
Off U.S. 101 near Trinidad
⚓ ✗ 🐟 👫 ⑨

The first time I saw Stone Lagoon, a low, still fog hovered over its surface, and I remember how much it felt like a place of mystery. Its secrets, it turns out, are known by few. Those few are usually people who have tried boat-in camping at the lagoon's secluded campground.

With U.S. 101 running right alongside the lagoon, complete with a parking lot and state park visitor center, you might think this place is about as mysterious as white bread. But when you get in a canoe or small boat and make your way over to the boat-in campground in Ryan's Cove, many hidden treasures can become yours.

The adventure starts with this little, primitive campground, out of sight of the highway, where the sites are set far enough apart to provide a degree of privacy. The trip includes access to a remote beach that's usually deserted and a section of the Coastal Trail, opportunities for low-speed boating or paddling to explore the lagoon's open/shut outlet, and a chance to catch sea-run cutthroat trout.

But there are other mysterious elements, such as the fact that the camp is exactly midway between Eureka and Crescent City, 43 miles north of Eureka, 43 miles south of Crescent City. In addition, it borders wetland habitat for the plover, a marine bird that has become quite rare. Because winter rains can raise the lagoon and then break a hole in the sand spit that contains it from the ocean, giant sturgeon will occasionally swim in, then be trapped, along with salmon, steelhead, and cutthroat. Like I said, mysteries.

What is not a mystery, however, is the fact that you can find a great campsite here. It is boat-in only, ideal for canoes, and after launching at the small ramp near the parking lot at the visitor center, it is a short ride across the lagoon to Ryan's Cove. Here you will find a half-dozen camps sprinkled in the woods, each with the basics, including a table and bear-proof food locker, but no piped water. Make sure you bring plenty of water. Also be certain to bring plastic garbage bags, so you can haul out all of your trash when you leave.

Boat-in camping is great because you can bring anything you want, just load it up and go, yet you still gain the seclusion similar to that provided by backpacking. A bonus here is that the town of Orick is only three miles to the north, so no matter what you need, you can probably get it quickly.

The lagoon covers 520 acres and is bordered to the west by a sand spit and miles of beautiful beach with no people. You can also reach a new section of the Coastal Trail that links up to Dry Lagoon to the south. Both of these hikes are great, flat walks with ocean views and nobody around.

On calm days, I love paddling my canoe around Stone Lagoon. The lagoon is fed by freshwater from McDonald Creek, and while filling, its outlet to the ocean is blocked by a natural sand barrier. Eventually the freshwater rises above the sand barrier and sometimes blows a hole to the ocean, and the lagoon becomes intermixed with fresh and saltwater. That is when the sea-run cutthroat and other species can make a run inside, often getting trapped when the sand barrier seals up. The best way I know to catch the cutthroats is to troll a Jake's Spin-A-Lure, gold with red dots, the same lure that works so well on cutthroat trout at Yellowstone Lake.

Upstream of the lake, a restoration project on McDonald Creek has been completed. The cows that caused the stream's destruction in the 1980s have been removed. Now, elk roam the habitat around the lagoon and trout are again spawning in the creek.

Who knows? The scratching sound outside your tent at night might just be a big elk looking for snacks. The mysteries never end.

Facilities: A primitive campground with six boat-in sites is available, each with a table, bear-proof food locker, fire ring with wide metal grill, and pit toilet. No piped water is available. Be prepared to rely completely on yourself, including bringing your own water. Stone Lagoon can turn brackish, making the water unfit for cooking or drinking.

Reservations, fee: No reservations; $7 fee per night.

Insider's note: Gas motors are permitted on the lake, but a 10-mile-per-hour speed limit is enforced. Food, drink, supplies, and telephone are available in Orick, located three miles to the north on U.S. 101.

Who to contact: Phone Humboldt Lagoons State Park at (707) 488-2041, or write to 15336 Highway 101, Trinidad, CA 95570.

Directions: From Eureka on U.S. 101, drive 43 miles north (15 miles north of Trinidad) to the Humboldt Lagoons Visitor Center on the left side of the highway. To reach the boat ramp, take the small dirt road at the north end of the parking area, which is routed to a small launch.

8. VIEW CREST LODGE COTTAGES
Humboldt Coast
Off U.S. 101 in Trinidad

Most cabins, lodgings, and campgrounds on the Humboldt coast have no ocean view, even though they are located close to the water. View Crest, on the other hand, didn't get its name by accident. Although there is a road to look across, the seven cottages here provide a variety of glimpses and views of the ocean and Trinidad coast, each one different from the next. The best? Cottage Number 5? Maybe. Everybody has their own opinion.

The first thing you notice upon arrival, though, is not the view but how nicely landscaped the entrance is. Very inviting. That is why people invite themselves right in. Then they discover that the cabins are clean, comfortable, and fully equipped, including the kitchen. Note that some of the cabins are positioned apart from the rest, and some are set up in duplex configurations. A bonus is that you can bring your doggy.

Besides the ocean views and the cute cottages, there is another feature that keeps people coming back time after time: the birds. Swallows often perform uncanny flying displays, hundreds of them, doing dipsy-doos in a swirling maze just before sunset. Many have nests at the cottages.

The aerial display can be your send-off for a great vacation at Trinidad, which may include trips to Patrick's Point State Park one mile north (see the story on Bishop Pine Lodge on page 41 for more on Patrick's Point), and farther north to Big Lagoon, Prairie Creek Redwoods State Park, and Redwood National Park. The best hikes in these places are described in the companion book to this one, *Easy Hiking in Northern California* (Foghorn Press).

One factor at View Crest that visitors should be aware of is that while it can be easy to arrange a stay here during the week, it can be extremely difficult during good-weather weekends. Once in the spring and twice in the fall we had three different weekend dates declined when we called in advance, because the place was already fully booked. Yet another time, on a midweek summer day, we were able to just drive right up at 5 P.M. and have our choice of the cottages.

Get the message? Right: For weekends, book your trip as far in advance as possible.

Facilities: View Crest Lodge has seven cottages, both separate units and duplexes. Each has a bathroom, a kitchen with cookware and utensils, and bed linens. Pets are permitted. Restaurants, a grocery store, a boat hoist, and fishing trips are available four miles south in Trinidad.

Reservations, fee: Reservations are available. Cabin rates range from $46.50 to $110 per night, depending on the size of the cabin, with no minimum stay.

Insider's note: A campground set in a redwood grove and an RV park are also available.

Who to contact: Phone View Crest Lodge at (707) 677-3393, or write to 3415 Patrick's Point Drive, Trinidad, CA 95570.

Directions: From Eureka, drive north on U.S. 101 for 20 miles to Trinidad and take the Trinidad exit. At the stop sign, turn left and drive west under the freeway a short distance to Patrick's Point Drive. Turn right on Patrick's Point Drive and drive four miles to View Crest Lodge on the right side of the road.

---

9. BISHOP PINE LODGE
Humboldt Coast
Off U.S. 101 in Trinidad

The Humboldt coast is the kind of place where you can forget everything. In fact, I did. I had such a good time exploring, hiking, beachcombing, and enjoying the views that when it was time to head off for the next adventure, I left my favorite pillow back at the cabin at Bishop Pine Lodge.

What? A favorite pillow? Sure, doesn't everybody have one? When I'm busy traveling, testing out cabins, it's one of two things that assures me a good night's sleep. You are not allowed to ask about the other.

What most people forget when visiting this area, however, is not their pillow but their problems. It's that kind of place. The Humboldt coast near Trinidad is highlighted by Patrick's Point State Park and its outstanding views, short hikes and beaches, forests with Sitka spruce, bishop pine, and redwoods, ocean fishing, whale watching...or just leaning against a rock, watching all that water out there.

Bishop Pine Lodge is located near the best of it, set midway between Patrick's Point State Park and the town of Trinidad, just a few minute's drive from each. The lodge consists of a series of small cottages and they are neat and well-kept. Well-behaved pets are allowed. Each cottage has a small kitchen, bathroom, and living area/bedroom, and although a television is provided, you can always drape a towel over it, or if it's in a cabinet, close the doors. Out here you will have no use for it.

The one element that didn't exactly thrill me was the over-luminous

---

paint job on the cottages, including front doors that are fire-engine red and bright green. In addition, remember that although the lodge is located near the ocean, it is set in the woods. Some newcomers are disappointed that there are no ocean views, or even a feeling of being close to the ocean.

But the place is quiet and comfortable, and after a good night's sleep with your favorite pillow, your first trip will likely be to Trinidad and the Seascape Restaurant. Try it out on a weekday morning, when it isn't too crowded and the cook has the time to really do a number, and you'll find the crab-and-shrimp omelette is OOTW (out of this world). Adjacent to the Seascape is a great little beach to the immediate north and the Trinidad Pier to the immediate south, and both make for nice walks. Ocean fishing trips are offered at the pier, and a boat hoist and primitive launch ramp are also available here.

Sooner or later, though, you will end up at Patrick's Point State Park. It is located a short drive north from Bishop Pine Lodge, requires a $5 entrance fee, and provides great coastal views, excellent short walks, and an aura that captures the best of the Humboldt coast.

The Rim Trail at Patrick's Point follows a two-mile route on the edge of the bluff around three sides of the park, with several short cutoff trails that can take visitors to coastal lookout spots. Our favorites were Palmer's Point and Wedding Rock, which provide a panorama of the ocean, adjacent coast, and even passing whales, and the parking area above Agate Beach, from which you can scan north across several miles of beachfront all the way to Big Lagoon.

Our suggestion is to hike the Rim Trail, then while en route, take off on each of the little side-trip trails, with each providing a different glimpse of this special place. This hike is like a foray into a new world, and before long you may notice that you have forgotten much of your old one, the one that had so many problems to solve.

If you're not careful, that's not all you'll forget.

Facilities: Bishop Pine Lodge has 13 cottages, each a different size with unique interior designs. Most have kitchens and all have bathrooms and telephones.

Reservations, fee: Reservations are advised and are often required in peak months. Fees range from $60 to $90 per night per couple.

Insider's note: Although you can luck out and have sunny weather, it is often foggy or rainy here, so it is a good idea to bring a variety of clothing.

Who to contact: Phone Bishop Pine Lodge at (707) 677-3314, or write to 1481 Patrick's Point Drive, Trinidad, CA 95570.

Directions: From Eureka, drive north on U.S. 101 for 20 miles to Trinidad and take the Trinidad exit. At the stop sign, turn left and drive west under the freeway a short distance to Patrick's Point Drive. Turn right on Patrick's Point Drive and drive 1.9 miles to Bishop Pine Lodge on the right side of the road.

10. EUREKA/ARCATA KOA CABINS
Humboldt Coast
Off U.S. 101 near Arcata

The log cabin provides a compelling image to many, and KOA campgrounds have experienced a rejuvenation across America by offering log cabins in miniature for camping.

The KOA on the Humboldt coast is a good example, with a series of six of these little cabins located along Highway 101 near all city facilities yet within reasonable driving range of many adventure destinations.

KOA stands for Kampgrounds of America, and they offer privately operated facilities that are clean, patrolled for safety, and consistent from site to site. But they have gotten carried away with this "K" fixation, as in Kampground, Kamping, and Kamping Kabins, and hey, as far as I'm concerned, I kan't take it anymore.

KOA Eureka is actually located north of Eureka, closer to Arcata, set just east of the highway, and their yellow-orange sign is easily visible to passing drivers. You turn in and discover that they have attempted to give the place a parklike feel, with a line of trees along the rear border of the park. The camping cabins (don't tell me how to spell) are small and cute, complete with a little porch and a swinging bench, and they come with electricity, heat, and beds. But don't forget your sleeping bag; no linens or blankets are available.

These cabins are actually prefabricated off-site, and when space is available at a campground, they are then shipped and assembled. That is why they are exactly the same at each KOA throughout the country. On a trip to Chattanooga, I discovered a KOA that had more than a hundred of these little cabins, which is one of the most peculiar sights you can imagine. A miniature city of tiny log cabins, all lined up.

Here on the Humboldt coast, the cabins can serve as a layover spot for Highway 101 cruisers touring the coast, and can also be used as a base camp for several nearby adventures. Those adventures include fishing for salmon and rockfish, and to the north, visiting any of a series of parks, including Patrick's Point State Park and Redwood National Park.

Fishing on ocean trips out of Humboldt Bay can be excellent in the summer and fall. King Salmon Charters, located on the shore of the bay

Hanging around on the front porch at the Eureka/Arcata KOA

just south of Eureka, runs party boat trips for salmon and rockfish. Typically the salmon fishing is best in midsummer, right around July 4th, and the deep-sea fishing for rockfish is best in late summer and fall, especially in September. Of course, weather is a vital factor when venturing on the ocean, and frequent storms in winter and strong winds out of the north in spring make July, August, September, and early October the best times to arrange a fishing trip.

Though rain is common in the winter, constant mild temperatures make the Humboldt coast a year-round destination for touring the coast and seeing the redwoods.

Patrick's Point State Park is an excellent side-trip destination. There are several short spur trails that cut off the Rim Trail and are routed out to great coastal lookouts. The best views are from Wedding Rock, where you can scan across the expanse of the Pacific Ocean and along the nearby coast with its rocky outcrops and beaches. On a clear day, it's breathtaking.

Most anybody visiting the Humboldt coast is going to head farther north, though, to see the giant redwoods. Both Redwood National Park and Prairie Creek Redwoods State Park are located along U.S. 101 as you head toward Crescent City. Some of the better hikes in this region are described in this book in the stories for Flint Ridge Walk-In Camp, Crescent City Redwoods KOA, and Patrick Creek Lodge, which are located amid these big redwood parks. They make the trip complete.

After a day of adventuring, you will return to your little log cabin at KOA Eureka and call it home for a night. If you stay long, pretty soon they'll have you spelling it with a K. Okay, okay—I surrender.

Facilities: KOA Eureka has six small log cabins, each with a porch with a swing, electric heat, and beds. A hot tub, two laundry rooms, shower facilities, a game room, and a small grocery store are available nearby. There are also 25 tent sites and 140 motor home sites.

Reservations, fee: Reservations are advised; cabin fees are $32 in the summer and $28 in the winter.

Insider's note: Ocean fishing trips can be arranged through King Salmon Charters at (707) 442-3474, and there is good hiking at Patrick's Point State Park, (707) 677-3570 and Redwood National Park, (707) 464-6101.

Who to contact: Phone KOA Eureka at (707) 822-4243, or write to 4050 North Highway 101, Eureka, 95503.

Directions: From Eureka, drive four miles north on U.S. 101 and look for the yellow-orange KOA sign on the right side of the road, next to Re-Sell Lumber.

If you are coming from Arcata, drive two miles south on U.S. 101 and look for the yellow-orange KOA sign on the left side of the road, next to Re-Sell Lumber.

11. MATTOLE RIVER RESORT CABINS
Lost Coast
Off Mattole Road near Petrolia

There is no place on earth like the Lost Coast, and on the Lost Coast, there is no place like Mattole River Resort.

The Lost Coast is located in remote southern Humboldt County, completely isolated and shielded by natural boundaries: the Pacific Ocean to the west, Humboldt redwoods to the east, Bear River Ridge to the north, and the King Mountain Range to the south. The road here is long and twisty, combining dirt, asphalt, and gravel. It's a destination you have to earn.

But when you crest the ridge and the Mattole River Valley comes into view, you suddenly realize you have entered a world that is much talked of but rarely seen. It is a gorgeous coastal setting, often a brilliant green in color, always fresh with the Mattole River running through its center, flowing on a meandering route to the sea. The coast itself is an unusual blend of remote farm country and ranchlands that extend to isolated beaches, rocky coastal outcrops, and tidelands where few ever venture.

In the center of the Mattole River Valley is the Mattole River Resort, five rental cabins in all, inexpensive but perfectly situated for adventuring on the Lost Coast. The cabins come with small kitchens, so once you've set up camp, you can turn this trip into a do-it-yourself special.

But I've got to tell you something. Every time I visit this area, I notice how the people here run at a different speed than the rest of the universe. Perhaps it is from being so isolated, that is, an hour-and-a-half drive from the nearest semblance of an urban area, Garberville. They not only do things when they want to, but the way they want to. That also applies to this resort. For instance, there are five cabins, but they are numbered 2, 3, 5, 6, and 9; there are no cabins 1, 4, or 8, while 7 is rented full-time. You figure it out. It's just the way things are out here.

Now let me provide you with a little inside knowledge. The best cabin here by far is Number 9. It has a wood-burning stove, skylights, decks in the back and front, and is totally secluded and separate from the other units. It is private, quiet, and pretty.

Once you have settled in and start running on Mattole River speed, which is 16 r.p.m. compared to 78 r.p.m. in San Francisco and 33 r.p.m. in the suburbs, you can plan your recreation. In addition to the pretty area drives to the coast, there is excellent hiking and biking in the summer and fall and fishing in the winter.

For hiking and biking: Drive out to the end of Lighthouse Road, where you'll find a trailhead for the Lost Coast Trail just beyond the Bureau of Land Management's Mattole Campground. From here, take the abandoned jeep trail for three miles out to the Punta Gorda Light Tower, a day trip with superb coastal views. Other great trips include hiking to Kings Peak in the nearby King Range, or biking on the quiet local roads in the Mattole Valley.

For fishing: The steelhead start arriving in January, and at times, will migrate en masse upstream all the way through March. The rains can be prodigious, however, rendering the river high and unfishable for weeks, and timing good stream conditions with a run of fish can make this an elusive victory. But when everything is right, the Mattole River can be one of the best rivers in California for steelhead fishing.

The weather is the one wild-card factor that can turn on you out here. It rains like crazy in the winter, can get fogbound on the coast in the summer, and the wind can blow furiously out of the north in the spring.

Fall brings the best weather, with short periods of perfection arriving without prediction the rest of the year.

Facilities: Mattole River Resort has five cabins, each with a bathroom and kitchen. Cookware, utensils, bed linens, and towels are provided. Small grocery stores are located nearby in the towns of Petrolia and Honeydew.

Reservations, fee: Reservations are available. Cabin rates range from $50 to $90, depending on number of beds and amount of privacy.

Insider's note: An excellent source of information on fishing for steelhead on the Mattole River is Bob Fuel at the Honeydew Store, (707) 629-3310.

Who to contact: Mattole River Resort can be reached at (707) 629-3445 or (800) 845-4607, or by writing 42354 Mattole Road, Petrolia, CA 95558.

Directions: From San Francisco, take U.S. 101 north past Garberville and Redway to the South Fork Road/Honeydew exit. Take South Fork Road and drive west (it becomes gravel/dirt at different points) for about an hour to Honeydew. In Honeydew, drive over the Mattole River Bridge, turn right on Mattole Road, and drive three miles. Look for the Mattole River Resort (white cabins, blue trim) on the left side of the road.

12. LITTLEFIELD RANCH CABINS
Ruth Lake
Off Highway 36 near Ruth

It's a winding, unending drive on Highway 36 way out here, but you end up in one of the most remote cabin settings in California. That is the main reason why people come here. The nearest mall seems like a thousand miles away.

The other reason people come here is to visit Ruth Lake, located just two miles away from Littlefield Ranch, the only lake of any consequence within decent driving range of Eureka. This is a long, narrow lake set at an elevation of 2,800 feet. Trout and bass fishing is decent—trout in the spring and fall, bass in the summer. There is a free boat ramp here, and the Ruth Lake Marina rents fishing boats along with houseboats, pontoon boats, and ski boats.

Littlefield Ranch is backed up against Six Rivers National Forest, just across a pasture (about 400 yards) from the Mad River. There is a path that starts near Cabin 3 that is routed into remote forest country, although there is no real destination, just "out there." To get an idea of how remote this area is, take the drive up the nearby Forest Service Road to the top of South Fork Mountain, where you get great views in all directions of this region of isolated western Trinity County.

One of the unique elements of Littlefield Ranch is that the cabins are set near a vintage barn. Vintage? Like vintage 1836, complete with hand-hewed poles and in decent shape. The cabins were built in the 1930s to house loggers, and they have been restored (the cabins, not the loggers), with many antique touches. Each has a small yard with a good number of trees.

For people who live on the coast or in the city, this place has everything their areas do not. There is no fog. There are no people. All is quiet. And while there is just about nobody driving on Highway 36 compared to the traffic jams of other places in summer, the twists and curves will have you slowing down anyway. But hey, that's why you came here in the first place.

Facilities: Littlefield Ranch has four cabins, with one, two, and three bedrooms. All have bathrooms and kitchens with cookware, utensils, and wood-burning stoves. One cabin has bed linens; otherwise bring a sleeping bag or your own sheets and pillows. Patio tables and barbecues are provided. Boat rentals are available at Ruth Lake two miles away. A grocery store is one mile away.

Reservations, fee: Reservations are required; cabin rates range from a low of $55 per night for a one-bedroom cabin to $80 per night for a three-bedroom cabin that sleeps 10 people.

Insider's note: Boat rentals can be arranged at Ruth Lake Marina, (707) 574-6529.

Who to contact: Phone Littlefield Ranch at (707) 574-6689, or write to Box 600, Ruth Lake, CA 95526.

Directions: From Eureka, drive south on U.S. 101 past Fortuna to Alton. At Alton, turn east on Highway 36 and drive about 50 miles to just past the town of Mad River. Turn right at the sign for Ruth Lake and drive 18 miles to the town of Ruth. Continue one mile past the Ruth Store and look for Littlefield Ranch on the left side of the road (just past the Ruth District Forest Service office).

If you are coming from Red Bluff, turn west on Highway 36 and drive about 60 miles (about 10 miles past the town of Forest Glen). Turn left at the sign for Ruth Lake and drive 18 miles to the town of Ruth. Continue one mile past the Ruth Store and look for Littlefield Ranch on the left side of the road (just past the Ruth District Forest Service office).

OTHER CABIN RENTALS IN HUMBOLDT COUNTY

Deer Lodge, 753 Patricks Point Drive, Trinidad, 95570; (707) 677-3554.

KOA Fortuna, 1660 Kenmar Road, Fortuna, CA 95540; (707) 725-3359 or (800) 404-0600.

Shasta-Trinity

** For locations of camps, see map on page 9. **

13. STEWART MINERAL SPRINGS CABINS
Shasta-Trinity National Forest
Off Interstate 5 near Weed

You probably figured there was a place like this near Mt. Shasta, a therapeutic retreat with mineral baths, saunas, massage service, Indian-style purification sweats—a place where the spirits of Shasta's fabled Lemurians seem to reign. Well, if you did, you figured right, and before you laugh it off as some New Age curiosity, consider first that the treatment here actually works. You will leave feeling like a whole new person.

Maybe it's the mineral baths. Maybe it's the influence of nearby 14,162-foot Mt. Shasta. Or maybe you just have too much stress in your life and you need to let it all go. Regardless, this is the place to do it in Northern California, remote enough that nobody gets here by accident, quality enough to make you want to come back.

Stewart Springs is located on the northern slopes of Mt. Eddy, adjacent to giant Mt. Shasta, set in the woods on property bordering Shasta-Trinity National Forest. There are five cabins available, along with other lodging possibilities, including rooms, small apartments, even tepees. You can plan a self-contained retreat, with cooking facilities provided in the cabins, and a woodsy restaurant on the premises.

Stewart Mineral Springs is an old resort, over 100 years old, yet it is still something of a secret. The magic is in the combination of hot mineral baths, saunas, or Indian sweats followed by a jump into cold, streaming Parks Creek, which flows through the property a short distance from the mineral baths. One of the perpetual challenges here is to go from one to the other, from the very hot to the very cold. If you survive it, heh, heh, you will feel invigorated for weeks.

There is also excellent hiking nearby, with a great, easy trip to Deadfall Lakes on the Pacific Crest Trail on the back side of Mt. Eddy. To reach the trailhead, turn left onto Forest Road 17 immediately after leaving Stewart Springs and drive nine miles to the parking area, well signed on the left side of the road. The hike is a five-mile round-trip, a perfect way to top off your visit.

And by the way, you may ask, what the heck is a Lemurian? Well, Lemurians, my friends, are a species of mysterious beings that are said to inhabit the inner world of Mt. Shasta, living in underground caves lined with gold. Phylos, the most famous Lemurian, is said to be able to materialize at will wearing a long, flowing robe, and occasionally inviting people into his golden temple to listen to soft music.

Like I said, you expect things like this near Mt. Shasta.

Facilities: Stewart Mineral Springs has five cabins, six apartments, and three tepees, along with dorm rooms, an A-frame house, and spaces for tent camping and motor homes. Kitchenette facilities are provided in the cabins and apartments, and a restaurant is located on the premises. Therapeutic mineral baths, massages, saunas, and purification sweats are available. Reservations are not required for mineral baths, but you must have an appointment for a massage or herbal body wraps.

Reservations, fee: Reservations are advised. The fee is $45 per night per cabin, $30 to $60 for an apartment room, $15 for a teepee. The fee for a mineral bath is $12 for guests at Stewart Mineral Springs, $15 for day-use visitors.

Who to contact: Phone Stewart Mineral Springs at (916) 938-2222 or (800) 322-9223, or write to 4617 Stewart Springs Road, Weed, CA 96094.

Directions: From Redding, drive north on Interstate 5 just past the town of Weed. Take the Edgewood exit, turn left at the stop sign, then drive a short distance (under the freeway) to Old Stage Road. Turn right on Old Stage Road and drive a short distance to Stewart Springs Road. Turn left and drive four miles to Stewart Springs.

---

14. DEADFALL LAKE BACKPACK SITES
Shasta-Trinity National Forest
Off Interstate 5 near Mt. Shasta

You can walk all 1,700 miles of the Pacific Crest Trail in California and not find a prettier lake with a shorter or easier walk than Deadfall Lake.

Pretty? Middle Deadfall Lake is a sapphire, pristine and quiet, set on the western side of Mt. Eddy in a mountain bowl at a 7,300-foot elevation. The water is deep and peaceful, and the lake is bigger than most expect, 25 acres. This is one of the true prize lakes of Northern California that you can only reach on foot.

A short, easy walk? Unbelievable: It is just 2.5 miles on a mostly flat trail, and for most hikers, a steady cruise of an hour or so will deliver you to its shoreline with nary a huff or a puff.

For a condensed version of a backpacking trip, Middle Deadfall Lake makes for an excellent destination. It is not only a short hike to a beautiful lake, but there are a few excellent lakeside campsites sprinkled about, the swimming is good, the fishing is fair, and several outstanding hiking side trips are available. Sound like it has it all? It does. And although Middle Deadfall Lake is located in remote Northern California, enough people know about it to make a midweek arrival advisable so you can have better prospects of claiming the best campsite.

The key is that the parking area and trailhead is located at a ridge-line, complete with markers for the Pacific Crest Trail. Most trailheads for the PCT are spur trails along streams in canyons, requiring long, uphill climbs, agonizing for the first day of a trip. Not this one. The trail laterals across the mountain slope with a gentle grade, and while routed in and out of forest, provides views across the mountain country to the west. When you near the lake, you will hop across a small creek, pass a trail junction, then continue straight ahead for another five minutes and top a small rim. Suddenly, there below you is Middle Deadfall Lake.

It is so pretty that the first order of business is usually just to find a good rock to sit on, maybe break out some trail snacks, relax, and enjoy being there. As you do, you will scan the area, and the vision for your adventure will clear right before your eyes.

Right off you will notice that the best campground is set in a small grove of trees on the back side of the lake, by far the most secluded and pretty spot for a tent. It is usually taken, however. Another good spot is near the lake's outlet stream. If either of these campsites is available, nab it.

Once you have your base camp set up, you will find yourself surrounded by a world of natural pleasures, with swimming or fishing often the first order of business. The water is clear and fresh, perfect for a refreshing swim. While the water temperatures are cool in midsummer and cold in early summer and early fall, it isn't numbing like the lakes in the high Sierra. During the early evening fishing for small brook trout is decent; casting with small lures such as the $^1/_{16}$-ounce Panther Martin spinner, black with yellow dots, gets the best results. Because this is bear country, be certain to eat your catch for dinner and burn (not bury) the fish heads and entrails.

Several excellent side trips are available for more hiking, including adventuring to find the two other Deadfall lakes. Upper Deadfall, set at 7,800 feet, is tiny, rarely visited, and requires some cross-country travel. Five-acre Lower Deadfall, located downstream at 7,150 feet, is decent for swimming. It gets far less attention than Middle Deadfall.

The best side trip is the climb up to the top of adjacent Mt. Eddy, 9,025 feet, which requires a 1,700-foot climb over the course of 3.5 miles from Middle Deadfall Lake, with decent trail most of the way. The view of Mt. Shasta from the Eddy summit is awe-inspiring; you will never forget it. But that's the way much of this trip is.

Facilities: Primitive camping areas are available near the shore of Deadfall Lake. You need to bring all equipment. A water purifier and backpacking stove are essential.

Reservations, fee: No reservation; no fee.

Insider's note: No mountain bikes are allowed on this trail or, for that matter, anywhere on the Pacific Crest Trail.

Who to contact: Phone Mt. Shasta Ranger District at (916) 926-4511, or write to 204 West Alma, Mt. Shasta, CA 96067. For a map of the area, send $3 to USDA-Forest Service, 630 Sansome Street, San Francisco, CA 94111 and ask for Shasta-Trinity National Forest. To obtain a topographic map, send $3.50 to Maps-Western Distribution Center, U.S. Geologic Survey, Box 25286-Federal Center, Denver, CO 80225 and ask for Mt. Eddy.

Directions: From Interstate 5 in Redding, drive north for about 60 miles, continuing past the town of Mt. Shasta to just north of Weed. Take the Edgewood exit, then turn left and drive a short distance to old Highway 99 (Old Stage Road). Turn right on Old Stage Road and drive a short distance to Stewart Springs Road. Turn left on Stewart Springs Road and continue about three miles to Stewart Springs. At Stewart Springs, veer to the right on Forest Service Road 17 and continue for about 10 miles to the trailhead parking area on the left side of the summit.

15. TOAD LAKE BACKPACK SITES
Shasta-Trinity National Forest
Off Interstate 5 near Mt. Shasta

As you make the drive to the trailhead for Toad Lake, you're bound to mutter something like, "How in the heck did this place ever get in this book?!"

Good question, because this can be the road through hell. It is long, twisty, and bumpy, at times jarring, requiring nearly an hour of driving in the mountains on dirt roads. The last quarter-mile is passable only by high-clearance vehicles, and four-wheel drive is recommended. Why do it? Because once you get the drive over with and park, you are at the threshold of a 15-minute backpack trip that rewards you with a pretty lakeside campsite, the best swimming hole in the Trinity Divide country, and several excellent side trips.

It is set high on the eastern flank of the Mt. Eddy Range, the big mountain directly west of Mt. Shasta. After parking, the first thing you will notice is the calm. Everything is so tranquil, especially compared to that tumultuous ride in, that it takes only a few moments for everything inside you to settle. After strapping on your backpack, you will hike up a wide path on a very gentle grade, and in short order, top a short crest and reach Toad Lake. The walk to the campsites is short enough that some hikers will make a repeat trip in order to bring in more gear and goodies.

Toad Lake, set at 6,950 feet, is green and pretty, covering 23 acres in a mountain bowl. Good campsites are located right where the trail feeds you to the lake, as well as along the shoreline to the right (north). The camps are set virtually at lake's edge, almost within jumping distance.

Jumping distance? That's right, jumping distance. Because on hot summer afternoons, there are few things better than jumping right into this lake. It's a great mountain lake for swimming, because the surface temperatures are warm in the summer months, and the surrounding mountain wall shields the lake from afternoon winds out of the north. In addition, you will discover there are pockets of cold and warm water; you might have warm water at your shoulders and a pocket of chilling water at your ankles. Sometimes it is just plain fun to bob around with a life jacket on, floating in and out of these warm and cold pockets.

Toad Lake is only fair for fishing, with a chance to catch small brook trout during the evening. Small? Yeah, dinkers galore.

Instead of fishing, most people plan several day hikes, using Toad Lake as their base camp. The best short trip is to nearby Porcupine Lake, a pristine alpine lake about a half-hour hike away. The route to Porcupine starts at the campsites, skirts around the lake in a counterclockwise direction, then makes a short climb to the rim of the bowl overlooking the lake. I've seen deer several times in this area. Here the route intersects with the Pacific Crest Trail, where you turn left and walk south for about 10 minutes, then turn right on the short cutoff trail to the lake. The lake is gorgeous, the water is clear, cold, and deep, and its shoreline is sprinkled with giant blocks of granite, a perfect lunch site.

Other more ambitious hikes are available as well. From the PCT, you can hike south for a few hours to an overlook of pretty Picayune Lake. Also from the PCT, you can turn north and make the all-day round-trip to the top of 9,025-foot Mt. Eddy, a climb of 2,000 feet, and get one of the most spectacular lookouts of Mt. Shasta imaginable.

Suddenly, that jaw-rattling drive in won't seem so bad after all.

Facilities: Several primitive backpack sites are provided along the shoreline of Toad Lake. Be prepared to rely completely on yourself. Bring a water purifier. The walk is short enough so that a return trip can be made to bring extra gear. Pets are permitted.

Reservations, fee: No reservation; no fee.

Insider's note: Lake Siskiyou is located near Mt. Shasta on the access road and has a campground, restaurant, coin-operated Laundromat, and other facilities.

Who to contact: Phone Mt. Shasta Ranger District at (916) 926-4511, or write to 204 West Alma, Mt. Shasta, CA 96067. For a map of the area, send $3 to USDA-Forest Service, 630 Sansome Street, San Francisco, CA 94111 and ask for Shasta-Trinity National Forest. To obtain a topographic map, send $3.50 to Maps-Western Distribution Center, U.S. Geologic Survey, Box 25286-Federal Center, Denver, CO 80225 and ask for Mt. Eddy.

Directions: From the town of Mt. Shasta on Interstate 5, take the Central Mt. Shasta exit and drive to the stop sign. Turn left, cross the highway, and continue to another stop sign at W.A. Barr Road. Turn left and drive past Lake Siskiyou and continue up the mountain (the road becomes Forest Service Road 26). Just past a concrete bridge, turn right and drive a short distance, then turn left on Morgan Meadow Road and continue for 10 miles to the parking area. The road is bumpy and twisty. The final quarter-mile to the trailhead is rough, and high-clearance, four-wheel-drive vehicles are recommended.

16. MT. SHASTA KOA CABINS
Mt. Shasta
Off Interstate 5 near Mt. Shasta

The view from the picnic table in front of K1, that is, "Kabin 1," is a superb panorama of 14,162-foot Mt. Shasta. If you're trying to eat a meal here, don't be surprised if a lot of your food ends up on the table instead of in your mouth, because you won't be able to keep your eyes off magic Shasta.

Mt. Shasta KOA is set at 3,500 feet in elevation, just on the outskirts of town, in a spacious parklike setting with log-style camping cabins nestled under trees on the edge of the KOA property. The trees make it surprisingly intimate, despite this being a big KOA with lots of motor home campers, set just a few blocks from downtown Mt. Shasta.

A number of visitors stay at KOA Mt. Shasta because it is so close to Interstate 5. Late arrivals are welcome, and it makes for an easy stop, camp, and get-up-and-go kind of place. But the area is too beautiful to not make at least one side trip, and so full of recreational opportunities that you could spend day after day adventuring.

At the least, make the drive up to Bunny Flat at Mt. Shasta, where at elevation 6,900 feet you can scan miles of charmed beauty, highlighted by views of Mt. Lassen, Castle Crags, and the Sacramento River canyon in one direction, and in the other, the main climber's route to the Shasta peak up Avalanche Gulch, past the Thumb and Red Banks. It is a spectacle, one of the best drive-to trips in Northern California. There are also good day hikes out of Bunny Flat, including the jaunt to Horse Camp, where most Shasta summit climbers will spend the night before making the one-day ascent.

The nearby Upper Sacramento River provides some of the best easily

There's one big reason to stay at the Mt. Shasta KOA

accessed fly-fishing for trout in California, especially during evenings in the early summer. In addition, nearby Lake Siskiyou is a jewel, almost always full to the brim, excellent in the summer for swimming and low-speed boating, with good trout fishing in the spring and early summer.

There are many other driving tours available nearby. Visiting Castle Crags, located just south of Dunsmuir along Interstate 5, is very popular, and provides a great view of Shasta as well as the Crags. Another great cruise is past Lake Siskiyou and up to Castle Lake, and again you get postcard views of Mt. Shasta, while visiting a pretty lake in a granite cirque with good hiking trails nearby.

No matter where you go here, you will keep getting pulled back to looking at giant Mt. Shasta. You just can't help it.

Facilities: Mt. Shasta KOA has four camping cabins, two one-room cabins, and two two-room cabins, each with a double bed and bunk bed with mattress (two bunk beds in the two-room cabins), small table, and electricity. No linens or pillows are available (bring your sleeping bag). A rest room with locking showers, a small store, a game room, a swimming pool, bike rentals, washers and dryers, and a dump station are available. There are also

41 motor home spaces with full hookups and 89 additional spaces for tents and motor homes. Leashed pets are permitted.

Reservations, fee: Reservations are accepted. There is a $29 fee per night for a one-room cabin, $37 fee per night for a two-room cabin, $17.95 fee per night for tent sites, $19.95 fee per night for motor home sites with no hookup, $22.95 fee per night for motor home sites with electricity, $24.95 fee per night for motor home sites with water, electricity, and sewer.

Insider's note: The drive up Everitt Memorial Highway to Bunny Flat is a must-do trip.

Who to contact: Phone Mt. Shasta KOA at (916) 926-4029 or (800) 736-3617, or write to 900 North Mt. Shasta Boulevard, Mt. Shasta, CA 96067.

Directions: From Redding, drive north on Interstate 5 for 58 miles to the town of Mt. Shasta. Continue past the first Mt. Shasta exit and take the Central Mt. Shasta exit. Turn right at the stop sign and drive to the stoplight at Mt. Shasta Boulevard. Turn left and drive one-half mile to East Hinckley Boulevard. Turn right on East Hinckley, drive a very short distance, then turn left at the extended driveway entrance to Mt. Shasta KOA.

17. CAVE SPRINGS/DUNSMUIR CABINS
Upper Sacramento River
Off Interstate 5 in Dunsmuir

The Upper Sacramento River is a living laboratory, once poisoned and now thriving, and trout fishers from throughout the West are coming here to experience its recovery.

This is the site of the worst inland toxic spill in California history and now it is also the site of the most remarkable rejuvenation ever documented. The spill occurred in July 1991 when a Southern Pacific freighter derailed a few miles upstream at Cantara Loop, sending a tanker wheels-up into the river, leaking a full load of all-purpose herbicide into the stream. Today some scientists are calling the river's recovery the "genesis effect," having seen the entire aquatic food chain become reestablished, including the population of rainbow trout.

That has put Dunsmuir Cabins—the best place to stay along the Sacramento River for visitors who want to fish, explore, hike, or even kayak this now famous trout stream—back in business.

Dunsmuir Cabins are located in the town of Dunsmuir, about an hour's drive north of Redding, and are set in different locations near the Sacramento River. They include a variety of units, ranging from California box construction cabins, which rent for $35 per night, to guest homes along the river that top out at $150 per night. The best way to get started on this trip is to call the owners, Louie Dewey or Joan Elam, at (800) 235-2028, and discuss what best fits your expectations.

The continued fascination over the historic spill and the evolving recovery make every trout you hook in the Upper Sacramento seem special. It can feel like the beginning of time, and for this river, it is. The best fly-fishing is to the north, from the Cantara Bridge on upstream, and to the south, from Castle Creek on downstream. Between those two areas is Dunsmuir, which is stocked with trout and where no fishing gear restrictions apply.

Most years, the river is cold but fishable by the opener in the last Saturday in April, then produces excellent caddis hatches by the end of May and stonefly by early June. In big snow years, the river can run high and swift well into June, then remain in good shape throughout the summer. By the way, your host, Louie Dewey, is an excellent fisherman and unless the water conditions are high from extreme snowmelt, can always put you on to trout.

Out of curiosity, many people now wish to visit the Cantara Bridge, the site of the train derailment and spill. This is now an exceptional fishing area, and a trail is available that is routed along the river from the CalTrout Staging Area at the end of Cantara Road (accessible via South Old Stage and Azalea roads north of Dunsmuir). The hike is described in detail in *Easy Hiking in Northern California* by Ann Marie Brown (Foghorn Press), and when we visited, a long freight train rolled through

The Cantara Loop, site of a toxic spill in July 1991, is now a thriving watershed

the loop, sending an eerie sensation down the canyon as well as down our spines. It was like "vuja de," my friend told me, a place you don't want to go all over again.

Other good hikes are available nearby at Castle Crags State Park, and of course, at Mt. Shasta to the north and in the nearby Eddy Range to the west. There are several excellent driving tours as well. The best three? 1—South of Dunsmuir, take the Castle Crags State Park exit and drive past the state park and continue up the mountain for awesome views of the Crags; 2—In the town of Mt. Shasta, take the Central Mt. Shasta exit and continue up the Everitt Memorial Highway all the way to Panther Flat at 7,400 feet elevation; 3—Drive to Lake Siskiyou and turn left for the drive up to Castle Lake, set at 5,450 feet, for incredible views of Mt. Shasta to the east.

But no matter what adventures visitors partake of by day, by late afternoon or early evening they are on the river with their fishing rods. After all, the trout are there, and you can't keep them waiting.

Facilities: Dunsmuir Cabins come in a wide variety of lodging styles, from box construction cabins to guest homes along the river.

Reservations, fee: Reservations are advised; fees range from $35 to $150 per night.

Who to contact: Phone Dunsmuir Cabins at (800) 235-2028 or (916) 235-2721, or write to 4727 Dunsmuir Avenue, Dunsmuir, CA 96025. For a map of the area, send $3 to USDA-Forest Service, 630 Sansome Street, San Francisco, CA 94111 and ask for Shasta-Trinity National Forest.

Directions: From Redding, drive 52 miles north on Interstate 5 to Dunsmuir. Take the Central Dunsmuir exit, which feeds onto Dunsmuir Avenue. Drive to 4727 Dunsmuir Avenue.

18. BOULDER LAKE BACKPACK SITES
Trinity Alps Wilderness
Off Highway 3 near Trinity Center

It was George Seifert, head coach of the 49ers, who first told me about Boulder Lake. It turns out that this is where George and his wife, Linda, often make one last trip at the end of summer for a final rest and rejuvenation before George returns as five-star general of the best football team in history.

If George can find peace and tranquillity here, then anybody can. After all, when you are expected to win the Super Bowl, you can become the most stressed-out person in California.

Boulder Lake requires a two-mile backpack hike that enters the Trinity Alps Wilderness. The lake is excellent for afternoon swims, evening trout fishing, and nightly stargazing. In addition, Goldfield Campground is available near the trailhead for late arrivals, and beyond Boulder Lake are a number of other destinations, including Little Boulder Lake (one mile by trail to the east), Lion Lake (three miles to the west), and Foster Lake (another four miles to the west).

If you arrive during a popular weekend and find the few campsites at Boulder Lake already taken, these lakes can provide a safety valve. Little Boulder Lake is a good side bet. The others are on a route that heads deeper into the wilderness interior to several other lakes and the headwaters of several streams, a good route for backpackers on lengthier trips.

The primary features of the region are Ycatapom Peak to the southeast, elevation 7,596 feet, and Sugar Pine Butte to the west, elevation 8,033 feet. The views of Trinity Lake are sensational from Ycatapom, although it takes an ambitious day hike to make it to the ridge to get them. The whole region is highlighted by very small alpine lakes, all set in rock bowls that make for fantastic swimming. Another bonus is that most backpackers don't start their trips here, but rather continue to the end of Coffee Creek Road for expeditions to the Caribou Lakes Basin and beyond.

Expedition? That's not the idea at Boulder Lake. After all, George Seifert goes there to relax. Perhaps you might, too.

Facilities: A few primitive backpack sites are provided along the shoreline of Boulder Lake. Be prepared to rely completely on yourself. Bring a water purifier.

Reservations, fee: No reservation; no fee. A free wilderness permit is required and can be obtained at the U.S. Forest Service District office in Weaverville.

Insider's note: Late arrivals can camp at drive-to Goldfield Campground, operated by Shasta-Trinity National Forest. It is located on County Road 104 (Coffee Creek Road), a short distance from the trailhead.

Who to contact: Phone Shasta-Trinity National Forest at (916) 623-2121, or write to Weaverville Ranger District, P.O. Box T, Weaverville, CA 96093. For a map of the area, send $3 to USDA-Forest Service, 630 Sansome Street, San Francisco, CA 94111 and ask for Shasta-Trinity National Forest. To obtain a topographic map, send $3.50 to Maps-Western Distribution Center, U.S. Geologic Survey, Box 25286-Federal Center, Denver, CO 80225 and ask for Ycatapom Peak.

Directions: From Redding or Eureka/Arcata, take Highway 299 to Weaverville. In Weaverville, look for the Forest Service office on the south side of the road and obtain your required wilderness permit there. From Weaverville, turn north on Highway 3 and drive past Trinity Lake. At the Coffee

Creek Ranger Station, turn west on County Road 104 (Coffee Creek Road) and drive approximately 6.5 miles to Goldfield Campground. (A trailhead is available here, but you can shorten the trip to Boulder Lake from six miles to two by continuing farther.) At Goldfield Campground, turn left and drive about three miles on a Forest Service road, then turn right on Forest Service Road 37N42Y and drive one mile to a parking area and trailhead. (A map of Shasta-Trinity National Forest is required to reach the latter.)

19. STEELHEAD COTTAGES
Trinity River
Off Highway 299 near Big Flat

Sometimes money does make a difference, especially if you don't plan on spending much, yet want a first-class vacation. There's a place on the Trinity River that solves this dilemma, where you can stay in a cabin at night then play in the river by day, rafting or fishing. The summer is outstanding for easy rafting here, and there's good bank-fishing access in this area, with the best fishing occurring in fall and winter, when the salmon and steelhead make their run upstream on the Trinity.

The price is only $42.90 per night to rent the cabin, and only $25 to rent an inflatable kayak for a day on the Trinity River, including all gear and a shuttle ride. Fishing is free, with a current state license, of course, and the bonus is that this area has many of the best shorefishing spots on the entire Trinity River. This is the appeal of Big Flat, a little one-store settlement along Highway 299, about an hour-and-a-half drive either from Eureka or Redding.

What makes this trip work in the summer is the rafting. You get a chance at pure exhilaration at a sport that is far easier to learn and safer than most people believe. In a survey I conducted of rafting companies in the West, this $25 trip at Big Flat on the Trinity River turned out to be the least expensive among hundreds of white-water adventures.

The Trinity River is located in Northern California west of Redding, starting as a trickle in the Trinity Alps and then flowing westward for 100 miles, eventually joining with the Klamath River in its journey to the sea. It is a fountain of beauty, rolling pure through granite gorges and abounding with birds and wildlife. Because flows are controlled by upstream dam releases, white-water rafting levels are guaranteed throughout summer.

Near Big Flat, the Trinity is a "pool-and-drop" river, that is, it consists of long, deep pools sprinkled with sudden riffles and drops, making it perfect for rafting. Class II and III rapids such as Hell Hole, The Slot,

Fishing for steelhead on the Trinity River

Zig-Zag, Fishtail, Pinball, and others occur every five minutes or so, providing short bursts of pure thrill, then short rests to regain your composure. In the lexicon of rafting, a Class I rapid is easy, Class III is exciting, and Class V is dangerous; on this section of the Trinity, most of the rapids are Class II. No matter how hard your heart may pound when your raft is flushed out of a surging river hole, it is extremely safe; the most dangerous part of the trip by far is driving here.

The biggest surge in white-water sports is in the popularity of inflatable kayaks, which look something like rubber bullets. They are perfect for the Trinity, providing the opportunity to have fun right away. Larger, more traditional rafts—either paddle rafts or the big oar boats, the latter requiring a guide—are also available. They have virtually zero chance of flipping on the Trinity.

The inflatable kayaks are my favorite. You can make a headlong run into a water chute, become partially submerged in the river, then come popping up as you head downstream, paddling away. You can feel like a salmon darting about the currents. On our trip, we rounded a bend, then suddenly came upon several turtles sunning themselves on rocks. We also saw migrating salmon, blue herons, and deer. The lucky few may even spot otters playing in the swirling eddies.

When you finish a day like this then bed down in your own private cabin, you'll practically glow from happiness. At the same time, you can grin over how little you have spent for so much fun. For a river trip with a cottage, this is the cheapest deal around.

Facilities: Steelhead Cottages has five cabins, each with a full bathroom and kitchen and propane heat. Picnic tables and barbecues are available, and a fish-cleaning station and horseshoe pits are nearby. A fish smoking facility is also available. A small grocery store is nearby.

Reservations, fee: Reservations are advised from August through November. Cottages rent from $42.90 for two to $75.90 for four.

Insider's note: For rafting information, phone Trinity River Rafting at (800) 307-4837 or Bigfoot Rafting at (916) 629-2263. For a free directory of all 50 river outfitters in California and the rivers they specialize in, phone (800) 552-3625.

Who to contact: Phone Steelhead Cottages at (916) 623-6325, or write to HCR1, Box 62, Junction City, CA 96048.

Directions: From Interstate 5 at Redding, turn west on Highway 299 and drive through Weaverville, continuing for 23 miles to Big Flat. Look for Steelhead Cottages on the right side of the road.

If you are coming from U.S. 101 at Eureka, drive north to Arcata. Just past Arcata, turn east on Highway 299 and drive through Willow Creek, continuing for 40 miles to Big Flat. Look for Steelhead Cottages on the left side of the road.

20. CEDAR STOCK RESORT CABINS
Trinity Lake
Off Highway 3 near Weaverville

For years, my pal Kurt Rogers hauled his waterski boat from the Bay Area to Shasta Lake and never said a foul word about the place. Then one weekend, just on a lark, he decided to try Trinity Lake instead. Guess what? He's never been back to Shasta.

You know why? Because of all the people at Shasta and the comparatively few numbers of them at Trinity. It can make a huge difference. So does being able to stay in a cabin, which is provided in various sizes by Cedar Stock Resort.

Like Shasta Lake, Trinity Lake is huge, provides good camping, houseboating, waterskiing, and fishing for smallmouth bass and rainbow trout, and has a trailhead for hiking to the Trinity Alps Wilderness nearby. But you get these adventures without a lot of people around, because while it is a 20-minute shot up Interstate 5 to hit Shasta from Redding, it's a one-and-a-half-hour circuitous drive to reach Trinity. By going the extra miles, however, you get the extra juice.

The cabins at Cedar Stock are available by the week from June 16 through September 2, when families usually visit the lake, with special two-day deals available from April 1 to June 15, when fishermen are more apt to visit. The costs during the summer season are $425 (4-sleeper cabin), $525 (6-sleeper), $625 (8-sleeper) and $725 (10-sleeper) for a week. One of the best deals is during the spring fishing season, when two people can rent a cabin and get a free fishing boat rental plus a $25 credit for dinner, all for $180 for two nights. Additional discounts are available during the off-season, with cabins renting for $50 to $95 per day.

There are a few things you should know, however. Maid service is not available, and you are charged extra for bed linens. I suggest you bring either your own sheets or sleeping bags, along with towels. While the cabins provide a stove with oven, sink, and small refrigerator, it is a good idea to bring a large ice chest so you have plenty of room for produce and beverages. All cabins are equipped with cookware, plus a nearby barbecue. A restaurant, grocery store, marina, and boat ramp are all close.

Trinity is a great waterski lake, by virtue of quiet water and few speedboats. It is big enough, with 145 miles of shoreline, to provide plenty of room for everybody. To stay out of northwest winds, most waterskiers prefer the sheltered western shoreline. Yet bass fishers prefer the hidden fingers and coves along the eastern shoreline, so they almost never get in each other's way.

The fishing can be excellent, best for smallmouth bass. Though it takes a knack to develop the feel for their bite, using plastic worms or grubs on the lake bottom can get them. These are big, strong smallmouth, mainly two- to four-pounders, and they really let it rip when they get hooked. The state record smallmouth, at nine pounds, one ounce, was landed at Trinity; you can see it at Brady's Sportshop on Main Street in Weaverville. It was caught by owner Tim Brady, who always has insider news as to what is working.

Trinity was built primarily as a water storage facility for farming, and in turn, the one problem here can be serious water drawdowns in late summer. In drought years, the place can end up looking like a dust bowl. But in typical years when there is a big snowpack in the Trinity Alps, the high runoff from snowmelt keeps the lake near full all the way through Labor Day weekend.

Full of water, that is. It never seems to be full of people. Just ask my friend Kurt.

Facilities: Cedar Stock Resort has housekeeping cabins sized to sleep 4, 6, 8, or 10 people. A kitchen, bathroom, cookware, and dishes are provided, and a barbecue is available nearby. A restaurant, a grocery store, a marina, houseboat and boat rentals, and a launch ramp are available.

Reservations, fee: Reservations are often required during summer. Fees vary according to time of year. From June 16 to September 3, a two-person sleeper cabin rents for $425 per month. From April 1 to June 15, a four-person sleeper cabin rents for $180 for two nights and includes a fishing boat and $25 credit toward dinner. In the off-season, a four-person sleeper cabin rents for $50 per night or $325 per week.

Insider's note: Bring your own sheets or sleeping bags for the cabins.

Who to contact: Phone Cedar Stock Resort at (916) 286-2225 or (800) 982-2279, or write to 45810 State Highway 3, Trinity Center, CA 96091.

Directions: From Interstate 5 at Redding, turn west on Highway 299, drive over Buckhorn Summit and continue to Weaverville. In Weaverville, turn right on Highway 3 and drive about 15 miles to Cedar Stock Road. Turn right on Cedar Stock Road and drive a short distance to the resort office.

21. TRINITY LAKE BOAT-IN SITES
Shasta-Trinity National Forest
Off Highway 3 near Weaverville

You want to get away from it all? While Trinity Lake is a long way from just about everything, you can get even farther away with a short boat ride to a little island where there are just three boat-in tent sites. Get away from it all? Why here you're practically on another planet.

And if fate has it that those three camps are already taken upon your arrival, no problem… because just a short boat ride away are two other boat-in camps, both intimate and uncrowded settings. So what you have here is a distant lake and little-known camps, a chance to beat the crowds with scant effort.

Trinity Lake is located north of Weaverville in Northern California, at the foot of the Trinity Alps. It is a big lake with some 150 miles of shoreline (the exact amount depending on water levels). Warm summer temperatures make it outstanding for water sports, especially all kinds of boating and waterskiing, and in quiet coves, swimming and fishing. Because Shasta Lake north of Redding is so much faster to reach for most visitors, Trinity Lake is sometimes lost in the shadow of its bigger brother.

It is a long way away, a one-and-a-half-hour drive from Redding, four-plus hours from Eureka, five-plus from Sacramento, and six-plus from San Francisco. But knowing you have your own island awaiting helps speed the miles away. Once you arrive at the lake, you will discover that there are a number of boat ramps within short range of the boat-in campgrounds, with one just north of the Trinity Dam, and three others in the Stuart's Fork cove, including one at Cedar Stock Resort and Marina. Take your pick.

From any of these, it is a short ride to your destination, tiny Ridgeville Island, set between the long-reaching peninsula in the center of the lake and a point on the western shoreline of the Stuart Fork arm of the lake. Here's more good news: If the three campsites are filled at Ridgeville Island, there are other boat-in campgrounds on each side of the island. Ridgeville boat-in camp (11 tent sites) is located directly to the east on the western shore of the nearby peninsula, while Mariner's Roost boat-in camp (seven tent sites) is located just west of the island on the shore of the East Stuart Fork arm of the lake.

All of the campsites are relatively primitive, with no piped water available, but vault toilets, picnic tables, and fire grills are provided. No reservations are available and the camp is free. What, you think they'd charge? Heck, then someone would actually have to show up now and then to collect the fee. Way out here? You gotta be kidding.

To really add to the enjoyment of your trip bring a light tarp that can be rigged with poles and ropes to provide a sunscreen. Shade can be hard to come by out here, and on those hot summer afternoons, the blazing sun at camps without a sunscreen can turn the occupants into creatures resembling boiled lobsters. Are we having fun yet?

That aside, Trinity can be great for recreation. The water warms by mid-June in the main lake body, ideal for waterskiing or swimming in the secluded coves along the lake's protected and remote eastern shore. The fishing is also quite good for trout and bass. The trout fishing is best at Stuart Fork and the northern headwaters of the lake, but the real sizzle is provided by smallmouth bass. The bass average two to three pounds, are exceptionally strong, and will pick up a grub that is "walked" very slowly along the bottom of the lake, 6 to 15 feet deep, best done in the east shore's coves. It takes a certain touch to catch these fish, but it is worth taking the time to learn the touch.

If you want to extend your trip and explore further, the area has unlimited potential. Trailheads for hiking, eventually leading into the Trinity Alps Wilderness, are located both up Stuart Fork and Coffee Creek (north of the lake). Just below Trinity Dam is Lewiston Lake, a pretty lake always kept brimful, with a 10-mile-per-hour speed limit so things stay quiet. Just below the Lewiston Dam is the Trinity River, offering a special section for trophy-sized brown trout, and farther downstream are excellent opportunities for rafting and inflatable kayaks.

Facilities: Primitive campsites are available, with vault toilets, picnic tables, and fire grills. There is no piped water.

Reservations, fee: No reservation; no fee.

Insider's note: Cabins are available at Cedar Stock Resort and Marina; phone (916) 286-2225. Several drive-to campgrounds are located along the western shoreline of Trinity Lake.

Who to contact: Phone Shasta-Trinity National Forest at (916) 623-2121, or write to Weaverville Ranger District, P.O. Box T, Weaverville, CA 96093.

Directions: From Redding, turn west on Highway 299 and drive 48 miles to Weaverville. Turn north on Highway 3 and drive seven miles to the Stuart Fork arm of Trinity Lake. Boat launches are located at Stuart Fork. Note: To bypass Weaverville and save about 15 minutes of driving time, from Highway 299, turn north at the Lewiston/Road 105 exit (some twisties), and continue 15 miles to Highway 3.

22. LAKEVIEW TERRACE CABINS
Lewiston Lake
Off Highway 299 near Weaverville

Lewiston Lake has just about everything. It's a treasure of a lake that is always full, with alpine beauty, good trout fishing, a pretty stream, the nearby Trinity Alps to explore, and cabins to stay in. But it is what Lewiston does not have—loud, high-powered jet boats—that makes it most special.

A 10-mile-per-hour speed limit guarantees quiet water, making your experience at Lewiston intimate and tranquil, yet retaining the prospects for great adventure. After I bought my canoe, it was one of the first places I visited, and within minutes of launching, I remember how we were paddling across the lake, the conifer-lined mountain slopes reflected in a perfect mirrorlike image on the lake surface, the only sound being the dipping of paddles, which left little whirlpools with every stroke. From the far shore of the lake, we could see the snow-covered Trinity Alps.

After an experience like that, nothing extra is needed to make for a great trip. But at Lewiston, you get that something extra: a chance for excellent trout fishing on the lake, the opportunity to go rafting on the Trinity River, hiking nearby on the edge of the wilderness—and you can crown it each night by staying in one of the cabins at Lewiston Lake.

Lakeview Terrace has cabins sized at one, two, three, and four rooms, along with an adjacent resort and RV park. There is also a swimming pool and a small Laundromat. By the way, the cabins are distant enough from the RV park to provide privacy. Each cabin has a picnic table and a barbecue, making them fine for evening celebrations.

Celebration? What would you be celebrating? Why catching trout, of course. At times, the trout fishing at Lewiston is fantastic, especially when the Trinity Dam Powerhouse, located at the head of Lewiston Lake, is running, pouring water and feed right down the chute and into the head of the lake. This attracts many big fish, from Lakeview Terrace on upstream to the powerhouse.

When the powerhouse is running, head upstream in a boat, anchor in the current, then use a nightcrawler for bait, either drifting it in the flow or getting it near the bottom. Guess what? As long as that powerhouse is running, you'll have great fishing for big rainbow and brown trout, 14- to 20-inchers, and sometimes, just sometimes, even bigger. Wow!

When the powerhouse is not running, well, the fishing is still fair, best during the evening near the tules near Lakeview Terrace. There can be an impressive surface rise near sunset here, so good that fly-fishers will drive long distances for the chance to cast a fly to it.

And if you are out there, whether in a canoe, one of the rental boats, or even a float-tube, not once will you cringe at the far-off roar of a high-powered V-8 engine echoing across the lake, followed a moment later by the arrival of a speedboat barreling in your direction at 50 miles per hour. It won't happen because there are none. There never will be. Lewiston Lake will always be quiet and peaceful.

It will also remain full. From a hydrologist's standpoint, it is technically the afterbay for Trinity Lake, so while neighboring Trinity goes up and down, so much that it can look like two different places in April and October, Lewiston stays put, high and stable. If it sounds like my kind of place, well, you are right on.

Facilities: Each Lakeview Terrace cabin has a living room, dining area, fully equipped kitchen, bath with shower, and one or more bedrooms. Picnic tables with barbecues are provided nearby. A small marina with boat and motor rentals, a swimming pool, and a small Laundromat are available.

Reservations, fee: Reservations are advised. Fees range from $36 to $80 per day or $216 to $480 per week, depending on size of cabin and number in party.

Who to contact: Phone Lakeview Terrace Resort at (916) 778-3803, or write to Star Route Box 250, Lewiston, CA 96052.

Directions: From Interstate 5 at Redding, turn west on Highway 299, drive over Buckhorn Summit and continue for five miles to the Lewiston-Trinity Center turnoff. Turn right on Trinity Dam Boulevard, drive about 10 miles (five miles past Lewiston), and look for Lakeview Terrace Resort on the left side of the road.

23. TSASDI RESORT CABINS
Shasta Lake
Off Interstate 5 near Lakehead

The first thing most people want to know about this place is what does "Tsasdi" mean. Extensive research reveals that in the tongue of the Wintu Indians, "tsasdi" means "place of heavenly gatherings in little tepees." Incredible, eh?

Just kidding. Actually, it is just the name of some guy who owned the place back in the 1980s; it is pronounced "*Sauz*-dee."

But it might just as well mean "place of heavenly gatherings," except instead of tepees, you can have them in cabins with a view of the Sacramento River arm of Shasta Lake. Tsasdi Resort features 20 cabins that are in good shape, with knotty pine walls and air-conditioning. The cabins are always clean and well-maintained by owners who live here year-round.

Don't get the idea that these are lakeside cabins; there is no such thing at giant Shasta Lake. These cabins are set on a hillside about 100 feet above the water, but there is direct lake access via a stairway that leads down to it. A bonus here is that if you have your own boat, you can dock it here for free as long as you stay.

Even in drought years when the lake level is drawn down, the boat docks and lake remain accessible. In fact, access remains good until the lake is down nearly 120 feet, which occurs only in late summer in drought years. Typically, there is plenty of water year-round, even in late summer and early fall.

Shasta, of course, is the number one boating recreation lake in California. It is a huge lake, with 365 miles of shoreline and five major lake arms, and it is the Sacramento River arm adjacent to Tsasdi that is the best for waterskiing. Shasta can have a surface temperature of 80 degrees, but the flows of the Sacramento River near Lakehead will keep it relatively cool and refreshing. That makes it perfect for all water sports.

In the early summer, just as the heat is starting to warm up the lake, many trout will head upstream to find cool water where the Sacramento River enters the lake. This is why this area can be one of the best in the lake for trout fishing, trolling from the Lakehead Bridge on upstream. Bass fishing can also be good here, but they tend to be quite small, primarily spotted bass. It is usually a morning affair, fishing the bottom of coves and points with plastic worms. It takes a special touch, but if you have it, you can catch 20 or 30 small bass a session.

But what this lake is best known for, of course, is hot weather, warm water, gobs of suntan lotion, and lots of boats. What is lesser known is that it is best enjoyed in one of the cabins at Tsasdi Resort, "place of heavenly gatherings." Well, it might not be an exact translation, but hey, close enough.

Facilities: Tsasdi Resort has 20 air-conditioned cabins sized at one, two, and three bedrooms, all with bathrooms and kitchens with microwaves. Bed linens, cookware, and utensils are provided. There is also an outside deck with a picnic table and barbecue. A swimming pool with a lake view is available. Free boat slips and a boat ramp are nearby. A grocery store is located in the town of Lakehead. There are no boat rentals at Tsasdi's, although they can be found nearby at Antlers, Lakeshore, or Sugarloaf marinas.

Reservations, fee: Reservations are available. Cabin rates are usually by the week in the summer, $575 for a cabin that sleeps four, $1,075 for one that sleeps nine. In the off-season, it is possible to rent a cabin by the night for as low as $45, $55, and $165, depending on the size of the cabin. Boat docking is free.

Who to contact: Phone Tsasdi Resort at (916) 238-2575 or (800) 995-0291, or write to 19990 Lakeshore Drive, Lakehead, CA 96051. For a trout fishing guide, call Gary Mirales at (916) 275-2278; for a bass fishing guide, call Bill Tuch at (916) 547-3582.

Directions: From Redding, drive 24 miles north on Interstate 5 to the town of Lakehead. At Lakehead, take the Antlers exit. At the stop sign, turn left, drive under the freeway and arrive at Lakeshore Drive. Turn left on Lakeshore Drive and drive two miles, then look for the sign for Tsasdi Resort on the right side of the road.

24. SHASTA LAKE BOAT-IN SITES
Shasta-Trinity National Forest
Off Highway 299 near Bella Vista

Could there actually be any secrets about Shasta Lake? After all, Shasta is the capital of boating and water sports in the western United States, the largest reservoir in California with the space and facilities to handle two million visitors a year, and millions upon millions of drivers cruise right by it on adjacent Interstate 5. So what could be left to tell, right?

Heh, heh. What few know is that hidden up one of the lake arms is a three-acre island with a boat-in campground and several little trails. It is well out of sight of any roads, and out of mind of most campers.

Ski Island is located on the Pit River arm of the lake about three miles upstream of the Pit River Bridge. There are 29 boat-in campsites here, each with a picnic table provided and vault toilets available. While there is no piped water, typical for boat-in camping, it's the last free camp at Shasta Lake. After all, to collect your fee, they'd actually have to send a boat out here, right?

Never let the number of people at Shasta Lake scare you off. This place is big enough to handle all comers, even on three-day holiday weekends, when you can always find many quiet coves to call your own for a day. When full, the lake has 365 miles of shoreline, 1,000 campsites at 18 campgrounds, 16 boat ramps, 11 marinas with boat rentals, 425 houseboats for rent, and five resorts with lodging, but just one boat-in campground. There are 22 species of sport fish in the lake, and 50-fish days are common for bass from late winter through spring or early summer. Captivating tours are offered, including one through the limestone caves of Shasta Caverns, and another right inside the massive Shasta Dam.

The reservoir is so huge that each of its arms has the qualities of a different lake. Amid all this bigness there is nothing quite like the smallness of picking out your own campsite on a little obscure island that gets overlooked by most.

Even the closest boat ramp to Ski Island is quite distant. The best place to launch is at Silverthorn Resort, the most outlying of the resorts at the lake, located in a cove on the Pit River arm of the lake, nearly 15 miles from Interstate 5 and some 25 water miles by boat from Shasta Dam. After launching, you head up the Pit River arm, three miles past the Interstate 5/Pit River Bridge.

The lake is fullest in April, May, and June, and some of the campsites are quite close to where you moor your boat, requiring a very short walk. In the fall, after the lake has been lowered to deliver water for irrigation in the Central Valley, the walk uphill to the campground can be lengthened considerably. Regardless, you still end up with a campsite right on an island at Shasta Lake.

This is a fantastic lake for boating. The water is warm, typically 70 degrees by Memorial Day weekend and sometimes even in the low 80s by the Fourth of July. Waterskiing, swimming, fishing, and just playing in the lake is great stuff. Even in the spring, when runoff is high, this part of the lake has less debris than the main lake body, so waterskiing conditions are good. In addition, the Pit River arm, as well as the adjacent Squaw Creek arm to the immediate north, is loaded with cove after cove, so there is an endless supply of places to hide away if you want—or fish for bass and crappie, which love these spots, too.

A bonus is that the nearby proximity of Silverthorn provides the opportunity to get whatever you have forgotten. When camping, you always forget something, right? Of course! No problem, just cruise on over and pick it up. A telephone is available there, too, and I have used it, by the way, to make an urgent call to my editor over the pressing problem of the moment....

"My cooler's outta ice, I left my money back on the island, and I can't figure out how to start this story...now what'll I do?"

Facilities: There are 29 boat-in campsites at Ski Island, each with a picnic table provided and vault toilets available. There is no piped water.

Reservations, fee: No reservations; no fee for camping. A $2 boat launch fee and self-registration is charged by the Forest Service.

Insider's note: An option for boat-in camping with a great boat-in trailhead is located up the McCloud River arm of the lake in a cove at Greens Creek.

Who to contact: For information about boat-in camping at Ski Island, phone Shasta-Trinity National Forest at (916) 275-1589. For information about Shasta Lake, phone the Shasta Cascade Wonderland Association at (800) 474-2782, or write to 14250 Holiday Road, Redding, CA 96003.

Directions: From Redding, drive north on Interstate 5 for three miles to Highway 299 East. Turn east on Highway 299 and drive five miles to Bella Vista. In Bella Vista, turn left on Dry Creek Road and drive seven miles to a fork in the road. Bear right at the fork and drive to Jones Valley Boat Ramp (a left at the fork will take you to Silverthorn Resort). After launching your boat, head west (to the left) for four miles to Ski Island. Land your boat on shore and pick your campsite.

OTHER CABIN RENTALS NORTH OF SHASTA LAKE

Pine-Gri-La, P.O. Box 100, Castella, CA 96017; (916) 235-4466.

OTHER CABIN RENTALS NEAR TRINITY LAKE

Becker's Bounty, Route 2, Box 4659, Trinity Center, CA 96091; (916) 266-2377 or (916) 266-3594.

Bonanza King Resort, Route 2, Box 4790, Trinity Center, CA 96091; (916) 266-3305.

Coffee Creek Ranch, Route 2, Box 4940, Trinity Center, CA 96091; (916) 266-3343.

Enright Gulch Cabins, 3500 Highway 3, Trinity Center, CA 96091; (916) 266-3600.

Ripple Creek, Route 2, Box 4020, Trinity Center, CA 96091; (916) 266-3505.

OTHER CABIN RENTALS IN THE TRINITY RIVER AREA

Bigfoot Cabins, P.O. Box 98, Junction City, CA 96048; (916) 623-6088 or (800) 422-5219.

Red Hill Motel & Cabins, P.O. Box 234, Weaverville, CA 96093; (916) 623-4331.

River's Edge, P.O. Box 1006, Meadow Vista, CA 95722; (916) 878-7928.

Trinity Canyon Lodge, P.O. Box 51, Helena, CA 96048; (916) 623-6318.

Ziegler's Trails End, P.O. Box 150, Hyampom, CA 96046; (800) 566-5266.

Lassen-Modoc

** For locations of camps, see map on page 9. **

25. CLARK CREEK LODGE CABINS
Lake Britton
Off Highway 89 near Burney

The cabins at Clark Creek Lodge were the hideouts of a variety of nefarious and celebrated characters, from gangster Al Capone during the bootleg whiskey days to former heavyweight boxing champ Jack Dempsey. More recently, people from the Bay Area have used it as their hideaway rather than their hideout, taking advantage of the privacy, fishing and boating at adjacent Lake Britton, the fantastic waterfall walk at nearby McArthur-Burney Falls State Park, and hiking and fly-fishing along the Pit River.

The lodge mixes a lot of the old with a little of the new. The old includes the lodge headquarters, built in 1921, and many of the cabins. The new includes a steak/seafood restaurant and bar. Put it together and you'll discover how two different worlds can ride the same orbit.

The cabins are rustic enough for the lodge owners to allow pets (not on the beds), but all have showers and most have at least small refrigerators. They don't have kitchens, so visitors learn to make do for food; some end up at the restaurant for dinner half-starved. The rooms don't have televisions, radios, or telephones, either, and for that, we shouted in chorus, "Hallelujah!" One more highlight: Bed linens are provided. "Hallelujah! Hallelujah!"

Lake Britton is very pretty, steep-sided and deep blue, with good trout fishing in the spring and fall, and surprising crappie action and a sprinkling of bass in the summer. The boat ramp at McArthur-Burney Falls State Park offers boat rentals of many varieties, including aluminum boats with motors, canoes, and paddleboats.

The park is better known, however, for its 129-foot waterfall, which is wide and cascading, with miniature waterfalls oozing out of the adjacent moss-lined walls. It's a dramatic sight year-round and is especially awesome in the early summer. There is a great lookout of the waterfall on the far side on the Burney Falls Trail, a hike described in more detail in the book *Easy Hiking in Northern California* (Foghorn Press). The trip takes only an hour and we recommend it.

By the way, the park rangers here are mighty clever, because they figured out how to make it impossible to see the waterfall without paying the $5 state park day-use fee. They realized that visitors could easily park along the highway, then make a two-minute walk past the entrance station to a great lookout spot for the waterfall. So what'd they do? The rascals signed the highway shoulder "No Parking" near the entrance, so with no place to park, you have to drive in past the kiosk. Gets you every time.

Another nearby adventure for hikers as well as fly-fishers is along the Pit River below the dam at Lake Britton. It is an excellent fishing area, where trout will rise to a carefully presented caddis fly. Anglers should note, however, that the wading can be slippery, deep, and tricky, and your casts must have a light touch with precision to inspire consistent rises. I've seen some people just give up, sit down on a rock, and watch the water run by.

Dramatic McArthur-Burney Falls drops 129 feet

Facilities: Clark Creek Lodge has cabins of various sizes with bathrooms and propane heat. There are no kitchens. Bed linens and towels are provided, and barbecue facilities are available. A boat ramp is located nearby at the state park. A dinner restaurant is on the property, which opens at 5 P.M. and is closed on Mondays.

Reservations, fee: Reservations are accepted, and the phone is attended during the evening. Cabin rates range from a low of $35 to a high of $50 per night, with a two-night minimum stay.

Insider's note: The Pacific Crest Trail is routed from McArthur-Burney Falls State Park north along the Hat Creek Rim to Grizzly Peak, and with no predictable water sources for 40 miles, is considered the worst section of the 2,700-mile route.

Who to contact: Phone Clark Creek Lodge at (916) 335-2574, or write to Route 1, Box 800, Burney, CA 96013.

Directions: From Redding, turn east on Highway 299 and drive to the junction of Highway 299 and Highway 89. Turn left (north) on Highway 89 and drive 10 miles, past McArthur-Burney Falls State Park and Lake Britton to North Clark Creek Road. Turn left on North Clark Creek Road and drive 2.5 miles to Clark Creek Lodge on the right side of the road.

26. MILL CREEK BACKPACK SITES
South Warner Wilderness
Off U.S. 395 near Alturas

The trick in uncovering secret and beautiful wilderness campsites in California that require very short hikes is venturing to the most remote areas imaginable. One of those areas is in Modoc County, way out in the northeastern corner of the state. You just plain don't get more remote than this, especially in the South Warner Wilderness.

Yeah, there's no fast way to get here. It's too far away and that keeps people out. But if you are willing to trade a protracted drive for an undemanding backpack trip to a pristine wilderness stream, then pack your sleeping bag, turn the key, and head out here, where few people roam.

What you get here is a short hike, as short as 1.5 miles to Mill Creek, then the chance of exploring upstream along another four miles of stream, with pretty little campsites sprinkled along the way. This is first-class easy hiking and camping, with decent trout fishing, and it comes with the option of a bonus day trip for the ambitious: A significant climb up to Warren Peak, 9,770 feet elevation.

How long to get here? Long. The nearest town is Alturas, about a 30-minute drive from the trailhead; then add another three hours from Redding, six hours from Sacramento, or seven hours from San Francisco. Yow! Right: It's a tortuous drive.

The payoff starts when you finally park at the Soup Springs Trailhead, located on the western border of the South Warner Wilderness. It is only a 1.5-mile hike to Mill Creek, climbing up and over a short hill, then down into a valley. Here you will find your destination, with such little effort compared to most wilderness backpacking trips that even the newest newcomers will yearn for more.

And more they can get. This is a small, pristine mountain stream and hiking up to its headwaters and beyond can add another dimension to the trip. When you first reach the stream, you will arrive at a junction with the Slide Creek Trail. Turn left here, continuing on the Mill Creek Trail, venturing up into Mill Creek Meadow. The trail meanders along the west side of the stream, climbing very gently for the most part for three miles.

Mill Creek is a pristine stream, much of it edging through the meadow. It is a good trout stream, but requires sneak-fishing techniques, approaching low and quiet, keeping your shadow and casting motion off the water. Do that during the evening bite and you have a chance to catch one of the more unique strains of rainbow trout, very dark and chunky, quite unlike their Slim Jim silvery counterparts of the high Sierra.

A great but grueling side trip to Warren Peak is also possible out of Mill Creek Meadow. To put it in perspective, consider that it is about four miles of hiking from the Soup Springs Trailhead up to the end of Mill Creek Meadow, all easy and pretty. It is another four miles to Warren Peak, but it is anything but a stroll, climbing 3,200 feet.

From the north end of Mill Creek Meadow, the trail begins to climb, steeply at times, up the western slopes of the Warner Range, for the first mile following the headwaters of Mill Creek. The trail then turns north away from the stream, junctions with the Summit Trail and climbs two miles to the peak.

Warren Peak is a great lookout and provides a perfect perspective to scan this unusual landscape. Both north and south is the Warner Range—rugged, high (compared to the adjoining lands), and remote—with rich woods and water along its nearby western slopes. Yet farther to the west is the high desert country of Modoc County, and to the east are miles and miles—as far as you can see—of the Nevada high wastelands, all of it dry, godforsaken country where it seems there isn't another soul in the universe.

Out here, that is often true.

Facilities: There are a series of primitive wilderness backpack campsites along Mill Creek. Plan on relying completely on yourself. Pets are permitted.

Reservations, fee: No reservation; no fee. A wilderness permit is required for overnight use and is available at the Warner Ranger District address below.

Insider's note: Because of early snowmelt here, this trail is one of the first to become accessible in mountain wilderness areas in Northern California.

Who to contact: Phone the Warner Ranger District at (916) 279-6116, or write to Modoc National Forest, P.O. Box 220, Cedarville, CA 96104. For a map of the area, send $3 to USDA-Forest Service, 630 Sansome Street, San Francisco, CA 94111 and ask for Modoc National Forest. To obtain a topographic map, send $3.50 to Maps-Western Distribution Center, U.S. Geologic Survey, Box 25286-Federal Center, Denver, CO 80225 and ask for Eagle Peak.

Directions: From U.S. 395 at the south end of Alturas, turn east on County Road 56 and drive six miles to the boundary of Modoc National Forest. Turn south on West Warner Road (Forest Service Road 5) and drive about 13 miles to the sign for Soup Springs Campground. Turn east on Forest Service Road 40N24 and drive 3.5 miles, just past Soup Springs Campground, to the end of the road, where there is a parking area. The trailhead is located adjacent to the parking area.

27. PADILLA'S RIM ROCK RESORT CABINS
Near Lassen Volcanic National Park
Off Highway 44 near Old Station

Padilla's Rim Rock is named after the Hat Creek Rim of the north Lassen volcanic plateau country, but is better known for its nearby proximity to Hat Creek and Lassen Volcanic National Park.

Hat Creek is a fine trout stream, well stocked along Highway 89 to the north, with access at several Forest Service camps along the road. But some people staying in cabins at Padilla's just walk right across the street and start fishing. The limit is five trout. (Note that the special wild trout section of Hat Creek, entirely catch-and-release using artificial lures with single barbless hooks, is located off Highway 299.)

Lassen Park, of course, is famous for its great hiking, ported thermal activity, wilderness lakes, and Lassen summit climb. Padilla's is located 14 miles from the northern park entrance at Manzanita Lake, where a catch-and-release fishery for large native trout provides a popular challenge. Hiking is excellent at Lassen, topped by the two-hour (one-way) summit climb with an outstanding view to the north of Mt. Shasta.

The cabins at Padilla's run the gamut when it comes to quality. Two new log cabins are really quite nice, and come completely furnished with everything but towels. The others range from fair to decent, including a few old cabins that are on what some would call the rustic side. But even these do fine if you're just looking for a notch up from a campground.

A little country store fronts the property, a cute little place that the owners call, "The biggest little store in Shasta County." A lot of trips have been salvaged thanks to that store, because no matter what you forget, they are likely to have it.

Facilities: Padilla's has 10 cabins of varying sizes and age. Bathrooms, kitchens with cookware and utensils, and bed linens are provided. Bring your own towels. A small grocery store is available on the property.

Reservations, fee: Reservations are accepted; cabin rates are $36, $48, $70, and $75 per night, depending on size and age of cabin.

Insider's note: For fishing information, phone Vaughn's Sporting Goods in Burney at (916) 335-2381.

Who to contact: Phone Padilla's Rim Rock Resort at (916) 335-7114, or write to 13275 Highway 89, Old Station, CA 96071.

Directions: From Redding, take Highway 44 east for 48 miles to the junction of Highway 44/89. Turn left (north) on Highway 44/89 and drive 14 miles to Old Station. Continue for two miles and look for Padilla's on the right side of the road.

28. MILL CREEK RESORT CABINS
Near Lassen Volcanic National Park
Off Highway 172 near Mineral

Like most people, we found out about the cabins at Mill Creek completely by accident.

We had heard about Drakesbad Resort in the remote Warner Valley area of Lassen Volcanic National Park, then discovered there is a one- to two-year waiting list at Drakesbad, and the way most people get in is by signing up on a list and waiting for a cancellation. That didn't fit our plans, but my old friend John Reginato, the former general manager of the Shasta Cascade Wonderland Association, told us about a place just south of Lassen Park in the national forest that was fairly remote and had good fishing and hiking nearby.

It turned out to be Mill Creek Resort and it is just unknown enough that cabins are usually available, yet sits in the middle of a great outdoor recreation area. It is east of Red Bluff in Lassen National Forest at 4,800 feet in elevation, just off remote Highway 172, a little loop road off the main highway that bypasses the Morgan Summit. The reason the place gets missed by so many is because nobody takes the Highway 172 bypass by accident; unless their destination is the little town of Mill Creek, they don't usually make the trip. In addition, there are no other businesses of any kind on little Highway 172. So right off, you have a relatively secret spot.

The resort has nine rustic cabins, all sized at one or two bedrooms, complete with a small kitchen and bathrooom. As cabins go, they are quite inexpensive, just $40 for a one-bedroom job, $70 for two bedrooms. The lodge has a small grocery store and a coffee shop, with the latter open from morning through evening.

A highlight here is nearby Mill Creek, and we mean the stream, not the town. From the town of Mill Creek, turn south on the Forest Service road and drive three miles to a parking area and trailhead. There is a great evening walk along the stream, which babbles and courses its way around rocks and into pools.

Mill Creek can provide fair fishing for trout, best when fly-fishing during the evening bite, usually with weighted nymphs and more rarely with small dry flies. If you are coming here primarily to fish, not hike, it is critical that you have a map of Lassen National Forest and a rulebook from the Department of Fish and Game. The reason is that there is some private land along Mill Creek, and if you spend several days exploring the river, you can risk crossing private property and raising the ire of somebody. The Forest Service map will keep you out of trouble. As for the DFG rulebook, some stretches of Mill Creek are catch-and-release, although a good chunk of it is stocked with trout that you can keep. The DFG plants about 2,000 rainbow trout that are 10- to 12-inches long each year in Mill Creek.

Sooner or later, however, you will find yourself making the 15-minute drive north to the entrance of Lassen Volcanic National Park, then exploring for at least a day or two.

There are several trailheads near the park entrance that make for great hikes. Just beyond the entrance, near the Southwest Information Center at the Southwest Campground, is the trailhead for a hike of about a mile out to Mill Creek Falls, which is great in early summer. If you drive farther into the interior of the park, you'll see the trailhead for Bumpass Hell on the east (right) side of the road (Highway 89), and here you can walk through a land of steam vents, boiling mud pots, and hot springs, all set in a prehistoric-looking volcanic setting.

When your adventures are complete at Lassen, instead of competing for a campground at the national park, you will have your little cabin waiting for you back in Lassen Forest at Mill Creek.

You may find the place by accident, but the good time that follows is no accident at all.

Facilities: Mill Creek Resort has nine one- and two-bedroom cabins with bathrooms, kitchens, and propane heat. One cabin has a fireplace. Bed linens, cookware, and eating utensils are provided. Pets are permitted. A small grocery store and coffee shop are available at the lodge.

Reservations, fee: Reservations are available. Cabin rates are $40 per night for a one-room cabin, $70 per night for a two-room cabin, with no minimum stay required.

Insider's note: For a recreation packet on the area, phone the Shasta Cascade Wonderland Association at (800) 474-2782. A map/brochure of Lassen Volcanic National Forest is available for free at the park entrance station when paying the $5 day-use fee.

Who to contact: Phone Mill Creek Resort at (916) 595-4449, or write to No. 1, Highway 172, Mill Creek, CA 96061. For a map of the area, send $3 to Office of Information, U.S. Forest Service, 630 Sansome Street, San Francisco, CA 94111 and ask for Lassen National Forest.

Directions: From Interstate 5 at Red Bluff, take the Highway 36 exit and drive east on Highway 36 to the town of Mineral. In Mineral, turn right on Highway 172 and drive six miles to the town of Mill Creek. In Mill Creek, look for the sign for Mill Creek Resort on the right side of the road.

29. LASSEN VIEW RESORT CABINS
Lake Almanor
Off Highway 89/36 near Chester

Some people go cabin camping for one reason: They can do all the things they can't do at home.

Dirty clothes on the floor? Who cares! Dirty dishes stacked up in the sink? Perfect place for them! Fishing equipment scattered everywhere? Easier to keep track of! A few empty bottles and cans? Easier to dispose of all at once!

Well, while not everybody is a slob when they go camping, you certainly have the chance to be one at Lassen View Resort at Lake Almanor. This is a place where you just tend not to worry about anything except the weather and having a good time. And while a fair number of families stay here in the summer, it is better known as the number-one fishing and hunting retreat around in the spring and fall, respectively. Guess what? Nobody turns into bigger slobs faster than a group of fishermen or hunters when they have the chance.

Lassen View Resort has 17 cabins in a campground setting, located on the eastern shore of Lake Almanor, a five-minute boat drive from one of the best fishing spots on the lake at Big Springs. This is a classic "fish camp," that is, it has everything for the angler, including cabins, a tackle shop, a store, and a small marina with boat ramp and boat rentals, Plus there are guides and all the blarney, er, I mean, advice, you can listen to.

Almanor is a very pretty lake, big (13 miles long) and often full, ringed by pines and firs, set at 4,600 feet in elevation near Lassen National Forest. Chester, the small town set at the north end of the lake, has supplies and a few restaurants, as well as a small airport. Nearby there are many other recreation options, including a remote and beautiful section of Lassen Volcanic National Park, Butt Lake, the Feather River, and thousands of acres of national forest.

Because there is no direct route to Almanor, unlike Tahoe or Shasta, the long, circuitous drive keeps some vacationers away. In addition, except for during midsummer, the weather scares off a lot of other folks. It gets very cold here in the winter, and hey, the lake can even freeze over by the end of January. That is why Lassen View Resort is typically open from May 1 through November 1.

But it's the chance for salmon and large trout that attracts most people to Almanor. I remember the first morning I spent fishing here. I caught five salmon that weighed a collective 25 pounds, and after each hookup, every one had runs of 35 and 40 yards, like they were trying to bore a hole to China. I just held on for the ride with my little spinning rod while guide Dan Barkhimer laughed at my predicament. What usually happens, I have since learned, is that you show up in the spring or early summer, spend a day or two locating the fish and figuring out the best strategies, then finally catch a few, sometimes just one or two, but they are apt to be five-pounders, maybe even bigger.

The best time for fishing is in May and June, then again in September and October. It can also be cold, rainy, and windy here in these months, although there are always periods of great weather, too. The best weather months are July and August, of course, but the fishing is only fair in the summer, decent for smallmouth bass. To make the resort attractive to families in midsummer, Lassen View sets up a volleyball net and a swimming and suntan dock on the shore of the lake, and occasionally holds evening bonfires.

What I like to do here is show up in May with some pals, then get up before dawn and eat a quick breakfast. I'll toss the dishes on the pile in the sink, wade past the clothes on the floor, gather up some fishing gear, and head out the door. By daybreak, we'll be cruising north to Big Springs, the sun sending its first glows on Mt. Lassen in the distance, and as we make our first casts, we'll be wondering how big a fish might take our hooks that day....

For people who know what is possible at Lake Almanor, that is all the enticement ever needed.

Facilities: There are 17 cabins available, ranging from two to five rooms. Stoves, refrigerators, all kitchen utensils, linen, and bedding are provided, and outside each cabin is a small deck, chair, picnic table, and fire ring with grill. A small grocery store, tackle shop, hamburger café, coin-operated washer and dryer are available. A boat launch, dock, swimming area, small marina with boat and motor rentals, gas, and fish-cleaning facility are nearby. Leashed pets are permitted in the campground. There are also 50 spaces for motor homes and 20 spaces for tents. In the campground, piped water, a rest room with showers, fire pits with grills, and picnic tables are available, with the size of facilities varying for each site. Restaurants are located in nearby Chester.

Reservations, fee: Reservations are advised; $56 to $80 fee per night for cabins.

Insider's note: Two fishing guides can just about guarantee your fishing success: Dan Barkhimer, for salmon and trout, and Mark Jimenez, for smallmouth bass, fly-fishing for trout, and nearby lakes. Either can be contacted through the Lassen View store.

Who to contact: Phone Lassen View Resort at (916) 596-3437, or write to 7457 Highway 147, Lake Almanor, CA 96137.

Directions: From Interstate 5 at Red Bluff, turn east on Highway 36 and drive about 75 miles to the junction with Highway 89. Turn south on Highway 89/36 and continue to the lake. As you approach the lake, continue straight on Highway 36. Drive through Chester and across the spillway at the north end of the lake. One mile past a lakeside rest stop, turn right (south) on County Road A13 and drive about four miles. The road will cross over the Hamilton Branch, then junction with Highway 147. Turn right and drive about one mile. Look for the large sign on the right side of the road for Lassen View Resort.

30. EAGLE LAKE CABINS
Lassen National Forest
Off Highway 36 near Susanville

With every blessing there seems to come an equal curse. So it is at Eagle Lake.

Eagle Lake has big trout, real big, like 18- to 20-inchers on average with five-pounders pretty common. The documented lake record was a smidgen over 11 pounds, and there are reports of even bigger fish. That is the blessing. The curse? Go forth and you will discover. It's the wind. It can really howl out here on the edge of the high desert in Lassen County, whipping huge yet shallow Eagle Lake to a froth, a common enough event to earn the respect of nearly every visitor.

What to do? No problem. You go and hide out in your cabin for a little extraneous recreation until the wind lays down, which will likely be the next morning, and then head out again.

Headquarters for Eagle Lake is the little town of Spaulding Tract, set on the western shore of the lake. This is where the Heritage Land Company operates a park with 30 cabins, all with bathrooms, kitchens, and propane heat. Some of the cabins have views of the lake. The place is more of a "fish camp" than anything else, with no linens or towels provided. You'd best bring a sleeping bag, a pillow, and plenty of towels or you'll discover yourself in a heck of a fix.

Eagle Lake is a big lake, with more than 100 miles of shoreline, and it is set at 5,100 feet in Lassen Forest near Susanville. From anywhere else but there, it is a long drive, and because of that many people never make the trip. But the place is unique, not only for its setting on the transition zone from forest to high desert, but for its alkaline nature that creates the perfect habitat for fast-growing Eagle Lake trout.

The boat ramp is located only a half-mile from the cabins, making it a snap to get from bed to the lake. It's a good thing, too, because with that wind, you need to be out very early. The vision of giant Eagle Lake trout should provide enough inspiration when your alarm clock goes off. Get out at dawn, get your fishing done and then get the heck off the water. Though there are days when it never blows (most common in the fall), in summer your fishing day is often over by 10 A.M. By 10:30 A.M., you're fishing on borrowed time; by 11 A.M., you're a fool; and by noon, if you're still out there and the wind is roaring, I'll start praying we don't have to fish you out of Davy Jones' locker.

The fishing is best in the fall, from mid-September to mid-October, when you can troll needlefish or other lures and catch surprising numbers of three- and four-pound trout, sometimes bigger. In the summer, from Memorial Day through July, the fishing is usually decent enough, not great, with the wind haunting late risers.

As the weather gets colder and colder as winter sets in, those big trout just seem to get hungrier and hungrier. You can even shorefish from the north end of the lake, using a nightcrawler for bait just outside the tules, and catch many huge trout. In late December, when the lake ices over, we've seen locals fishing through the ice, catching one after another. My pal John Korb made one trip where he saw a fellow use a weighted nymph to catch and release 17 trout in three hours, the biggest a seven-pounder.

How cold does it get here in the winter? Well, it got so cold in the winter of '95 that this cat kept licking itself to stay warm. In the spring, its litter was born wearing miniature sweaters.

Facilities: There are 30 cabins in various sizes, each with a bathroom and kitchen. Cooking utensils, dishes, and silverware are provided, but no bedding or towels. Bring your own sleeping bag and towels. A boat ramp is available one-half mile away. A small store is located at a nearby RV park and a grocery store is available in Spaulding Tract.

Reservations, fee: Reservations are rarely required. Cabin fees range from $45 per night to $85 per night, depending on the size of the cabin but not the number of people in a group. Weekly rates are available, typically costing $250 with a $50 cleaning deposit.

Insider's note: The fishing season at Eagle Lake is different from other areas of California. It runs from Memorial Day weekend through December 31.

Who to contact: Phone Eagle Lake Cabins (Heritage Land Company) at (916) 825-2131, or write to 686-920 Spaulding Road, Eagle Lake, CA 96130.

Directions: From Redding, drive east on Highway 44 to Highway 44/89. Turn right on Highway 44/89 and drive 45 miles to Highway 36. Continue east on Highway 36 for about four miles to County Road A1. Turn left on County Road A1 and drive to Spaulding on the shore of Eagle Lake. In Spaulding, turn right on Spaulding Road and drive 1.5 miles. Look for the sign for Heritage Land Company on the right side of the road.

31. SPANISH SPRINGS RANCH CABINS
Ravendale
Off U.S. 395 near Susanville

From my vantage point in the saddle, I could just make out the silhouette of a lone rider on horseback. My own horse, Rusty, let out a snort. Apparently he wanted an apple or something. "Good horsey," I said, patting him on the neck. But no amount of "good horseys" could calm Rusty. Perhaps he too had spotted the approaching stranger, and it had made him nervous.

From this distance, I couldn't tell if the stranger was armed or not. I did see the reflected gleam of a concho on the seat, er saddle, likely stolen from a bandolero south of the border. He was a big man, and silent, too, and he rode his horse calmly and slowly as if taunting me, cutting a route down the hillside and under an oak tree toward where I had taken my stand, all the while alternating his stare from the trail and back to me.

A light, cold breeze made my neck tingle. I checked my supply of bullets, but they were gone. Wait a minute, I didn't even have my six-shooter. I was a sitting duck.

Finally the stranger approached, pulled his horse to a stop, and after eyeing me from 10 feet, spoke slowly and with a fixed glare. He had a slight drawl to his voice.

"Man, my butt is sore," he said. "How's yours?"

It turned out to be Gary Voet, fellow outdoors writer, an outlaw riding horseback on the Modoc plateau country. Outlaw? Yeah, the guy had stolen my apple and given it to his own horse, Spot. No wonder Spot did whatever Gary said. He didn't even have to say, "Good horsey."

"The sun be gettin' a little low in the sky," Gary said, speaking slowly and surely, letting you know just by the way he talked that he had survived great hardship, maybe even drank water out of a hoof print during the drought. "We'd best be gettin' back to the ranch."

The ranch, in this case, was Spanish Springs Ranch, a huge spread in northeastern California's Madeline Plains, high-desert sagebrush country where there are still miles and miles to roam on horseback, cows to tend, and steaks to eat.

We rode in and dismounted, attempting to walk as if our butts didn't hurt, and then sauntered in to the ranch house. Out here in Modoc country, they eat steak and not chicken, they drink beer in a bottle and not wine, and they get up too damn early in the morning for my taste. But when you're playing cowboy or cowgirl, there are sacrifices that just have to be made.

After our prodigious appetites had been satisfied, our group broke up to get a little shuteye. After all, the morning comes early out here. Some people stayed in log cabins, others in suites with mini-kitchens, and still others in private rooms in the bunkhouse. In the darkness, I was just about to drift off to sleep when I heard a coyote yip in the distance. It was lonely. I thought about yipping back, but I had much to think about: consider the business of tomorrow.

What to do? We could roam off and try to find the herd of buffalo at the ranch. We could go for a trail ride, maybe head up on the hills for a panoramic view that stretches hundreds of miles across the high desert. Maybe see if we could spot antelope or do some fishing.

In the fall during the waterfowl season, Spanish Springs provides an excellent location for hunting geese. This is also when the major cattle drives and horse drives are scheduled, when it really does feel something like the Old West, complete with sore butt. Other possible activities include a hay wagon ride, archery, trapshooting, swimming, and tennis.

And by the way, when you come here, I suggest you bring an extra apple. With an apple, you have a lot better chance of getting your horse to walk, turn, and stop than trying the "Good horsey" strategy.

Facilities: Spanish Springs Ranch has four log cabins, 14 suites with mini-kitchens, six duplex units, and three private rooms in a bunkhouse. Bathrooms and bed linens are provided but kitchens are not available except in the suites. All meals are provided ranch-style. Pets are allowed at the main ranch but not at the working cattle ranch.

Reservations, fee: Reservations are available. Cabin rates are $145 per day, including all meals and activities (such as horseback riding). A room in the bunkhouse is $115, a duplex room is $120 and the suites are $125, all including meals and activities. From October 1 through April 30, weekend getaway specials are $299 per couple, including meals, lodging, and activities.

Insider's note: Overnighters and trail riders are always welcome. The cowboy cattle drives at Spanish Springs Ranch are scheduled during spring and fall and last seven days and six nights.

Who to contact: Phone Spanish Springs Ranch at (916) 234-2050, (800) 272-8282, or (800) 560-1900, or write to P.O. Box 70, Ravendale, CA 96123.

Directions: From Red Bluff, turn east on Highway 36 and drive 107 miles to Susanville. From Susanville, turn east on U.S. 395 and drive 17 miles to Litchfield. From Litchfield continue north on U.S. 395 for about 30 miles. Look for the signed entrance road (three flagpoles and lighted sign) to Spanish Springs Ranch on the right side of the road.

OTHER CABIN RENTALS NEAR EAGLE LAKE

Eagle Lake RV Park & Cabins, 687-125 Palmetto Way, Eagle Lake, CA 96130; (916) 825-3133.

Sonoma-Mendocino

** For locations of camps, see map on page 9. **

32. BELL GLEN RESORT COTTAGES
Eel River
Off U.S. 101 near Leggett

"What the heck do you do in Leggett?" a friend asked me.

The best answer to that is: "Absolutely nothing."

Because the best way to spend your time here is to indulge yourself, taking trips to the 24-hour sauna, swimming in the adjacent South Fork Eel River, reading a book or doing whatever else you can think of on the cottage decks overlooking the redwoods, and enjoying the food, quiet, and tranquillity.

Sure, there are many great adventures available nearby, most notably visiting the redwood parks or fishing the Eel River, but when you settle down in one of the cottages at Bell Glen Resort, you will find ambition replaced with heavenly languor. In other words, you can do nothing, and that's not only just fine, it can be your only pursuit here.

It works because Bell Glen has six cottages that rate "adorable," complete with teddy bears (no kidding). It's the first time I've gone camping with a teddy bear, but I liked it. Other features include a cottage with a "tub for two" (now this is getting interesting) and another with a small Jacuzzi on the deck (this is getting really interesting). The resort also has low-cost cabins and hostel dorm rooms in a variety of configurations.

Bell Glen Resort is located in Leggett, near the junction of highways 1 and 101 in northern Mendocino County, amid the southern range of the Redwood Empire. To the immediate north is Standish-Hickey State Recreation Area (camping, hiking), Smithe Redwoods State Reserve (access to the Eel River), and Richardson Grove State Park (hiking in giant old-growth redwoods). The northern Mendocino coast is only a 35-minute drive away via Highway 1.

In the summer, the river is reduced to a trickle, sprinkled with warm pools ideal for swimming. One of the best spots is a short walk just below the cottages. The hole is 14 feet deep, perfect for swimming all summer. In the winter, it can be a good fishing spot as well.

Many summer swimming holes become fishing holes when the Eel River attracts salmon and steelhead in late fall and winter. In fact, in the winter, the stretch of South Fork Eel River from Leggett on downstream to Garberville can provide some of the better steelhead fishing in California, although river conditions and fish migrations are unpredictable. Shorefishing access is best in Cooks Valley and south of Benbow. As steelhead are a migratory fish, timing is everything. It's an "interception fishery" where you get one chance for each fish as they swim upstream.

Sure, there is actually a lot to do near Leggett year-round. But with the setup at Bell Glen Resort, you may not want to do anything at all.

Facilities: Bell Glen Resort has six unique cottages, each with a bathroom and bed linens but no kitchen. Each cottage has a private redwood deck and view of the Eel River, and two cottages have a tub sized for two. Another cottage has a Jacuzzi on the deck with a privacy curtain and another has a fireplace. Included each day is breakfast, wine, and maid service. A sauna and Jacuzzi (both swimsuit optional) and a nearby swimming hole (swimsuit required) are available. A restaurant and small pub are located at the resort. A community kitchen is also available.

The resort also has a hostel/dorm (six buildings) with a community kitchen and bathhouse. Pets and smoking are not permitted inside the buildings.

Reservations, fee: Reservations are available. Cottage rates are $95 to $140 per night for two people, depending on accommodations, with discounts for the third night. Hostel rates are $15 per night per person, including a do-it-yourself breakfast.

Insider's note: Maps with 11 self-guided day trips are provided to guests by owner Gene Barnett.

Who to contact: Phone Bell Glen Resort at (707) 925-6425, or write to 70400 Redwood Highway 101, Leggett, CA 95585.

Directions: From San Francisco, take U.S. 101 north for 185 miles (44 miles past Willits) to Leggett. When you reach Leggett, continue north on U.S. 101 for two miles, and look for the sign for Bell Glen Resort on the left side of the road.

33. HOWARD CREEK RANCH CABINS
Mendocino Coast
Off Highway 1 near Westport

Why can't life be like this all the time? Imagine this: A beautiful cottage with an ocean view, a 30-second walk to a long, pristine beach, a hot tub and sauna, a wood stove fired up when you want it, and more, all set on the remote north Mendocino coast, one of the most divine stretches of ocean frontage anywhere.

While life can't be like this all the time, it can last for as long as you decide to stay at one of the cabins at Howard Creek Ranch. For a lot of people, a vacation here is like a fantasy. When they get back home, they ask, "Did that really happen?" The answer is yes, it really did.

When you drive north of Fort Bragg on Highway 1, you will notice how with each passing mile, there are fewer and fewer people. By the time you reach Westport, about a 20-minute drive, the number of people has dwindled to a handful, the coastal beauty is spectacular, and when you drive another three miles to Howard Creek Ranch, it can feel like you are entering the front door of paradise.

The place has three cabins, including one with a small, private Jacuzzi on a deck. Four rooms in a renovated barn and four more in the lodge are also available. A hot tub and sauna are available, and the way it usually works is that they are used on an individual couple basis, with guests taking turns so privacy is always retained. Everything near the cabins is cozy, pretty (flowers everywhere), and quiet. Yet the grounds cover 40 acres with a year-round creek, ocean views, horses, and a few cows.

The property adjoins Westport Union Landing State Beach, about a 30-second walk from the cabins across the road and down to the beach. It's a long sandy beach, and at low tide you can walk it for three miles. No, yer not dreamin'. From the cabins, the ocean is close enough not only to see, but to hear.

You will notice horses roaming and grazing at the ranch, and sure enough, one of the bonuses here is that you can go for a horseback ride, not only a private ride at the ranch, but even right down on the beach. In addition, you can also arrange for a horse-and-carriage tour on the dirt roads of the ranch. What? You say riding a horse makes your butt sore? No problem: You can schedule for a personal, professional massage.

This is camping? Sure. You haven't camped like this before? Then you've got a lot to learn.

Facilities: Howard Creek Ranch has three cabins, four rooms in a lodge, and four rooms in a renovated barn. Each cabin has a bathroom (one has a nice outhouse), microwave, refrigerator, and wood stove. One cabin has a Jacuzzi on its deck. Full ranch-style breakfast is provided. Barbecues are available. A hot tub and sauna (swimsuits optional) are available, usually on a private basis. A grocery store is available three miles to the south in Westport.

Reservations, fee: Reservations are advised. Cabin rates are $55, $115, and $145 per night, depending on the level of accommodations, two-night minimum on weekends. Rates for rooms range from $69 to $145 per night, two-night minimum on weekends. Horseback rides cost $30 per hour. Horse-and-carriage rides are $10 per person.

Insider's note: The Sinkyone Wilderness is accessible to hikers on the Lost Coast Trail. The southern trailhead is located at Usal Campground. Few people know the exact directions: From Howard Creek Ranch, drive north on Highway 1 for 10 miles to Milepost 90.99. Turn left onto County Road 431 (a dirt road, often unsigned) and drive six miles to the Usal Campground and trailhead.

Who to contact: Phone Howard Creek Ranch at (707) 964-6725, or write to P.O. Box 121, Westport, CA 95488.

Directions: From San Francisco, take U.S. 101 and drive 141 miles north to Willits. In Willits, turn west on Highway 20 and drive 35 miles to Fort Bragg and Highway 1. At Highway 1, turn north and drive 15 miles to Westport. In Westport, continue for three miles north. At Mile Marker 80.49, look for Howard Creek Ranch on the right side of the road.

---

34. SURFWOOD HIKE-IN CAMP
MacKerricher State Park
Off Highway 1 near Fort Bragg

One of the most pleasant shocks of exploring the Mendocino coast was discovering Surfwood Hike-In Camp. It came as a total surprise, a secluded and beautiful walk-in campground that gets overlooked by most people simply because it takes a one- to three-minute walk to reach one of the 10 campsites.

MacKerricher State Park provides a huge and popular series of campgrounds, 142 sites in all, and it always seems to be full during the summer. In addition, this is the only state park on the Northern California coast that has just about everything: a beautiful beach set in an ocean cove, tidepools on a reef that extend out to a harbor seal rookery, a small lake stocked with rainbow trout, a forest with deep-grained bishop pines, two great hikes, and one excellent bicycle route. In addition, day-use access (and a nice brochure) are free. Imagine that. With all this, MacKerricher is hardly a secret, one of most popular parks on the coast, despite its geographical isolation.

But guess what? These 10 hike-in camps get overlooked anyway. We visited on an August weekend, right during the peak vacation season, with warm, blue-sky weather that had locals and out-of-towners filling the parking lots and drive-in camps. But at Surfwood Hike-In Camp, only four of the 10 campsites were taken, and of the remaining six that were available, five of them were very special. But they were empty!

Campsites 7 to 10 require about a three-minute walk and provide glimpses of the ocean. Campsites 2 to 6 require a one- to two-minute walk and are secluded in lush greenery and forest. Only Campsite 1 is a dud, located about 30 feet from the parking area, right next to the rest room. Each campsite has a flat tent site, picnic table, and food locker, with water available at the rest room adjacent to the parking area.

The trail in is flat, making it easy to make repeat trips to the car in

Fishing from a rubber raft on Lake Cleone near Surfwood Hike-In Camp

order to haul in whatever gear you need. Once you have your camp set, you can take the trail farther out and within minutes it will route you to the parking area for a protected beach and the trailhead for the Headlands Trail.

This is a short walk, much of it on a raised, wooden boardwalk, which extends to a seal-watching station and tidepools, one of the best places on the Pacific Coast to see harbor seals. Just a short distance away, the seals lay on rocks sunbathing, occasionally turning their heads to get a glance at arriving onlookers. Just below the viewing station, there is a short rock bluff that provides a perfect viewing perch. Below that, there is an expanse of tidepools, and during a period of calm, the pockets of seawater are remarkably clear.

There are several other first-rate adventures at this park. Our favorite was the hike around Lake Cleone (1.1 miles); The trail peeks in and out of forest and across a pretty marsh, and often provides views of this little lake; much of the trail is wheelchair-accessible on a raised wooden boardwalk.

One of the best bike rides anywhere is also here, on an old logging road known as the "Haul Road," which has been converted to a bicycle route that extends the entire eight-mile length of this coastal park. When the historic trestle just south of the park at Pudding Creek is restored, it will be possible to ride from the mouth of Ten Mile River all the way south to Fort Bragg, a distance of ten miles.

Fishing for trout at Lake Cleone is poor to fair, with the lake stocked with small rainbow trout a few times every summer by the Department of Fish and Game. Fishing from the rocks at Laguna Point is a better bet, although snags are common. During our visit, we saw a big cabezone landed here. Bird-watching can be excellent, both at the lake and at Laguna Point.

But what makes everything work here is the Surfwood Hike-In Camp, offering a chance at seclusion and beauty, with many adventures so close by.

Facilities: MacKerricher State Park has 10 walk-in campsites, each with a picnic table, food locker, and flat tent site. Piped water and a rest room is available within a two- or three-minute walk. There are also 142 drive-in campsites.

Reservations, fee: No reservation; $14 fee per night. For a drive-in campsite, reservations are advised; phone Destinet at (800) 444-PARK ($6.75 reservation fee).

Insider's note: Wildflowers and mushrooms are abundant throughout the park, but picking them is illegal.

Who to contact: Phone MacKerricher State Park at (707) 937-5804 or (707) 865-2391, or write to P.O. Box 440, Mendocino, CA 95460.

Directions: From San Francisco, take U.S. 101 and drive north to Willits. At Willits, turn west on Highway 20 and drive to Highway 1 at Fort Bragg. At Fort Bragg, turn north on Highway 1 and drive three miles, then turn left at the park entrance. At the entrance station, obtain a park brochure, drive ahead a short distance, then turn left and drive three-tenths of a mile (past Lake Cleone). Turn left at the signed turn for the access road to Surfwood Campground. Drive a short distance and turn right at the parking area for Surfwood Hike-In Camp.

35. MENDOCINO COAST WALK-IN CAMP
Van Damme State Park
Off Highway 1 near Mendocino

Van Damme State Park is hardly a secret. Its drive-to campground always seems to be full in the summer months, often with campsites reserved weeks ahead of time. But what is not so well known is a series of 10 walk-in campsites that require a 1.75-mile backpack hike. They are so quiet that they make the drive-in campground seem like a war zone.

This allows you to experience the best of Van Damme, hiking or biking the Fern Canyon Trail, visiting the Pygmy Forest, exploring Little River, yet ending the day in the seclusion of a pretty hike-in camp. It offers the best of coastal backpacking, with only the effort of a 45-minute walk. For a backpacking trip, the idea of walking less than an hour to reach your destination is kind of like planning a rocket launch to the moon and instead taking a ride around the block.

Start your trip with your telephone, calling for trail conditions and campsite availability. In winter, heavy storms can down trees across trails here, or even cause Little River to flood, closing the trail. When paying your camp fees at the park entrance kiosk, always get an update. That completed, park your vehicle at the trailhead for the Fern Canyon Trail, located near the campfire center. From here it is 1.75 miles to the hike-in campsites.

This is a scenic walk, passing through coastal forest often dripping with moisture, either from fog in midsummer or rain in the winter. The trail starts near sea level, then rises gently to the east. There are a series of little bridges that crisscross the Little River on the canyon bottom, adding a special touch to the trail.

That is why this is one of the most popular trips on the entire Mendocino coast. Bicycles are allowed on it as well. Note that during the awesome winter of 1994-95, this route was largely washed out by flood waters, and park officials hope to reopen the route in the winter of 1996.

The adjacent Pygmy Forest gets a number of curious visitors. You get there by hiking to the loop at the end of Fern Canyon Trail, or by driving 3.5 miles on nearby Little River Airport Road; the road is well signed off Highway 1, and the turnoff is a short distance south of the entrance to the state park. The Pygmy Forest is like a bonsai festival, with lots of curious little trees of various sizes. The trail is set on a raised, wooden boardwalk, routed in a loop that takes only about 15 minutes to complete and is wheelchair-accessible.

One key to making this trip work well is your timing. In the summer, do not expect to be able to drive in during the evening, spend your first night at a drive-in campsite, then head off to your backpack camp the following day. It doesn't work that way because the drive-in sites are usually full. Instead, be sure to arrive early enough so you can head out into the wilds right off, at least by 5 P.M. in summer months. From San Francisco, figure on about three hours driving time. And remember, always call first before heading out.

Facilities: Van Damme State Park has 10 hike-in, primitive campsites. There is no piped water. A food locker and level tent site are provided. No trash pickup is provided, so plan to pack out everything. The park also has 74 drive-in campsites, but in summer months, a reservation is usually required.

Reservations, fee: No reservation; $14 fee per night. To reserve a drive-in campsite, phone Destinet at (800) 444-PARK ($6.75 reservation fee).

Insider's note: The best weather on the Mendocino coast is typically in mid-August through mid-October. In addition, in the winter there is often a period of no rain and blue skies in late December/early January.

Who to contact: Phone Van Damme State Park at (707) 937-5804 or (707) 445-6547, or write to P.O. Box 440, Mendocino, CA 95460.

Directions: From San Francisco, drive north on U.S. 101 to Cloverdale. Take the Highway 128 exit, then turn left at the stop sign and drive west on Highway 128 to Highway 1. Turn north on Highway 1 and drive 8 miles. Van Damme State Park is on the right (east) side of the road.

---

36. THE INN AT SCHOOLHOUSE CREEK
Mendocino Coast
Off Highway 1 in Little River

As I write this, I am sitting on the deck of a cottage overlooking the ocean, taking turns gazing into the little screen of my portable computer and then off into the distance at the cobalt-blue horizon of the ocean. We're dipping tortilla chips in our favorite green salsa, chasing it with cold water, with sunbeams blessing everything around us. It seems almost like a fantasy. Some job, eh?

This morning after breakfast, we spotted a little "puff of smoke" on the sea surface, the spout of a passing whale, before we hiked to a water-

Highway 1 winds down the misty, fog-enshrouded Mendocino Coast

fall deep in the redwoods and took a stroll along an ocean bluff with rocky sea stacks and sea tunnels below. This evening, after we finish this story and the chips (not necessarily in that order), it's off to another waterfall. Hey, how did I get a job like this?

A better question is: How do you get a life like this? The answer is to make the 150-mile drive north of San Francisco to the Mendocino coast, stay at The Inn at Schoolhouse Creek, then break out your hiking boots for plenty of stellar walks and hikes through forests, along streams, and one on of the most beautiful stretches of coastline in America. There are also excellent driving tours on Highway 1, and for the ambitious, a chance for spectacular scuba diving in shallows, sea kayaking in coves, and coastal fishing for salmon or rockfish.

The Inn is a great place to stay because instead of hotel or condo-style lodging, there are six cottages, several with ocean views, along with another half-dozen rooms in a separate unit. The cottages are cozy, clean, and intimate, with wood stoves, small kitchens, full baths, and, hooray, no television or telephone. Rose, Heather, and Fuchsia cottages all have decks with ocean views; Cypress and Willow have ocean views (but no decks); and Hawthorn has a forest-view deck and ocean glimpses. The price varies from a low of $85 per night to a high of $130 per night; reservations are advised.

The Inn is located in the town of Little River, three miles south of the town of Mendocino and about 10 miles south of Fort Bragg. Within a 15-minute drive is Van Damme State Park, the Mendocino Headlands, Russian Gulch State Park, Caspar State Beach, and Jug Handle State Reserve. A bit farther south is Navarro River Redwoods, and just north is Fort Bragg, Noyo Harbor, and Jackson State Forest. So there are a wide number of choices for recreation within a very short distance.

The fastest and easiest way to get a slice of this life is to drive to the town of Mendocino and take the short drive out to the Mendocino Head-lands. The views, sunsets, and whale-spout viewing are all spectacular here, and there is a short, flat walk along the bluff that provides a con-tinuous lookout at the best of it.

A more secluded hike with an additional payoff is the five-mile round-trip in Russian Gulch State Park to see 36-foot Russian Gulch Falls. This is a divine waterfall, starting in a chute, then staircasing in three steps, finally cascading off a huge boulder into a pool. The entire setting can be stunning, with ferns, giant downed logs and a forest canopy.

There are many great hikes and other adventures in this area, too. The best are the short trail to the sea tunnels and Devil's Punchbowl at Russian Gulch State Park, and the half-mile Chamberlain Creek Trail to a 50-foot waterfall at Jackson State Forest. There are other options,

Rocky sea stacks in Jug Handle State Reserve, near The Inn at Schoolhouse Creek

however. Like going to the secluded cove and beach at Jughandle, sportfishing out of Noyo Harbor at Fort Bragg, and sea kayaking or snorkeling on calm days amid the sea tunnels, sea stacks, and coastal rock formations just north of Mendocino.

Or you can do what I'm doing right now. Sitting on a deck (with or without a computer), gazing off at miles of ocean. Hey, did we polish off the chips already?

Say, just how did I get a job like this?

Facilities: The Inn at Schoolhouse Creek has six cottages with wood stoves, small kitchens, and bathrooms; most have decks and ocean views. There are also six inn-style rooms, most with ocean views. A telephone is located at the office, a short walk away.

Reservations, fee: Reservations are strongly advised. The fee ranges from $85 to $130 per night for cottages, $75 to $100 for rooms.

Insider's note: The best time for whale watching is from Christmas through Memorial Day.

Who to contact: Phone The Inn at Schoolhouse Creek at (707) 937-5525, or write to 7051 North Highway 1, Little River, CA 95456.

Directions: From San Francisco, drive north on U.S. 101 to Cloverdale. Take the Highway 128 exit, then turn left at the stop sign and drive west on Highway 128 to Highway 1. Turn north on Highway 1 and drive 6.5 miles. Look for The Inn at Schoolhouse Creek on the right (east) side of the road.

37. SERENISEA COTTAGES
Mendocino Coast
Off Highway 1 near Gualala

If your fantasy is sitting in a hot tub on the edge of an ocean bluff, gazing at the sea, listening to the breakers, maybe even making a wish on a shooting star, then it just might happen. Because there is a place where dreams like this come true, and it is called Serenisea.

Four cabins are perched on a bluff point, not far from the cliffside hot tub, an intimate and dramatic setting on the remote Sonoma coast just north of Gualala. If you can't figure out what you're supposed to do out here, well, you ain't got a clue.

For the clueless, there is a trail that starts near Cabin 2 and takes about three minutes to get down to the ocean, where you will find a rocky/sandy beach, set amid some outcrops. If you still don't have a clue, you can play tag with the waves or something. This is also a prime spot for snorkeling and diving, good for abalone in season. But the hot tub is a lot warmer, and if you've got a clue, you can't beat the company.

During the day, the cliff at Serenisea is a great place to watch for the spouts of passing whales. In the winter, the nearby Gualala River attracts a fair run of steelhead and is popular for kayaking. Just south of the town of Gualala is Gualala Point Regional Park, where there is an excellent easy walk amid giant coast cypress trees with a lookout of both the Gualala River and the coast.

Sound good? Nah. I'll stick to the hot tub.

Facilities: Serenisea has four cottages on the property, each one quite different. Bathrooms, kitchens, cookware, utensils, bed linens, and towels are provided. Wood stoves and gas heating are also provided. A hot tub (swimsuit optional) is available. Smoking, children and pets are permitted. Small stores are located nearby in Gualala and Anchor Bay to the north. A boat ramp is available adjacent to Point Arena Pier. Also available from Serenisea are 23 completely furnished vacation homes in the Gualala area, most with decks and hot tubs.

Reservations, fee: Reservations are required; fees for the cottages range from $75 to $179, with two-night minimum stays required on weekends. Rates for vacation homes in the area range from $95 to $180 per night.

Who to contact: Phone Serenisea at (707) 884-3836 or (800) 331-3836, or write to 36100 Highway South, Gualala, CA 95445.

Directions: From San Francisco, take U.S. 101 north to Petaluma. In Petaluma, take the East Washington exit, and from there, turn west on Bodega Avenue (it merges), and continue through Petaluma for 26 miles to Bodega

Bay, where the road merges with Highway 1. Continue north on Highway 1 past Bodega Bay and Sea Ranch to Gualala. At Gualala, continue north for three miles and look for Serenisea on the ocean side of the road.

38. LAKE SONOMA BOAT-IN SITES
Santa Rosa/Sonoma
Off U.S. 101 near Healdsburg

One little idea, one little law, and just like that, Lake Sonoma offers one of the best camping experiences available anywhere in California's foothill country.

That one little idea was to impose a five-mile-per-hour speed limit—no-wake zones—in many large areas of this lake. With that law, you instantly have guaranteed quiet water. In turn, a series of 14 boat-in camps are available, dotted about the lake, which offer peace and quiet and excellent swimming and fishing. The whole experience can be absolutely great.

Lake Sonoma is located north of Santa Rosa, west of U.S. 101, near the little town of Healdsburg. It was created when the Army Corps of Engineers built a dam on Warm Springs Creek, a major tributary to the Russian River, backing water up two major canyons. The result was a reservoir that extends nine miles north on the Dry Creek arm and four miles west on Warm Springs Creek (speed limits enforced on two miles), plus miles of secluded coves. That makes it ideal for all water sports, with water warm enough for excellent waterskiing and jet-skiing, yet enough quiet places for swimming, fishing, or just floating around and playing in the coves. In addition, the lake is bordered by an 8,000-acre wildlife area and has 40 miles of hiking trails.

Get the picture? Right: This is a big lake, set in the rich foothill country of Sonoma County, with plenty of room for everybody. That includes people looking for little-known campsites.

The boat-in camps are primitive, with no piped water, but with chemical toilets, garbage cans, tent sites, picnic tables, fire rings, and lantern poles (you can hang your food on them), and they are free. You can construct your camp in any style you like. With a boat, you can bring anything you desire to make the trip fun. Because it gets hot out here in the summer, be sure to bring some kind of sunscreen. A light tarp rigged with poles and ropes works quite well.

Using the boat-in camp as your base of operations, you are ready to have fun, and this end of the lake is outstanding for both fishing and swimming. Shaded coves provide good fishing spots for redear sunfish, largemouth bass, and catfish. It really can be fun to use live minnows for bait during a quiet evening, then watch your line being tugged or your bobber dance when a big fish wanders by for an apparently easy dinner. Minnows are available at the Dry Creek Store, located on the access road just south of the lake.

In the summer, the water often reaches 75 to 80 degrees on the surface, making it wonderful to swim and play in. With the speed limit in effect, you don't have to worry about getting run over by a high-speed boat. If you love waterskiing, hey, no problem, because another huge portion of the lake is set aside with no speed limits. So take your pick: If you want a quiet spot, you can find it; if you want to let it rip in a powerboat, you can do that, too.

There's a full-service marina, boat ramp, and large parking area, usually the starting point for most trips here. The marina has rentals available, including boats with motors, canoes, and paddleboats. In addition, a visitor center operated by the Army Corps of Engineers—with maps and brochures, information about camping, boating, and hiking, and recreation officers who can answer any questions you may have—is located below the dam.

The best plan is to stop at the visitor center first and get information on boat-in campsite availability. Since there are only 14 sites, they sometimes fill up on good-weather Saturdays during summer. If so, the Liberty Glen Camp provides an option, with 118 developed campsites, piped water, and rest rooms with showers. Parking spots, tent sites, food lockers, and picnic tables are provided at each site. All sites are taken on a first-come, first-served basis.

But what I like best is setting up camp in a cove at a boat-in site well up the Dry Creek arm, watching the evening shade cover the lake and the pools left on quiet water by rising fish, and wondering why more people don't relish such simple pleasures.

Facilities: There are 14 primitive boat-in sites at different locations around the lake. There is no piped water. Chemical toilets, garbage cans, tent sites, picnic tables, fire rings, lantern poles (you can hang your food on them) are provided. A full-service marina is available at the lake, with rentals for boats with motors, canoes, and paddleboats.

Reservations, fee: No campground reservations are available; no fee for the boat-in sites. A $2 fee for launching boats is charged. Campers at the drive-in Liberty Glen Campground are charged $12 per night.

Insider's note: The boat-in campsites tend to fill up most weekends as soon as warm weather arrives in the spring. It is advisable to plan for a Friday arrival. Note that dogs are permitted here, as long as they are leashed.

Who to contact: For maps, brochures, or information, phone the Army Corps of Engineers at (707) 433-9483, or write to Lake Sonoma, 3333 Skaggs Springs Road, Geyserville, CA 95441. For marina or fishing information, phone Lake Sonoma Marina at (707) 433-2200.

Directions: From San Francisco, drive north on U.S. 101, continuing 12 miles past Santa Rosa to Healdsburg. At Healdsburg, take the Dry Creek exit, turn left and drive 11 miles. After crossing a small bridge, the visitor center will be on your right side. To reach the boat ramp, continue past the visitor center for about three miles, cross the main bridge at the lake, then turn left to the public boat ramp.

39. JIM'S SODA BAY RESORT CABINS
Clear Lake
Off Highway 29 near Kelseyville

If you think there are no fish left, an early summer trip to Clear Lake can provide a glimpse into a different world, one in which you can actually catch something. No matter what, it sure beats going to an aquarium.

What? No fish? I meet hundreds of people every year who say they never catch anything. "None left," they say. Randy Cross, the former 49er, told me he thought that there was just one fish, "and it is passed around for pictures."

At Clear Lake, there are fish left. In fact, there are a lot of them. Big ones. Bass, crappie, bluegill, catfish. And they can bite like a pit bull taking a chomp out of a burglar wearing porkchop underwear.

It just so happens that Jim's Soda Bay Resort, complete with cabins, private boat ramp, and dock, is located amid some of the lake's best fishing spots. Jim's sits on the western side of the lake near Kelseyville at Soda Bay. The shoreline near here to the north is lined with tules and carved with coves and sloughs, one of the fishiest looking places you can imagine (more on that later).

In addition to being ideal for fishing, Jim's is a good place to make your headquarters for a visit to Clear Lake for several reasons. You see, one of the problems at Clear Lake is the varying quality of lodging and campgrounds; there are some real dogs out there. But this is one of the better ones, small with tidy cabins and clean grounds. There are just six cottages, all air-conditioned, and two (cottages 2 and 4) have porches with lake views. They are fully equipped, including kitchen, bedding, and towels, and each has a patio with a barbecue and an outside table. You also have access to a small beach, boat ramp, and boat dock, which is private and used exclusively by guests.

Clear Lake's warm, calm waters make it perfect for waterskiing, swimming, and other water sports in late spring and early summer. In late summer and fall, hot weather and the lake's high levels of nutrients—phytoplankton and algae—often set off major algae blooms that can cause a soupy green mess, no fun for swimming.

But that green mess is the stuff that makes Clear Lake so great for fishing. The algae provides food for minnows, and lots of minnows means lots of sport fish.

What attracts most anglers is the bass fishing. One year, Clear Lake was even rated the top bass lake in America, with not only lots of fish, but sizable numbers of big ones. The shoreline and sloughs near the state and county parks are often good spots where you can pepper casts along the tules, keep on the move, and catch your share. At the northwest end of the lake, there are also lots of old pilings and docks where bass and crappie will hold. For the latest information on fish location, techniques, and lure choice for this area of the lake, call Lakeport Tackle at (707) 263-8862.

Then there is another option. On a warm summer morning, you can anchor up along the tules, fasten a red worm under a bobber, and toss it out. Before you know it, that bobber will start to dance. Just like that, you will have a bluegill on. It is one of the best ways to get children hooked on fishing, catching bluegill after bluegill, strong little fellows that provide a nice tussle.

And if you think there are no fish left, it is quite a thrill to watch that little bobber start to jump around. It's proof that you don't have to go to an aquarium to see a fish after all.

Facilities: Jim's Soda Bay Resort has six air-conditioned cottages, each with a bathroom and full kitchen. Cookware, utensils, bed linens, and towels are provided, and each unit has an outside table and barbecue. A boat ramp, dock, small beach, and swimming area are available nearby for guests only. Fishing boats and pontoon boats may be rented.

Reservations, fee: Reservations are available. Cabin rates range from $50 to $59 per night.

Insider's note: A good source of fishing information for this area is Lakeport Tackle, (707) 263-8862.

Who to contact: Phone Jim's Soda Bay Resort at (707) 279-4837, or write to 6380 Soda Bay Road, Kelseyville, CA 95451.

Directions: From San Francisco, take U.S. 101 north for 15 miles to Highway 37. Turn right on Highway 37 and drive 23 miles to Vallejo. Turn left on Highway 29/Napa and drive to Lower Lake. At Lower Lake, turn left on Highway 29 and drive about eight miles to Soda Bay Road. Turn right at Soda Bay Road and drive four miles past Konocti Harbor Inn and continue for another four miles. Look for Jim's Soda Bay Resort Cabins on the right side.

40. MURPHY'S JENNER INN & COTTAGES
Sonoma Coast
Off Highway 1 in Jenner

For some reason, a lot of people think you have to suffer before you are rewarded.

That logic is often applied to vacations, where some feel you are required to be in a hurried panic before departing, drive endlessly to some far point of the earth, and arrive very late, hungry and exhausted. That accomplished, you are allowed to start having fun the next day.

Here at the Murphy's Jenner Inn, none of that applies. As far as vacations go, there is no cause for hysteria prior to departure, because you get to stay in a cabin rather than a tent, and the drive is pretty short, allowing you to arrive fresh and well fed. In other words, you start having fun before you even get here.

This is because Jenner Inn is located at the mouth of the Russian River on the Sonoma Coast, one and a half hours from San Francisco, two and a half hours from Sacramento, and only 45 minutes from Santa Rosa. You just turn the key of your car, point her to Sonoma, and before you know it, you're here.

When you arrive, you find little cottages and homes set on a coastal foothill at the mouth of the Russian River. This is Jenner-by-the-Sea, with the main inn set below a prominent rock outcropping, the adjacent cottages and homes nuzzled into the hillside. Jenner Inn offers six cottages, three homes with rooms for rent, and two private vacation rental homes. For the cottages, the cost ranges from $120 to $175 per night.

Rosebud and Rosewater are waterfront cottages with ocean and estuary views, as well as an adjacent grassy yard, which slopes down to the water. This makes for an excellent put-in spot for kayaks or canoes. River-sea Cottage has an exceptional view of the bird refuge on Penny Island and the place where the Russian River meets the sea. Whale Watch Cottage has a great view of the ocean, Tree House is set for a river lookout, and Mill Cottage provides scenes of a meadow and stream. There are absolutely zero telephones or televisions, so you will quickly embrace the natural harmony of the coast.

No matter which way you turn, there are many side trips and adventures available. To the south is Sonoma Coast State Beach (five minutes on Highway 1), Bodega Bay (20 minutes), and Point Reyes National Seashore (an hour). To the north on Highway 1 is Fort Ross (20 minutes) and Salt Point State Park (30 minutes). To the east on Highway 116 is

Sonoma coastline near Salt Point State Park, north of Jenner

the Russian River, the Russian River wine country (30 minutes), and Armstrong Redwoods State Park (30 minutes).

The closest quality adventure requires just a short drive south on Highway 1 to Shell Beach/Sonoma Coast State Beach. Shell Beach is a beautiful place, and with the trail to Arch Rock and good beachcombing at low tides, you can spend hours here. If you want to hike, just across from the entrance to Shell Beach, on the east side of Highway 1, is the coastal trailhead for the Pomo-Ohlone Trail. The trail climbs up the foothills, providing beautiful views of the ocean to the west, and eventually gains the ridge for more great views, including those of Goat Rock at the mouth of the Russian River and a sweeping lookout of the coast.

We've learned that Shell Beach can get a lot of visitors, especially on those rare perfect blue-sky days when the wind isn't howling. Yet even then, the Pomo-Ohlone Trail is usually all but ignored. So if you want to avoid people, yet still have great views and coastal beauty, this trail provides an insurance policy for getting all that.

But once you discover how easy it is to make the trip here, how quiet and tranquil the surroundings can be, you are not apt to be in any great rush to do anything. You might just want to hunker down and watch the cormorants glide by, the sea lions play tag, or the water lap at the shore. This is one place where you don't have to suffer first to justify having a good time.

Facilities: Murphy's Jenner Inn has six cottages, three homes with rooms for rent, and two private vacation rental homes. Each cottage is unique, but most feature a kitchenette and full bath, with decks, hot tubs, and fireplaces available. There's a telephone at the office. No pets are allowed.

Reservations, fee: Reservations are advised; fees for the cottages range from $120 to $175 per night. Two-night minimum stays are required on weekends.

Insider's note: For a free recreation travel packet about the Russian River region, phone (800) 253-8800.

Who to contact: Phone Murphy's Jenner Inn at (707) 865-2377 or (800) 732-2377, or write to 10400 Coast Highway 1, Box 69, Jenner, CA 95450.

Directions: From San Francisco, take U.S. 101 north to Petaluma. In Petaluma, take the East Washington exit, and from there, turn west on Bodega Avenue (it merges) and continue through Petaluma for 26 miles to Bodega Bay, where the road merges with Highway 1. Continue north on Highway 1 past Bodega Bay for about 15 miles, drive over the bridge that crosses the Russian River, and enter the town of Jenner. Look for Murphy's Jenner Inn on the right side of the road.

41. POMO CANYON WALK-IN SITES
Sonoma Coast State Beach
Off Highway 1 near Bodega Bay

I still can't believe it. I showed up at Pomo Canyon Campground and it seemed like there wasn't another soul on the planet. Not a single camp was taken. No hikers were on the trails. Not even a single car was in the parking area. And this was in early June, on a clear, warm day, the kind you dream about on the Sonoma Coast.

It might make sense if Pomo Canyon was a dive of a place, but it's more like divine. In fact, it is one of the prettiest, most secluded campgrounds within a 100-mile radius of San Francisco, and in addition, it offers a stellar hike through redwoods up to a ridgeline with great views of the coast, then down to pristine Shell Beach.

The camp is well hidden from Highway 1 tourists, located south of the mouth of the Russian River yet set a few miles inland from the highway, in a canyon at the base of coastal foothills. That is likely why so many people miss it. You turn on obscure Willow Creek Road, and in about five minutes, arrive at a gravel parking area with a small sign designating the Pomo Canyon Campground.

From here, two trails are routed into a redwood forest to a series of 20 walk-in sites, with some campsites as close as 30 yards and others as far as a quarter-mile hike with a climb. The access points are located directly behind an information board; note that the access trail/dirt road directly behind the information board is relatively level, while the access trail to the right (Pomo-Ohlone Trail) requires a climb. Each site has a picnic table, fire grill, and flat tent site, the latter a nice touch by the State Parks Department since the entire camp is set on a slope. The camp has pit toilets and piped water available, and like at most camps, reaching them requires a short walk.

This is a real pretty camp, providing a sense of being far away in mountain redwoods. While there are no monster redwoods, the second-growth forest is dense and quiet, always shaded and cool, with a good amount of space between the campsites. It is very easy to forget how close you are to the ocean. That can make it something of a stunner if you hike the Pomo-Ohlone Trail, which provides dramatic coastal views from its ridgeline lookouts in the course of 1.6 miles to the top, or 2.5 miles all the way to Shell Beach.

From the parking area, the Pomo-Ohlone Trail starts to the right of the information board, immediately entering redwoods and passing several walk-in campsites, then rising quickly through the forest. There are several groups of what some call "cathedral trees," clusters of young redwoods seemingly linked together, often in circles.

The trail continues to rise, steeply at times, climbing out of the redwoods and emerging atop coastal foothills. From late winter to early summer, wildflower blooms are decent here, including golden poppies, blue-eyed grass, and lupine. Within 40 minutes, you will reach a rock outcropping off to the right, and with it, a great lookout of the mouth of the Russian River, Goat Rock, and, at last, the coast. This is also a great picnic spot.

If you continue on, you will enter another redwood forest featuring more cathedral trees, then emerge and climb over the crest, where you are rewarded with a panorama of the Sonoma coast. On the hike down to the beach, some walk with their arms outstretched, palms open, absorbing the vastness of the sea, which seems to stretch on forever here.

The trail feeds right across the highway to Shell Beach, one of Sonoma's prettiest beaches, worth seeing and exploring on a trail heading north all the way past Arch Rock. But alas, this is no secret, and, at least in the summer, you'll have to share it with the onslaught of visitors looking for a stop on their tour of Highway 1.

Meanwhile, you can just head back to your secret camp, taking the Pomo-Ohlone Trail, perhaps stopping now and then on the steady climb across the foothills to admire the beautiful views—and the new world you have discovered.

Facilities: There are 20 walk-in sites, each with a picnic table, fire ring with grill, and a flat tent site. Piped water and pit toilets are available nearby. No pets are permitted.

Reservations, fee: No reservations; $9 fee per night, $2 for each extra vehicle per site.

Insider's note: The Pomo-Ohlone Trail is named after the Pomo and Ohlone Indians, who developed it as a trade route between the inland valley and the coast.

Who to contact: Phone Sonoma Coast State Beach at (707) 875-3483, or write to 3095 Highway 1, Bodega Bay, CA 94923.

Directions: From San Francisco, take U.S. 101 north to Petaluma. In Petaluma, take the East Washington exit, and from there, turn west on Bodega Avenue (it merges) and continue through Petaluma for 26 miles to Bodega Bay, where the road merges with Highway 1. Continue north on Highway 1 past Bodega Bay for about 10 miles. Turn east (right) on Willow Creek Road (if you cross the Russian River, you have gone too far) and drive for about three miles to Pomo Canyon Campground.

42. HUCKLEBERRY SPRINGS CABINS
Russian River
Off Highway 116 near Monte Rio

"This can't be the way," I muttered to myself. "There can't be any resort cabins way out here. Got to be the wrong way."

Of course, I could have asked directions back in Monte Rio. But being a male humanoid, that would be sacrilege; no man ever asks directions unless it's a final resort. It was hardly a final resort. I still had my little brochure map, and I was still pointing my truck in the direction it indicated, so I drove, hoping I would somehow find the place.

After passing through Monte Rio, the little town along the Russian River, I made the assigned right turn at Tyrone Road, though it's so small that I just about missed it. It turned out to be a narrow patch of asphalt that passed a few houses, then climbed and turned to gravel, then dirt, narrowed even more, passing through a forest of some oaks and redwoods. There was no sign of any resort. "This can't be the right way," I said.

But it was, it turns out. A moment later, posted on a tree on the right side of the road, was a small sign that read, "Huckleberry Springs," and in a few minutes, despite all my misgivings, I was pulling into a small parking place next to the lodge headquarters.

It also turns out that this is one of the most secluded settings for cabin rentals in California, with four unusual little cabins secreted away in the woods in the foothills south of the Russian River. The place is quiet and remote, yet at the same time, set close enough for canoeing, hiking, and fishing, or just playing in the river. The only reason it rates a 9 instead of a 10, by the way, is because you must drive to take part in the area's outdoor recreation.

The cabins at Huckleberry Springs are like nothing I've seen anywhere. The Cherry Barrel, believe it or not, is literally that—a giant barrel that has been converted into a room, with a pine ceiling and a skylight, along with a bathroom, making it the most unusual cabin imaginable.

Another, Spring Hill, is reached via a five-minute walk up a steep hill. You are rewarded with a little custom-made cottage with a deck and a view of the valley, a bed set high in a loft accessible by a built-in ladder, and a skylight. It is absolutely quiet, and if you're lucky, you might even see shooting stars at night through the skylight.

The cabins do not have telephones (whew!), but they do have small televisions with VCRs (that's okay, you can ignore them). At lodge headquarters, a telephone is available, along with a library of videotapes, and scaled-down restaurant-style dining. A small pool is also available, and along the trail up to the Cherry Barrel, there is a gazebo with a hot tub.

There are many activities in the Russian River region, of course: Canoeing, sunbathing, hiking, horseback riding, wine tasting, winery tours, golf, fishing, and touring through redwoods (at Armstrong Redwoods State Park) and along the coast. A free recreation travel packet is available by phoning (800) 253-8800.

The fastest way to have fun is to rent a canoe with a friend and take your time paddling down the river, stopping along the way to picnic, swim, sunbathe, or fish. The best bet for newcomers is to leave from Forestville at Burke's Canoe Rentals, then take the 10-mile paddle downstream through redwoods and lush greenery to a private beach in Guerneville, where Burke's will provide a shuttle ride back. Many other options are available, of course.

From Huckleberry Springs, a great side trip is a drive along the Russian River to the coast at Highway 1. You can make it even better by hiking the Pomo-Ohlone Trail, detailed in the story about Pomo Canyon Walk-In Sites on page 105.

On the other hand, you could just loll around at Huckleberry Springs, maybe swimming, hot tubbing, eating and drinking, then retreat to your cabin and be happy you didn't give up on the directions it took to get there.

Facilities: Four cabins are available, each with a bathroom, television, and VCR. No telephones are provided in the cabins. At the lodge, a telephone, video library, and restaurant-style dining are available. A small swimming pool and spa with gazebo are also available.

Reservations, fee: Reservations are required; $125 to $145 per night.

Insider's note: For a free travel packet detailing recreation in the Russian River region, phone (800) 253-8800.

Who to contact: Phone Huckleberry Springs Country Inn at (800) 822-2683 or (707) 865-2683, or write to P.O. Box 400, Monte Rio, CA 95462.

Directions: From San Francisco, drive north on U.S. 101 to the Rhonert Park area, then take Highway 116 west. Continue on Highway 116 past Sebastopol and Guerneville. Four miles past Guerneville, at an intersection with a stop sign, go straight (Highway 116 veers to the right) and enter Monte Rio. Turn left on the Bohemian Highway, drive a short distance over the Russian River, then turn right on Main Street. Continue on Main Street through Monte Rio. One mile past the firehouse, turn right on Tyrone Road. Drive one-half mile, then bear right on Old Beedle Road and continue for one mile to Huckleberry Springs.

---

43. WASHINGTON STREET LODGING
Napa Valley
Off Highway 29 in Calistoga

Yeah, it's a mighty long stretch to call this "camping," but hey, it gives you an excuse to go to Calistoga, right? And any excuse to go to Calistoga is a good excuse.

This is the place where souls get recharged, bodies get rejuvenated, and your brain takes a vacation. How? By taking advantage of the town's hot springs, mud baths, towel wraps, massages, and quality dining. In 24 hours, Calistoga finds a way to get inside you and realign your senses.

As for the "camping," it consists of staying in one of these cute little cottages at a place called Washington Street Lodging. We figure it's camping because there is no television or telephone, but hey, we just had to come up with some kind of reason to stay here. It's called Washington Street Lodging because ...you guessed it!...it's on Washington Street, about two blocks from the main drag in Calistoga.

The cottages are clean, quiet, cozy, pretty inside and out, and believe it or not, you can bring your pet. Hey, we said this was camping, right? The first thing you notice when you arrive is that the entire property is loaded with blooming flowers, and the place is well-kept. After settling in, you will notice that the headwaters of the Napa River run right by the

Hiker in Bothe-Napa Valley State Park near Washington Street Lodging

place. Although it's more like a creek, the riparian woodlands here provide a nice feel and setting, especially in the early evening. One special feature of cottages 3 and 4 is the small deck overlooking the creek.

The only downer is for late risers during the spring, fall, and winter. Directly across the stream, behind the cottages, is an elementary school yard, and they have playtime every morning for 20 minutes starting at

8:15. The shrieks can be irritating if you are trying to sleep. In summer, it's not a factor, of course.

Peace is what you come here for, and for the most part, it is peace that you will get. Calistoga has nine hot spring spas, all with mud baths and a variety of treatments that will make your skin glow. The full treatment, which includes a mud bath, hot mineral soak, towel wrap and massage, will have you surrendering to the final euphoria. "Problems? What problems? I don't have any problems." Taking a mud bath is like sinking into a cauldron of ooze, the hot soak will permeate and loosen every tight muscle in your body, and then the warm towel wrap will have you practically levitating with tingles. Finish it off by getting worked over by a masseur and your mission will be near complete; you will gleam for days. Even the most tightly wound souls will yield and suddenly, in just a few hours, none of your problems will seem quite so important.

After reaching this state of harmony, the best way to integrate it into the real world is to visit one of the area's parks for a hike in a natural setting. There are three state parks nearby, two to the south of Calistoga, Bothe-Napa and Bale Grist Mill, and one to the north, Robert Louis Stevenson. The most appealing trip is to Bothe-Napa, located on Highway 128/29, which offers redwoods and a walk along Ritchey Creek. The most demanding hike, with spectacular views when the air is clearest in the spring, is the 10-mile round-trip to the top of 4,343-foot Mount St. Helena in Robert Louis Stevenson State Park; the 2,000-foot climb covers a five-mile span. The trailhead is along Highway 29, eight miles north of Calistoga. In the winter, this mountaintop is sometimes flecked with snow from passing storms, and visiting it can seem like a dream.

After getting a treatment at Calistoga and staying in a cottage at Washington Street, somehow it all fits just right.

Facilities: Washington Street Lodging has six cottages, each with a small kitchen with microwave and bathroom with shower. Pets are permitted.

Reservations, fee: Reservations are strongly advised, both for cottage rentals and for treatments at any of the spas. Cottages are roughly $100 per night. Full spa treatments are about $75, with some less expensive options.

Insider's note: Triple-S-Ranch, located five miles north of Calistoga, also offers cabins from April through December. Phone (707) 942-6730.

Who to contact: For reservations or a free brochure, phone Washington Street Lodging at (707) 942-6968, or write to 1605 Washington Street, Calistoga, CA 94515. Various hot springs resorts in Calistoga include: Calistoga Spa Hot Springs, (707) 942-6269; Calistoga Village Inn & Spa, (707) 942-0991; Dr. Wilkinson's Hot Springs, (707) 942-4102; Golden Haven Spa, (707) 942-6793; Indian Springs, (707) 942-4913; Lavender Hill Spa, (707) 942-4495; Lincoln Avenue Spa, (707) 942-5296; Mount View Hotel & Spa, (707) 942-6877; Nance's Hot Springs, (707) 942-6211.

Directions: Take Interstate 80 to Vallejo, then take the Highway 37 exit and drive west into Vallejo. At a major lighted intersection, turn north on Highway 29, drive past Napa, and continue about 30 miles to Calistoga. At the flashing light, turn right on Lincoln Avenue and drive into downtown Calistoga. Turn left (north) on Washington and drive two blocks to 1605 Washington, on the left (west) side of the road. Limited parking is available near the cottages. On Washington Street, park only on the east side of the road.

OTHER CABIN RENTALS IN THE CLEAR LAKE AREA

KOA Cloverdale, P.O. Box 600, Cloverdale, CA 95425; (707) 894-3337 or (800) 368-4558.

KOA Willits, Box 946, Willits, CA 95490; (707) 459-6179.

The Narrows Lodge Resort, 5690 Blue Lakes Road, Upper Lake, CA 95485; (707) 275-2718 or (800) 476-2776.

OTHER CABIN RENTALS ON THE MENDOCINO COAST

KOA Manchester Beach, Box 266, Manchester, CA 95459; (707) 882-2375.

Wishing Well Cottages, 31430 Highway 20, Fort Bragg, CA 95437; (707) 961-5450.

Plumas-
Sierra Foothills

** For locations of camps, see map on page 9. **

44. BUCKS LAKE CABINS
Plumas National Forest
Off Highway 89 near Quincy

I was just a 12-year-old when I became an outlaw.

It was at Bucks Lake, where I'd discovered this great fishing spot along the shore. I'd cast out my lure, and just like that, a beautiful rainbow trout would strike; then I'd set the hook and fight that dancing trout as if I'd been transported to heaven. The limit was 10 then, and in back-to-back days, I filled my stringer with beautiful limits, feeling about as proud as I'd ever been.

So proud, in fact, that I started bragging about it at the little grocery store, and suddenly discovered a game warden with willing ears.

"Where'd you get them?" he asked.

"Right out there," I answered, pointing to the spot.

"That area is closed to fishing," said the game warden, explaining that it was where the weekly trout plants are made. "I'm afraid I'm going to have to take you to jail."

I started crying, figuring my life was over, that I would never see my family again. But then the warden put his arm around me and said, "Well, it looks like you have already learned your lesson and you don't have to go to jail after all. Just make sure you check the rules from now on wherever you fish."

Well, I've never broken the promise, but every time I return to Bucks Lake, I look at the spot along the shoreline and remember that experience. I also remember how much fun I had on that first trip to the mountains, trout fishing, camping, going out in a boat, and playing tag with the squirrels.

Bucks Lake is still a great place for such an adventure, one of the best places you can drive to in the northern . The lake is set at an elevation of 5,237 feet in Plumas National Forest, 17 miles from the town of Quincy. The bonus here are the small cabins, some with lake views, and a lodge/inn with lake-view rooms, along with seven campgrounds set in the pines, most within short walking distance of places to go casting for rainbow trout. Facilities at the lake include a small but complete marina with boat rentals, a general store (yes, the same one), and a restaurant with bar.

The air is clear and clean up here, tinged with the scent of pines, and the lake is full and blue-green, with all the streams running pure. Since Bucks Lake is surrounded by national forest, you can drive, hike, and explore as much as you could desire. An old route called the Oro-Quincy Road is also available, a 20-mile-per-hour gravel road that runs through national forest all the way from Bucks Lake through the little towns of Berry Creek, Merrimac, and Letterbox en route to Oroville.

But what makes Bucks Lake a winner is the trout fishing, and not just for 12-year-old outlaws. It is one of the most consistent producers of rainbow trout in Northern California, with the best spot by Rocky Point near where Bucks Creek enters the lake. Another good spot is in the old river channel near where Mill Creek enters the lake, and if you troll deep in the early morning, you have a chance to catch a large Mackinaw trout.

The lake record is a three-foot, 18-pound Mackinaw trout, caught in May of 1995, but other big fish caught in the same time period include a 16-pound brown trout and several 16-pound Mackinaws (caught and released). The catch rate for rainbow trout and brook trout, averaging 12 to 16 inches, has also been quite good, particularly during the evenings near the two inlets.

The cabins operated by Bucks Lakeshore Resort and Bucks Lake Lodge are cozy, set in the pines, and accommodate up to eight people. Timberline Inn also faces the lake and is backed up against the forest, a woodsy-looking place with 12 modern rooms, but cooking and pets aren't allowed. There are seven campgrounds near Bucks Lake, five with water and two without, and all are operated on a first-come, first-served basis.

At this elevation, the nights start to cool off by September, dropping to the 40s most nights with daytime temperatures in the 70s. It feels about perfect, not too hot, not too cool, and the trout like it, too. There's excellent fishing by boat during the last two hours of light.

It's so good, that if you're not careful, it might just turn you into an outlaw.

Facilities: Bucks Lake Lodge has cabin facilities, Timberline Inn, and a campground. Bucks Lakeshore Resort has cabins with accommodations for up to eight people. A small marina, boat ramp, boat-and-motor rentals, and general store are available. There are also seven campgrounds nearby.

Reservations, fee: Reservations are advised for cabins; fees range from $50 to $79 per day, $250 to $495 per week. No reservations are available for campsites.

Insider's note: An outstanding source of fishing information is Al Bruzza of the Sportsmen's Den in Quincy; phone (916) 283-2733.

Who to contact: Phone Bucks Lakeshore Resort at (916) 283-6900, or write to P.O. Box 266, Quincy, CA 95971. Phone Bucks Lake Lodge at (916) 283-2262 or (800) 481-2825, or write to P.O. Box 236, Quincy, CA 95971.

Directions: From San Francisco, take Interstate 80 east to Sacramento. In Sacramento, turn north on Interstate 5 and drive three miles to the junction with Highway 99. Turn north on Highway 99 and drive 13 miles to the junction with Highway 70. Turn north on Highway 70 and drive to the junction with Highway 89. Turn south on Highway 89 and drive 11 miles to Quincy. In Quincy, turn right at Bucks Lake Road and drive 17 miles to Bucks Lake.

45. LAKE OROVILLE BOAT-IN SITES
Sierra Foothills
Off Highway 70 near Oroville

From an airplane, Oroville looks like a multilegged monster, with five lake arms spanning across 167 miles of shoreline. When the lake level is up in spring and early summer, it is a great boat-in camping destination, including the only boat-in camp in California with piped water, Craig Saddle.

But there is a lot more here that isn't available anywhere else. There are actually rest rooms on floats bobbing around, a rare convenience for boaters anywhere in America, as well as floating tent platforms located in no-wake zones. The tent platforms are a flat surface on a pontoon anchored in the lake, where a boater can tie up his boat, then actually pitch a tent on the platform, right on the lake.

Crazy? Yeah, but it works. Four boat-in campgrounds make it work even better.

In all, there are 86 campsites at four boat-in campgrounds: Craig Saddle (18 sites), located on a point between the Middle and South Fork Feather arms; Foreman Creek (26 sites), located straight north across the lake from the Bidwell Marina; Goat Ranch (five sites), located on the upper end of the North Fork; and Bloomer Camp (35 sites), located on the North Fork. A fee of $7 is charged for each night.

Oroville is located at 900 feet in elevation in the foothills north of Marysville, so warm, sunny weather is the standard for most of the summer. It is one of the major water storage reservoirs in the West, filled with both rain runoff and snowmelt from the northern Sierra, and the emerald-green lake sparkles in contrast to the oak grasslands that surround it. In big snow years, melting snow in July will keep the lake nearly full, even though water releases from the lake are high to provide irrigation for Central Valley farmers. In lean snow years, the lake level starts dropping in July, since the farmers take the water regardless of its recreation value.

Most people visiting Oroville head first to Bidwell Marina, register for their campsite, buy whatever they have forgotten for the trip, then launch their boats. The best boat ramp on the lake is here, as well as a full-service marina.

After launching, the preferred destination for most is Craig Saddle Boat-In Camp, the one with piped water. Head straight out into the lake, then turn right (east), pass under a bridge, and note a shoreline point straight ahead. Head up the South Fork Feather arm, then curve just inside that point and you will discover a cove, the site of the boat-in campground.

If you want a smaller, more remote setting, but one that has no piped water, Goat Ranch Camp is located on the upper end of the North Fork arm, on the west side of the lake, about a five-mile boat ride from the ramp at Bidwell Marina. An insider's note is that a cartop-only ramp is located right "around the corner" at Spring Valley.

Because Oroville gets hot weather, it is like a big bathtub in the summer, with surface water temperatures often in the high 70s to low 80s. That makes it great for swimming, waterskiing, and powerboating. However, there are occasional conflicts between fishers and waterskiers (and jet-skiers), typically when a high-speed boater breaks the law by powering too close to shore or in a cove. The whole thing is often ridiculous and can turn asinine if alcohol is involved. My suggestion is for waterskiers to stay in open water, out of the coves, and for fishers to carry a cellular phone and punch 911 if they are confronted by a lawbreaker.

Fishing for bass can be fantastic at Oroville in April and May, when a team of two anglers might catch and release 60 or 70 bass per day. The best of it is always in the backs of coves, particularly where there is floating wood debris. The bass hide under that wood.

One note of caution: The weather gets hot out here in the summer and anybody who isn't prepared for it will get burned like a boiled lobster. It is critical to bring a sunscreen for your camp.

That done, Oroville offers some of the best boat-in camping in the West. The lake is big, warm, and friendly, with plenty of facilities, good weather, and room for everybody.

Facilities: There are 86 campsites and four boat-in campgrounds. Craig Saddle Boat-In Camp is the only one of the four with piped water. Each site has a picnic table and fire ring; a pit or vault toilet is available.

Reservations, fee: No reservation, except for Bloomer Camp (a group camp); phone Destinet at (800) 444-PARK ($6.75 reservation fee) to reserve Bloomer. For the other camps, fees are $7 per night, plus an additional $3 per day for boating use on the lake.

Insider's note: No fires or barbecues are allowed anywhere at Lake Oroville except inside permanent fire rings.

Who to contact: Phone Oroville Visitors Center at (916) 538-2219, or write to 917 Kelly Ridge Road, Oroville, CA 95966. Phone State Park District Headquarters at (916) 538-2200. Phone Bidwell Marina at (916) 589-3165, or write to 801 Bidwell Canyon Road, Oroville, CA 95966.

Directions: From San Francisco, take Interstate 80 east to Davis. Turn north on Highway 113 and drive to Marysville. In Marysville, turn east on Highway 20, drive through Marysville, then turn north on Highway 70. Continue north on Highway 70 to the town of Oroville. Take the Oro Dam Boulevard exit, turn right and drive 1.6 miles to Highway 162 (Olive Highway). Turn right and drive about five miles to Kelly Ridge Road. Turn left at Kelly Ridge Road and drive to Bidwell Marina.

46. BULLARDS BAR RESERVOIR BOAT-IN SITES
Sierra Foothills
Off Highway 20 near Marysville

California has 373 lakes you can drive to, but Bullards Bar Reservoir shines like a lone beacon in a field of darkness when it comes to boating, camping, and water sports.

Not only are there two developed boat-in campgrounds at Bullards Bar, but the rules allow boaters to create their own primitive campsites anywhere along the lake's shore. You know how rare that is? Well, put it this way: there are 372 lakes in California that don't have both kinds of camping, and most have neither.

This reservoir is the prettiest of the dozens in the Sierra Nevada foothills, always big, clear, and kept nearly full with water pouring in from the North Fork Yuba River. It is set at a 2,300-foot elevation and has 55 miles of shoreline, so it is big enough to provide plenty of space for all users, including waterskiers, swimmers, and anglers.

The developed boat-in campgrounds are Madrone Cove and Garden Point, each providing picnic tables, fire grills, and vault toilets. Reservations are required. Madrone Cove boat-in camp is located on the west side of the lake, while Garden Point boat-in camp is farther north on the North Yuba River arm, also set on the western shore. Both provide shaded campsites. The surrounding area is far more wooded than at other reservoirs in the foothills, such as massive Lake Oroville to the north (see story on page 116) or Collins Lake to the near west, and it gives the lake a more intimate setting than most reservoirs.

The best spots for do-it-yourself boat-in sites are located at points and the backs of coves, which tend to be flatter than the rest of the lake. Because the lake's shore is steep in many spots, and the water level is rarely full right to the brim, do-it-yourself boat-in campers will usually pick a spot that is actually exposed lake bottom, searching for ground that is as flat as possible. Alas, it is never quite flat. My first time here I rolled all over the place in my sleeping bag and never did figure out how to get comfortable.

Bringing a shovel is critical, for it will allow you to dig out a flat spot for your tent or sleeping bag. In addition, bring a light tarp with poles and ropes so you can stake up a good sunscreen, imperative during the hot summer months. A legal requirement for do-it-yourself boat-in camping is that you bring your own portable chemical toilet. These work great and solve what used to be an inevitable problem for both campers and lake managers.

Bullards Bar changes seasonally, so timing is everything when it comes to recreation. In the spring, especially after big rain years, a lot of debris is washed into the lake via the Yuba River, a common problem at many big lakes. The surface is usually clear of most debris by May. That is also when the water temperature starts to warm, with the surface usually reaching 70 degrees by Memorial Day weekend. By then, the lake is ideal for powerboating, waterskiing, and swimming. The steep shoreline makes it poor for wading or for kids playing in the water, but to cool off I just put on a life preserver and bob around like a cork. By the end of July, the water temperature is very warm, sometimes close to 80 degrees, and the lake level often starts dropping as water is fed from the reservoir to farmers in the Central Valley.

Another unusual element at Bullards Bar is the fishing. Instead of trout or bass, the best prospects are often kokanee salmon, which some believe are the best-tasting freshwater fish in California. Kokanee are bright silver, typically 10 to 13 inches, and will not touch still bait. They will usually take only trolled lures trailed behind flashers. Some people have even caught kokanee on a piece of corn (right out of the can) trolled with flashers.

With a little luck, you can have it all—boating, waterskiing, and playing in the water in the afternoon, maybe catching a few kokanee in the early evening—then have a fish fry at your boat-in campsite by dusk. You really can have it all.

Facilities: Madrone Cove has 10 boat-in campsites. Garden Point has 20 boat-in campsites. Picnic tables and fire grills are provided and vault toilets are available. There is no piped water. If you are going to make your own campsite, a chemical toilet is required. Bring a shovel to dig out a flat spot for a tent. A tarp, poles, and ropes are advised for making a sunscreen.

Reservations, fee: Reservations are required; $10 fee per night.

Who to contact: Phone Emerald Cove Resort at (916) 692-3200, or write to P.O. Box 1954, Nevada City, CA 95959.

Directions: From Sacramento, drive north on Highway 70/99 to Marysville. At Marysville, turn east on Highway 20 and drive 12 miles. Look for the sign for Bullards Bar Reservoir and turn left at Marysville Road. Drive 10 miles north on Marysville Road, then turn right on Old Marysville Road and drive 14 miles to reach Bullards Bar Reservoir. Turn just before the dam to reach Emerald Cove Marina.

47. LONG VALLEY RESORT CABINS
Plumas National Forest
Off Highway 89 near Quincy

Every time I mention the words "Middle Fork Feather," several of my pals cringe as if I just revealed their most treasured secret.

That is because the Middle Fork Feather River is one of California's great trout streams, but to be honest with you, the best spots are still pretty much secret, requiring long, grueling hikes in and out of canyons that will have you wheezing like Pete Rose racing to make his last bet.

But there is a better way to get a taste of it, by combining a stay at one of the cabins at Long Valley Resort with a Middle Fork Feather fishing trip. Plus you can hike at nearby Plumas-Eureka State Park, and have access to four golf courses in Graegle as well as a half-dozen drive-to lakes in the Lakes Basin and some 50 lakes in the whole region. That is because Long Valley Resort is set along Highway 70/89 in Plumas Forest country, at elevation 4,300 feet.

From Long Valley Resort, the easiest access to the Middle Fork Feather is to drive a half-mile north on Highway 70/89, then turn left on Sloat Road. From there, drive about a mile, then turn right, drive over the railroad tracks, continue a short distance to the river, and drive over the river. Here the road turns to dirt and traces along upriver for a spell; this is where you can get fishing access.

When Long Valley Resort is your headquarters, this stretch of river provides a quick and easy hit. Then the next time you hear someone say, "Middle Fork Feather," well, you might just be cringing yourself.

Facilities: Long Valley Resort has five cottages, four with two bedrooms and three beds. Each has a bathroom, a kitchen with cookware and utensils, and bed linens and towels. Weekly maid service is included. A grocery store/café is available within a half-mile.

Reservations, fee: Reservations are available. Rates are $55 per night with a two-night minimum, or $350 per week, with a charge of $6 per day per additional person (more than two).

Insider's note: The best fishing lure for trout on the Middle Fork Feather River is a $1/16$-ounce Panther Martin spinner, yellow spots on black body with gold blade.

Who to contact: Phone Long Valley Resort at (916) 836-0754, or write to P.O. Box 30003, Cromberg, CA 96103. For a map of the area, send $3 to Office of Information, U.S. Forest Service, 630 Sansome Street, San Francisco, CA 94111 and ask for Plumas National Forest.

Directions: From San Francisco, take Interstate 80 east to Sacramento. In Sacramento, turn north on Interstate 5 and drive three miles to the junction with Highway 99. Turn north on Highway 99 and drive 13 miles to the junction with Highway 70. Turn north on Highway 70 and drive to the junction with Highway 89. Turn south on Highway 70/89 and drive 11 miles to Quincy. Continue through Quincy, drive 15 miles, and look for Long Valley Resort on the right side of the road.

48. DAVIS LAKE CABINS
Plumas National Forest
Off Highway 70 near Portola

Ten deer were knee-deep in a meadow, nibbling their dinners. In an adjacent clearing, a dozen mountain quail were hopping around, pecking for evening morsels. Nearby, the gold sunbeams of dusk refracted across Davis Lake, the surface dimpled by hatching bugs and rising fish.

This was the scene at Davis Lake, where all can seem magical at dusk, the time when wildlife, birds, and fish lose their inhibitions and spring to life. For at least a short while, even human visitors are allowed access to this special world. But then again, all can seem magical everywhere in Plumas National Forest, one of America's greatest recreation destinations. Oddly, many people do not even know where Plumas is or what is here.

Plumas has some 30 lakes you can reach by car, another 25 that you can reach by foot, 2,000 miles of trout streams, 42 campgrounds, and six lakes with cabin rentals: Davis, Gold, Sardine, Salmon, Packer, and Almanor. It is located in California's northern Sierra, a region about 50 to 70 miles northwest of Reno. With access by two-lane highways 70 and 89, Plumas is often obscured by the easier-to-reach Tahoe area to the south.

My trip started at Davis Lake, where we rented a cabin, which was actually more like a custom home. Davis, set at elevation 5,775 feet, gives rise to one of the most productive aquatic systems in the Sierra, and with it, one of the most prolific fisheries as well. In spring and fall, the rainbow trout are big and eager, while in summer, there are scads of large-mouth bass, a rare combination.

Like I said, the cabins are more like small homes, beautiful and exquisitely maintained. Although there is no television or telephone, they are almost too nice; a lot of people have lived in homes nowhere near this elegant. They are set on a hill sprinkled with pines, located about a quarter-mile from the Grizzly Creek Store at the southern end of the lake, about a 10-minute drive from the boat ramp.

The best time of year is late spring to early summer, then again in late summer to early fall, when the big rainbow trout awaken as hungry as German shepherds. The key is the huge daily temperature swing during the spring and fall, when temperatures can range from 25 degrees at daybreak to 75 degrees in the afternoon. The cold nights cool the lake down, yet the warm afternoons will inspire insect hatches and kindle the kind of trout bite that many anglers yearn for.

The trout here can come huge in the fall, with 15- to 18-inchers typical, and the chance at a big one going five pounds or better. Does it take a secret trick to take them? Oh yeah, you better believe it. What works is trolling an olive green woolly bugger, no weight, no flashers, on the northwest side of the lake outside of Freeman Creek and Grizzly Creek. The exact woolly bugger you need here is only available at the Davis Lake Store, a little country shop and the only store at the lake.

Plumas County: One of the top three regions in California for outdoor recreation

Davis Lake has great aquatic richness, so much that it gets heavy weed and algae growth in midsummer, making it unpleasant for swimming. But all the aquatic growth is why the lake is able to support a good bass fishery, one of the few lakes in the Sierra to do so.

I rate Plumas as one of the three best regions in California for fishing, camping, boating, hiking, and hunting; the others are Inyo in the southeast Sierra and Mt. Shasta in Northern California. The bonus at Plumas is that the entire county has only 20,000 residents, so even on weekends, the roads are clear, there are no lines anywhere, and the lakes don't get fished too hard.

Best of all, Plumas County fulfills exactly what most people desire from the great outdoors: beautiful country, lots of wildlife, good fishing, cabin rentals, and many campgrounds at lakes and streams with excellent hiking, backpacking, and hunting. What more could you ask for?

Facilities: Davis Lake Cabins offers three custom cabin suites of different sizes. Each has a fine kitchen, a living room, and sleeps two to eight people. A small store with a telephone is located about a two-minute walk away.

Reservations, fee: Reservations are advised, and require a deposit of half your fee. The fee is $78 per night for a one-bedroom for two people, $120 per night for a two-bedroom for four people. For each additional person, the fee is $10 per adult and $5 per child. Prices are slightly higher in winter.

Insider's note: For a free travel packet, phone the Plumas County Visitor's Bureau at (800) 326-2247. For fishing information, call Al Bruzza at the Sportsmen's Den in Quincy at (916) 283-2733.

Who to contact: Phone Davis Lake Cabins at (916) 832-5372, or write to P.O. Box 1385, Portola, CA 96122. For a map, send $3 to Office of Information, U.S. Forest Service, 630 Sansome Street, San Francisco, CA 94111 and ask for Plumas National Forest.

Directions: From San Francisco, take Interstate 80 east to Truckee. At Truckee, turn north on Highway 89 and continue through Sierraville (a left turn is required here) and to Sattley. At Sattley, turn right on County Road A23 and drive 13 miles to Highway 70. At Highway 70, turn left and drive one mile to Grizzly Road. Turn right on Grizzly Road and drive seven miles to an unnamed, paved road (look for the sign: "Services, 1 mile"). Turn left on that road, drive over the Davis Lake Dam, and you will arrive at the Grizzly Creek Store. Just past the store, turn left on Davis Way and drive up the hill for a short distance (it's well signed for Davis Lake Cabins) and look for the cabins on the right.

---

49. ELWELL LAKES LODGE CABINS
Lakes Basin, Plumas National Forest
Off Highway 89 near Graegle

First, let's end the confusion. There is no Elwell Lake. Rather there is nearby Mt. Elwell, 7,812 feet in elevation, and the lodge is named for the dozens of lakes in its shadow, including 23 within a three-mile radius of the lodge.

The cabins, both housekeeping cabins and tent cabins, provide a perfect base camp for exploring this area, whether you're hiking, fishing, boating, or windsurfing. Highlights include beautiful Long Lake, located three-quarters of a mile away, where the lodge provides unlimited use of boats and motors for guests, and of course, the Mt. Elwell Trail.

For newcomers to the lodge, climbing Mt. Elwell is like being baptized. It is a three-mile hike one-way to the top, requiring a climb of 1,100 feet. Your reward is a spectacular view of the Lakes Basin, a landscape of granite, pine forest, and lakes dotted about, looking like gem after gem.

Note that nearby Gold Lake Lodge, located less than a half-mile to the north, as well as other lake and cabin settings in the area, provide many more opportunities. Before planning your adventure, check out the stories on those places in this book, on pages 124-130.

Facilities: Elwell Lakes Lodge provides cabins and tent cabins. Cabins are fully equipped with a bath, a kitchenette, a barbecue, weekly linen, use of a boat on nearby Long Lake, and full use of lodge facilities. Tent cabins have facilities available nearby.

Reservations, fee: Reservations are required. Fees vary according to the size of the cabin. A small cabin for two people is $55 per night. A large cabin for up to six people is $93 per night. Tent cabins rent for $12 per night for one person, with each additional person costing $6 per day. Weekly rates are available.

Insider's note: This is one of the best cabin locations in California for hiking to nearby mountain lakes.

Who to contact: Phone Elwell Lakes Lodge at (916) 836-2347, or write to P.O. Box 68, Blairsden, CA 96103. For a map of the area, send $3 to USDA-Forest Service, 630 Sansome Street, San Francisco, CA 94111 and ask for Plumas National Forest. For a topographic map, send $3.50 to Maps-Western Distribution Center, U.S. Geologic Survey, Box 25286-Federal Center, Denver, CO 80225 and ask for Gold Lake.

Directions: From San Francisco, drive east on Interstate 80 to Truckee. In Truckee, turn north on Highway 89 and drive past the town of Clio to the Gold Lake Highway near the southern end of Graegle. Turn left on the Gold Lake Highway (Forest Road 24) and drive up the mountain. Turn right at the signed turnoff for Elwell Lakes Lodge (if you reach Gold Lake, you have gone too far) and drive a short distance to the lodge.

50. GOLD LAKE LODGE CABINS
Lakes Basin, Plumas National Forest
Off Highway 89 near Graegle

Nothing is perfect, right? But when you first hear about Gold Lake, it is possible to conclude, "I have found perfection."

Gold Lake is the centerpiece of the Lakes Basin Recreation Area, a beautiful sky-blue lake set in a rock basin in the northern Sierra, at a 6,400-foot elevation. It is by far the largest of the many lakes in the region, and the trout here can get huge. Plus there are several trailheads around the lake for outstanding hikes to smaller nearby lakes, and a pack station and stable is available near Gold Lake.

Perfect, right? There's more. Gold Lake Lodge, located about a half-mile north of Gold Lake near the Sierra crest at a 6,620-foot elevation, provides both "rustic" and "standard" cabins, and a restaurant serving dinner and breakfast. Nearby Elwell Lakes Lodge (see story on page 123) provides an alternative.

Perfect? Unfortunately, it's not. The one bugaboo that surprises new-comers all summer long is the wind at Gold Lake. The lake's location near the Sierra crest often causes what is called the venturi effect, especially in the afternoon, when wind is funneled through the mountain gap over the lake, picking up speed as a large mass of air is forced through a relatively small gap in the mountain ridge. In turn, that wind often causes whitecaps and waves at Gold Lake, even when nearby lakes such as Salmon, Packer, and Sardine have scarcely a ripple.

That is why anglers must get on the lake very early, prior to the wind picking up, or have boats large enough to handle rough water. My pal Allan Bruzza at the Sportsmen's Den in Quincy has proved that the wind actually helps the fishing here by keeping the big trout far less wary than at lakes that are glass-calm, and has caught both brown trout and Mackinaw trout weighing more than 10 pounds here. Bruzza also taught me a secret, that there is one protected cove that is calm even when the rest of the lake is raging. Of course, the wind is great for windsurfing and sailing in dinghies, at least until it really howls.

The cabins at Gold Lake Lodge are situated largely out of the wind and close to excellent short hiking trails to nearby lakes. There are two styles of cabins: "standard" have full baths; "rustic" do not, but offer detached facilities nearby. For double occupancy for two nights, the difference in price is $15 per night, $125 for a rustic and $140 for a standard. The price includes full dinner and breakfast.

A bonus at Gold Lake Lodge is that the owners, Ann and Pete Thill, keep the only boat available at nearby Big Bear Lake. This pretty lake is a half-mile walk from the lodge and provides good trout fishing, often with higher catch rates than at Gold Lake, though the trout are far smaller.

This is one of several excellent short hikes available here. The trail from Gold Lake Lodge to the north shore of Big Bear Lake (6,485 feet) is slightly downhill, losing about 200 feet, and from there, it is a short distance to Little Bear Lake, then about a quarter-mile to Little Cub

Frazier Falls, near Gold Lake Lodge Cabins

Lake. You can then take a half-mile loop that skirts the southern shore of Long Lake (which is quite beautiful), then turn left and pass Silver Lake and Round Lake (6,714 feet) before heading back to the lodge. This great loop hike passes six lakes in all and covers about three miles.

Just about perfect, eh? Well, of course, there's so much more to do here. The hike to the observation point for 100-foot-tall Frazier Falls, full and beautiful most of the summer, is only about a half-mile. Several other smaller waterfalls are also nearby. In all, there are more than 30 natural mountain lakes in the Lakes Basin, along with 11,000 acres of wilderness full of streams, meadows, and the Sierra crest, most of it accessible by trail.

Perfect? Just about.

Facilities: Gold Lake Lodge has both "rustic" and "standard" cabins. Standard cabins provide a full bath; rustic cabins do not, but have facilities available nearby.

Reservations, fee: Reservations are required. Fees are $80 per night, single occupancy, for a rustic cabin or $100 per night, single occupancy, for a standard cabin; $125 per night, double occupancy, for a rustic cabin or $140 per night, double occupancy, for a standard cabin. There is a two-night minimum, with weekly rate discounts.

Insider's note: Gold Lake can be windy, but a cove in the lake is well protected from afternoon winds.

Who to contact: Phone Gold Lake Lodge at (916) 836-2350, or write to P.O. Box 25, Blairsden, CA 96103. For a map of the area, send $3 to USDA-Forest Service, 630 Sansome Street, San Francisco, CA 94111 and ask for Plumas National Forest. For a topographic map, send $3.50 to Maps-Western Distribution Center, U.S. Geologic Survey, Box 25286-Federal Center, Denver, CO 80225 and ask for Gold Lake.

Directions: From San Francisco, drive east on Interstate 80 to Truckee. In Truckee, turn north on Highway 89 and drive past the town of Clio to the Gold Lake Highway near the southern end of Graegle. Turn left on the Gold Lake Highway (Forest Road 24) and drive up the mountain. About a half-mile past the Lakes Basin Campground, turn right at the signed turnoff for Gold Lake Lodge and drive a short distance to the lodge.

51. PACKER LAKE LODGE CABINS
Lakes Basin, Tahoe National Forest
Off Highway 49 near Bassetts

What a place: old lakefront log cabins, good trout fishing, low-speed boating, one of the best trails in California for hiking, and it is all set in Tahoe National Forest, where serenity reigns. No, you have not gone to heaven. You have instead gone to Packer Lake.

The lodge features 14 cabins, including low-cost log cabins (a bit on the raw side) all the way up to newer cabins with all-electric kitchens, bathrooms, and everything you need except for food. A bonus is the small fishing boat that is supplied as part of the package for all cabin guests.

Packer Lake is set at a 6,218-foot elevation, located at the foot of the dramatic Sierra Buttes. The trout fishing is decent at Packer Lake, but there are an additional 15 lakes with fishing within a five-mile radius in the Lakes Basin Recreation Area. Take your pick.

The most dramatic adventure of all, however, is hiking to the awesome and thrilling lookout at the Sierra Buttes. The trailhead is at the Packsaddle Campground, and from here you must make a climb of 2,369 feet over the course of about five miles. The trail traces the mountain rim to the lookout, topped off by a stairway with 176 steps that literally juts out into open space, a climb that is an eerie yet unforgettable experience. The view is astounding, hundreds of miles in all directions.

Who knows? Maybe you have gone to heaven.

Facilities: Packer Lake has 14 cabins varying in size and accommodations. Most have bathrooms and kitchens, with bed linens and towels provided, but a few available at reduced rates do not. A small fishing boat is included in cabin rentals. A small dock, primitive boat ramp, and additional rental boats and canoes are available. A small restaurant is on the property.

Reservations, fee: Reservations are required. Cabin rates are $53 per day for a one-room sleeping cabin with no kitchen and bath, and $90 to $110 per day (depending on size) for cabins with a kitchen. Weekly rates are $345, $560, $630, and $715, depending on accommodations and size.

Who to contact: Phone Packer Lake Lodge from May to mid-October at

(916) 862-1221, or write to P.O. Box 237, Sierra City, CA 96125. From November through May, call (415) 921-5943, or write to 2245 Beach Street, Apartment 2, San Francisco, CA 94123. For a map of the area, send $3 to USDA-Forest Service, 630 Sansome Street, San Francisco, CA 94111 and ask for Tahoe National Forest.

Directions: From San Francisco, take Interstate 80 east to Truckee. At Truckee, turn north on Highway 89 and drive 20 miles to Sierraville. At Sierraville, turn left on Highway 49 and drive about 10 miles to the Bassetts Store. Turn right (north) on Gold Lake Road and drive one mile. Look for the signed turnoff for Packer Lake/Sardine Lake. Turn left here, drive a short distance, and at the fork, bear right (left goes to Sardine Lake) and drive two miles to Packer Lake.

52. SARDINE LAKE CABINS
Lakes Basin, Plumas National Forest
Off Highway 49 near Bassetts

Staying in a cabin at Sardine Lake might seem just too good to be true. Unfortunately, it often is.

It is one of the prettiest mountain cabin settings anywhere. The lake is small but gorgeous, blue-green and sheltered, with the rim of the Sierra Buttes providing a dramatic backdrop. The cabins are cute and cozy, set near the lake in a pine forest, with a first-class restaurant along the shore and a small marina within a short walking distance.

How could this be too good to be true? Because it is darn near impossible to get a reservation and actually spend a week here. These cabins are reserved so far in advance that the only way to arrange a stay is to sign up on a waiting list, then hope for a cancellation. Some people, having fallen in love with the place, book the same cabin, for the same dates each year, even years ahead of time.

Which leads to an admission: You see, uh, ahem, oh, eh, I didn't actually stay here. Visited here? Yes. Hiked here? Yes. Fished here? Yes. Boated here? Yes. But stay in one of the great little cabins? No. In fact, when word circulated in Plumas County that I was writing this book, the owners at Sardine Lake actually requested to be left out, because they didn't want to turn more people away. Sorry. This place is just too good to keep secret.

If you have never been here, your first glimpse of the place can be quite stunning. Though the lake is small, it is pristine, almost divine, set at 6,000 feet in elevation, and the contrast between the calm blue-green lake surface and the granite mountain backdrop can provoke great feeling

The snowy Sierra Buttes behind the Sardine Lakes

in all who see it. There is no substitute for natural beauty, and there is no substitute for Sardine Lake.

Because it is a small lake, a five-mile-per-hour speed limit is in effect, perfect for little boats such as my canoe. A primitive, narrow dirt boat ramp is located just beyond the parking area, but it works well enough. The lake is well stocked with rainbow trout, which provide good fishing for trollers, with five-fish limits quite common on the days I have been here. Shoreline bait-dunkers do fair enough, but the best of it is to be had from a boat. That is why aluminum boat rentals are popular here, especially for people who are renting cabins (the lucky stiffs).

Because most people catch trout, a lot of them think they have discovered some secret spot at the lake, and upon departure, enjoy confiding this great secret to newcomers. Actually, it seems that most of the lake can provide good fishing. As you depart from the marina, the entire left side and back wall are good, with both an inlet and steep dropoff often holding good numbers of trout. See? Now I've done it, too. I tell ya, we fishermen just can't help it. But that's what happens when you catch a lot of fish.

The hiking here is also exceptional, with several excellent short hikes. One is the Sand Pond Interpretive Trail, which has wheelchair accessibility, and another leads to Upper Sardine Lake. The latter includes a hidden waterfall on the stream that connects Upper Sardine Lake to Lower Sardine Lake.

As for the cabins, they are cuter than an Easter basket full of bunnies. They are small, cozy, and quiet, set in pines within a short distance of the lake, restaurant, and marina. At the restaurant they ring a dinner bell, then serve meals family-style. Reservations are required, and there is occasionally space for visitors not staying in the cabins.

You take one look at this place, the mountain beauty, the little cabins, the fishing and hiking, and right off you know you'd like to try it out. Me, too. Some day I'd really like that. Let's see, three years from now, end of July, midweek...wonder if they'll have a cabin available....

Facilities: Sardine Lake Lodge provides lakeside cabins with beds with linens, kitchenettes, and bathrooms. A restaurant, marina with boat rentals and fish-cleaning station are available. A primitive dirt boat ramp is accessible only to small boats on trailers.

Reservations, fee: Reservations are required. However, cabins are reserved so far in advance that usually you must sign up on a waiting list, then hope for a cancellation. The fee is $470 per cabin per week.

Insider's note: Several maps show the jeep road on the right side of the lake linking up with the trail that is routed up to the spectacular Sierra Buttes. These maps are in error; although it was once a route, it is now impassable. The trailhead to reach the Sierra Buttes is out of the Packsaddle Campground near Packer Lake.

Who to contact: Phone Sardine Lake Lodge at (916) 862-1196, or write to Box 216, Sierra City, CA 96125. For a map of the area, send $3 to USDA-Forest Service, 630 Sansome Street, San Francisco, CA 94111 and ask for Plumas National Forest. For a topographic map, send $3.50 to Maps-Western Distribution Center, U.S. Geologic Survey, Box 25286-Federal Center, Denver, CO 80225 and ask for Gold Lake.

Directions: From San Francisco, drive east on Interstate 80 to Truckee. In Truckee, turn north on Highway 89 and drive for 30 miles just past the town of Sattley to Highway 49. Turn left on Highway 49 and drive over Yuba Pass to the town of Bassetts. At Bassetts, turn right on the Gold Lake Highway and drive about two miles. Turn left on Packer Lake/Sardine Lake Road and drive a short distance, then veer to the left at the Y and drive one mile to Sardine Lake.

---

53. SIERRA SHANGRI-LA CABINS
Yuba River, Sierra Nevada
Off Highway 49 near Downieville

The Yuba River is one of the prettiest rivers to flow westward out of the Sierra Nevada. The stretch of river near Downieville is especially gorgeous, flowing from the drops of melting snow from the Sierra crest, with deep pools and miniature waterfalls, often edged by slabs of granite and punctuated with boulders. In the spring it can be a wild and cold force of water, running blue-white during peak snowmelt. In the summer and fall, it greens up, warms considerably, and takes on a more benign demeanor in its routed canyon course.

From the cabins at Sierra Shangri-La, you can watch the changing faces of this dynamic river. The North Fork Yuba passes within ear range of the cabins here. Several have views of the river canyon, but from all of them you will feel the magnetism of moving water.

The reason more people don't know about the Yuba, or the secluded cabins near its banks, is because of its remoteness. There is no direct way to get there. Even with the best route on Highway 49, you will discover that calling it a "highway" is a mighty long stretch. In fact, it's ridiculous. This two-laner is constructed like a narrow pretzel, probably built on an old stagecoach route where grades had to be lengthened by curving the roads in order to give the horse teams a breather.

That keeps the area largely a secret. Yet here on the canyon bottom at 3,100 feet in elevation is Sierra Shangri-La and its eight cabins. The cottages with the best river views are BlueJay, LaVista, Flycaster, and Jim Crow, while three rooms in the upper level of the lodge also provide great views. By the way, the resort gets its name from the nearby magnificent Shangri-La wall of river stone.

This stretch of river can be excellent for fishing for both rainbow trout and brown trout, and is decent for swimming (see insider's note) and rafting out of Goodyear's Bar.

The North Fork Yuba has a mix of native trout as well as a bonus of 12,000 that are planted each year in early summer. It can be a lot of fun to cruise along the river, stopping at the turnouts to fish for 20 or 30 minutes per spot. Fishing access is good, although some of the better spots have been taken over by goldmining operations. Some of these guys get testy if you fish too close to them, or act like you might actually be interested in absconding with their piddling amounts of gold. Yeah, surrrre, heh, heh, heh.

There is one profound element you will notice here. Hang around the river for a while, and you will relax and get happy probably faster than in any other setting. My outdoor writer friend Ann Marie Brown believes this phenomenon is the result of being close to the influence of a clean and refreshing course of moving water, which seems to carry your troubles off downstream and cleanse your spirit. Maybe that's her secret for being able to write so fast. Never seen anything like it.

A good dose of Yuba River may not turn you into a high-speed writer, but regardless, you won't see anybody leaving Sierra Shangri-La after a week's stay with anything but a big, happy smile on their faces.

Facilities: Sierra Shangri-La has eight cabins of various sizes, each with a bathroom, a kitchen, and a wood stove. Bed linens are provided. No pets are permitted. A lodge with family-style dining is available on the property. Three bed-and-breakfast rooms with river views are also available.

Reservations, fee: Reservations are available. Cabin rates are $54 to $150 per night, depending on the size of cabin, season, and length of stay. A minimum stay of a week is required in July and August ($580 per week for a couple). The three bed-and-breakfast rooms at the lodge are rented by the night and start at $54.

Insider's note: The resort has a good swimming hole on the North Fork Yuba within walking distance of the cabins. Another good one is upstream at Union Flat Campground near Quartz Point, six miles east of Downieville on Highway 49.

Who to contact: Phone Sierra Shangri-La at (916) 289-3455, or write to P.O. Box 285, Downieville, CA 95936. For a map of the area, send $3 to USDA-Forest Service, 630 Sansome Street, San Francisco, CA 94111 and ask for Tahoe National Forest.

Directions: From San Francisco, take Interstate 80 east through Sacramento to Auburn. In Auburn, take Highway 49 north to Nevada City. In Nevada City, continue on Highway 49 (it jogs left in Nevada City, then narrows) for 42 miles to Downieville. In Downieville, continue three miles east on Highway 49 and look for the sign for Sierra Shangri-La on the right side of the road.

54. ROLLINS LAKE CABINS
Sierra Foothills
Off Interstate 80 near Colfax

What I remember most about the first time I flew over the Sierra foothills, besides how tired my arms were, was the surprising number of lakes set in the canyonlands. Rollins Lake is one these, tucked away in the foothills at 2,100 feet in elevation north of Colfax off Interstate 80. Here at Rollins Lake, right where the foothills meet the forest, a resort with cabins offers the opportunity for a surprising variety of water sports and recreation.

This area is not only where the valley grasslands rise and give way to conifers, but where the snow line starts in winter as well. The result is a reservoir that crosses the spectrum, from very hot in summer to very cold in winter, with great transition periods in the spring and fall. The summer heat makes it excellent for waterskiing, boating, and swimming, and the spring and fall transitions are great for fishing for trout and bass. In spring and early summer, when afternoon winds are common out of the west, the lake is also popular for small sailboats and windsurfing.

With its nine well-furnished cabins, Rollins Lakeside Inn is the focal point at the lake. Each of the cabins is complete with everything you need, including all cookware and bed linens, as well as everything you don't need, such as television with cable. No problem with the latter. Just throw a towel over it.

Rollins Lake has two extensive lake arms that cover 26 miles of shoreline, as well as long stretches of open water near the lower end of the lake. That makes it excellent for waterskiing, with water surface temperatures ranging from 75 to 80 degrees in the summer. Most anglers choose to fish well up the lake arms, either for bass in the coves during the morning and evening bites in the summer, or for trout near where the feeder streams enter the lake. The latter is where the lake's water is coldest; trout are naturally attracted there during the hot months by cool water temperatures, oxygenated flows, and an abundant food supply.

There are several other lakes in the immediate region, including Englebright, Collins, and Scotts Flat, but only Rollins has cabin rentals.

Facilities: Rollins Lakeside Inn has nine cabins, each with a kitchen, bathroom, cookware, utensils, and a barbecue on the porch. A swimming pool and a game room with a pool table are also available. A boat ramp and marina with boat rentals (aluminum boats with motors, canoes, and paddleboats) are located about a half-mile away.

Reservations, fee: Reservations are available. Cabin rates are $70 to $125 per night, depending on size of cabin, with weekly rates of $450 to $650.

Insider's note: 30 boat-in campsites and four drive-to campgrounds provide an option at Rollins Lake.

Who to contact: Phone Rollins Lakeside Inn at (916) 273-0729, or write to P.O. Box 152, Chicago Park, CA 95712.

Directions: From San Francisco, take Interstate 80 and drive east through Sacramento. Continue for about 60 miles to Highway 174 at Colfax. Take Highway 174 (a winding two-laner) east for about 3.5 miles to Orchard Springs Road. Turn right on Orchard Springs Road and drive about a mile to Rollins Lakeside Inn.

OTHER CABIN RENTALS IN PLUMAS AND SIERRA COUNTIES

Chalet View Lodge, Highway 70, Box 20575, Graegle, CA 96103; (916) 832-0335.

Feather River Park Resort, Highway 89, Box 37, Blairsden, CA 96103; (916) 836-2328.

Gold Lake Beach Resort, Gold Lake, 1540 Chandler Road, Quincy, CA 95971; (916) 836-2491.

Gray Eagle Lodge, Gold Lake Road, Box 38, Blairsden, CA 96103; (916) 836-2511 or (800) 635-8778.

KOA Auburn, 3550 KOA Way, Auburn, CA 95602; (916) 885-0990.

KOA Placerville, 4655 Rock Barn Road, Single Springs, CA 95682; (916) 676-2267.

Layman Resort, Highway 70, Box 8, Blairsden, CA 96103; (916) 836-2356.

Salmon Lake Lodge, Box 121, Sierra City, CA 96125; (408) 771-2622.

For a free travel packet on the region, phone the Plumas County Visitors Bureau at (800) 326-2247.

OTHER CABIN RENTALS IN THE YUBA RIVER AREA

Yuba River Inn, P.O. Box 236, Sierra City, CA 96125; (916) 862-1122.

River Pines Resort
(530) 836-2552

San Francisco Bay Area

** For locations of camps, see map on page 9. **

55. LAWSONS' RESORT COTTAGES
Dillon Beach
Off Highway 1 near Tomales

It doesn't take long to become enchanted with Dillon Beach, the oceanside community set at the mouth of Tomales Bay. The cottages here provide sweeping ocean views, access to excellent beach walks, clamming (in season), beachcombing, and charter boat fishing operators just a mile away.

If you can arrange to stay here during the week, then do so. Although this area is a popular Bay Area spot for weekend getaways, during the week the place attracts relatively few people. So not only will you get to enjoy great coastal beauty and recreation, but you won't have to contend with the masses. The cottage rental rates are also lower during the week.

The cottages, as well as the seven vacation homes, are completely furnished with everything but food and drink. Weather is always a wild card, with fog common in the summer, but surprisingly no matter how rough the ocean is, Tomales is often calm, sheltered from west winds by Inverness Ridge at Point Reyes National Seashore. That makes Tomales Bay great for sea kayaks and small boats.

Other great features include some of the best clamming beds on the Bay Area coast; Lawsons' will show you exactly where to find them. If you want to clam, plan your trip for a minus low tide. Fishing is also excellent, and charter boats make runs for rockfish year-round and for salmon during the summer. Some of the best spots on the coast for catching rockfish are at Cordell Bank. Salmon often school outside nearby Tomales Point in midsummer, and halibut enter Tomales Bay in late summer and fall.

Facilities: Lawsons' Resort has three cottages, plus seven vacation homes. All are completely furnished, including kitchens with cookware and utensils, bed linens and towels, and wood stoves. A small store is available. Smoking and pets aren't permitted.

Reservations, fee: Reservations are advised. The weekend rate for a cottage that sleeps six is $300 for two nights. Discount rates are available on weekdays. A two-night minimum stay applies on weekends.

Who to contact: Phone Lawsons' Resort at (707) 878-2204 or (707) 878-2710, or write to P.O. Box 97, Dillon Beach, CA 94929.

Directions: From San Francisco, take U.S. 101 north to Petaluma. In Petaluma, take Washington Boulevard and drive east (it turns into Bodega Avenue) for 10 miles. Turn left at Tomales Road (if you reach the town of Two

Rock, you've gone a mile too far) and drive six miles to the town of Tomales at Highway 1. At the stop sign, turn right on Highway 1 and drive a quarter-mile to Dillon Beach Road. Turn left on Dillon Beach Road and drive four miles to Lawsons' Resort.

56. WILDCAT BACKPACK CAMP
Point Reyes National Seashore
Off Highway 1 near Olema

You can explore over 50,000 miles of hiking trails in the Bay Area and not find more dramatic natural wonders than you will discover on this hike over the course of just 5.1 miles. You will pass great coastal lookouts, a series of hidden lakes, a stunning waterfall (especially after a good rain), exceptional rock formations, and a pretty beach. And waiting at the end is a backpack campground set on an ocean bluff.

What more could you ask for? Wait! Don't answer that! Heh, heh, heh. Actually, if you have a special love for the coast in its most natural state of beauty, this trip will come close to your idea of perfection.

What makes it work is Wildcat Camp, reached via a one-way hike of about two to three hours. The camp has 11 primitive sites set in a meadow on an ocean bluff, and unlike most backpack camps, piped water and pit toilets are provided. This is an environmentally sensitive area where minimum-impact camping styles are required, and that means no fires, camping only in designated sites, and being absolutely certain to leave not even a trace of litter behind. To do so, pack a camping stove for cooking, obtain the required site permit, and bring along an extra plastic garbage bag to pick up every piece of litter you create or come across.

Start by securing a reservation for one of the campsites by phoning park headquarters at the Bear Valley Visitor Center at (415) 663-1092. Access and camping are free, but if you head in blind and camp without a permit, you will be subject to a fine and expulsion. Park headquarters also offers a free hiking map, a great bonus, and the rangers always seem friendly and helpful.

While there are several ways to reach Wildcat Camp, our favorite is the Palomarin Trailhead, located on the coast north of Bolinas. This is also the southern trailhead for the 15-mile Coastal Trail, which is routed across much of Point Reyes National Seashore's most remote and beautiful country. The best of it is included on the walk out to Wildcat Camp.

In the first two miles, the trip starts by dipping down into a ravine, then climbing out about 500 feet to a coastal bluff, where you reach a junction with the Lake Ranch Trail. Turn left, staying on the Coastal Trail, and you will skirt past the northern shoreline of Bass Lake, then a mile later, Pelican Lake. These lakes are always stunners the first time you see them, larger than you might anticipate, especially Pelican Lake, which usually fills each year by early February.

From here the trail drops down to Alamere Creek, where another surprise awaits. The creek runs down a canyon, pours right over an ocean bluff in a clean cascade—about a 40-foot drop—then hits the beach and runs right into the ocean. Alamere Falls is one of those rare waterfalls that run into the sea. Like all waterfalls in the Bay Area (where there is no snowmelt, of course), this one is best seen in the winter and early spring, especially after two or three days of sustained rains. Its size can vary dramatically, from an awesome cascade in the late winter to a thin silver seep in the summer.

From Alamere Falls, it is two miles to Wildcat Camp, with the trail making a short climb, then heading along the grasslands above Wildcat Beach past tiny Ocean Lake, making another short climb around larger Wildcat Lake, then dropping you down to the campground.

With your base camp set, you can begin to explore the network of more than a half-dozen trails intersecting within a few miles in the hills to the east. At night, you'll hear the call of the sea and coastal breezes, feel the giant presence of the ocean, and as you drift off to sleep, you will know that everything is right with the world.

Facilities: There are 11 primitive sites, with piped water and pit toilets. There are also four group sites nearby, which can hold 25 people each. For cooking, backpack stoves are required. No mountain bikes or pets are permitted.

Reservations, fee: Reservations and a backcountry camping permit are required. Parking, access, and camping are free.

Insider's note: No fires are permitted.

Who to contact: Phone Point Reyes National Seashore at (415) 663-1092, or write to Superintendent, Point Reyes National Seashore, Point Reyes, CA 94956. They can also provide you with a free trail map. To obtain topographic maps of the area, send $6 to Maps-Western Distribution Center, U.S. Geologic Survey, Box 25286-Federal Center, Denver, CO 80225 and ask for Bolinas and Double Point.

Directions: From San Francisco, drive north of U.S. 101 to San Rafael. Take the Sir Francis Drake Boulevard exit and drive west about 20 miles to the town of Olema. Turn left on Highway 1 and drive 8.9 miles south to Bolinas Road, which is usually not signed. Turn right and drive 2.1 miles to Mesa Road. Turn right and drive 5.8 miles to the Palomarin Trailhead.

57. STEEP RAVINE CABINS
Mt. Tamalpais State Park
Off Highway 1 near Stinson

It happens over and over again. You call the Destinet camp reservation line and get a busy signal. But you keep at it. Then when you finally get through, you proceed to tackle the automated phone system, powered by hope, only to discover that all the cabins at Steep Ravine are booked for weeks.

Sound familiar? You ain't lyin'. If you've plowed this turf, you know that while the Steep Ravine cabins may not be well known to the general public, they are the favorite spot of enough people to keep them locked up most of the time.

But there is a solution, although it requires planning and fortitude. First you must schedule when you want to stay here as far ahead as possible—reservations are available seven months in advance. For a weekend in August, for instance, you can book your trip in January. Do that and you get booked. Do anything else and you stand a chance of missing out. A good chance. Like I said, it happens over and over.

Steep Ravine Cabins are located on an ocean bluff at Rocky Point on the Marin coast, close enough to hear the waves. These are primitive cabins, with a wood stove, picnic table, and flat wood surface for sleeping. You bring everything else. Officially, they are called "environmental campsites"; when you call Destinet for reservations, ask for "Mt. Tamalpais State Park Environmental Campsites at Steep Ravine." That works.

The cabins cost $30 per night, plus a $6.75 reservation fee. A gate on the access road, located on the ocean side of Highway 1, keeps the camp secluded and relatively hidden from many people.

It can be a spectacular setting, one of the best anywhere on the Pacific Coast. Even on foggy days there are passing ships, fishing boats, and lots of marine birds, especially in the summer when pelicans and murres are so abundant here. On clear days, the sunsets can be breathtaking. You will never forget the sight of that big fireball dipping into the ocean, inch by inch. In the winter, you might even spot passing whales, tipped off by their spouts, which look like little puffs of smoke.

While it can be enjoyable to do absolutely nothing here but enjoy this scene, there are also several exceptional hikes nearby, including an easy romp down to the beach, and on the other side of Highway 1, a hike up Steep Ravine, one of my favorite places on this planet.

There are two beach walks from the cabins. The closest is down to the cove just north of Rocky Point and to Redrock Beach. The walk is short, with the trail routed right out of the camp. The other trail is on the south side of Rocky Point and reaches a tiny but secluded beach. To get there, you walk back up the access road, turn right, then look for the trail on the right down to the cove.

If you finally get booked for a cabin, then discover it is drizzling, raining, or downright storming, don't cancel out. Instead, take advantage of what can be a wondrous experience. Wondrous? What can be wondrous about getting wet? The Steep Ravine Trail, that's what. Just across the highway, with a small jog to the right, is a trailhead for Steep Ravine. From this trailhead, the route follows along Webb Creek, where you make a steady traipse uphill with a perfect view of the creek, with several small cascades in sight upstream. Rain brings everything to life here—ferns, sorrel, and redwoods. I've seen the place on a sunny summer day, and I've seen it in a howling late winter storm, and with some decent rain gear, I'll take the latter anytime.

The first time I saw the Steep Ravine Cabins was when I was salmon fishing, and we approached just offshore of Rocky Point. Suddenly I spotted these neat little wood shacks set on the bluff, and I made a mental note to check up on them. Imagine my amazement to discover that "all you have to do" to stay here is make a reservation.

All you have to do, eh? Well, while that isn't as easy as it sounds, it's well worth going through the planning to finally rope one of these cabins.

Facilities: There are 10 cabins, each with a wood stove, picnic table, and flat wood surface for sleeping. There are also six walk-in campsites. Piped water and firewood are available.

Reservations, fee: Reservations are required. Reserve through Destinet at (800) 444-PARK ($6.75 reservation fee). The cabin fee is $30 per night; walk-in campsites are $9 per night.

Insider's note: Directions on how to get through the gated access road are included in the reservation confirmation.

Who to contact: Phone Mt. Tamalpais State Park at (415) 388-2070, or Marin District Headquarters at (415) 456-1286, or write to Mt. Tamalpais State Park, 801 Panoramic Highway, Mill Valley, CA 94941. A map/brochure of Mt. Tamalpais State Park is available for $1 at the Pantoll Ranger Station, or by mail from the address above. A more detailed hiking map of the area is available for a fee from Olmsted Brothers Map Company, P.O. Box 5351, Berkeley, CA 94705.

Directions: From San Francisco, take U.S. 101 north into Marin. Take the Stinson Beach/Highway 1 exit and continue to the coast at Muir Beach overlook. Turn north on Highway 1 and drive about four miles to the Rocky Point access road (gated) on the left side of the highway.

Mt. Tamalpais State Park

Off Highway 1 near Mill Valley

If I ever get stuck in San Francisco, feeling jammed out by a series of meetings, traffic snarls, and lack of parking spaces, there is still nothing that can undermine my faith in the good this world can provide. You know why? Because I know that in just 45 minutes I can be at the Pantoll Walk-In Camp, set at the threshold of the best network of hiking trails in the Bay Area.

Pantoll Campground is located at 1,500 feet in elevation on the western slopes of Mt. Tamalpais in Marin County, a place of spectacular and diverse beauty. Within a few miles are breathtaking coastal views, an intimate redwood canyon with a stream, hilly grasslands sprinkled with deer and other wildlife, and more than a dozen hikes that rate a 10.

But what separates it from other trailheads on Mt. Tam is the walk-in campground. By camping, you can be at one of the perfect vantage points to watch the sun rise or set, without a big rush to either get there at dawn or get out at dusk. There may be no better place on earth to watch a sunrise than from the nearby East Peak Lookout.

After parking at the Pantoll parking area, then registering at the adjacent ranger station, it is about a 100-yard walk to your campsite. There are 16 sites for tents, and each comes with a picnic table and fire grill; piped water and flush toilets are available. A $14 fee is charged in the summer months, $12 in the off-season. No reservations are available, but because a short walk is required—and the camp is not on the state park Destinet reservation system—many people stay away. Most of the time you can have your pick of the camp, although it always fills during summer weekends. If there is any question about campsite availability, call Mt. Tamalpais State Park at (415) 388-2070, or Marin District Headquarters at (415) 456-1286.

Once your campsite is secure, you can start exploring the surrounding land, an expanse of enchantment for hikers. There are two stellar hikes that start right at Pantoll, Steep Ravine and Matt Davis/Coastal Trail. The trail into Steep Ravine is pure heaven, heading down into a canyon with a pretty stream (with several cascades after good rains), luxuriant undergrowth and a towering redwood canopy, all pristine and beautiful. The Matt Davis/Coastal Trail is routed out eventually across open hills where the views of the Marin coast and ocean are breathtaking, like the whole world is within reach of your open palms. At either of these places, some visitors feel as if they are being filled by divine energy.

But that is how Mt. Tamalpais is. A lot of people say it is one of the few places anywhere that projects a feeling of power. That is why campers at Pantoll should take advantage of their proximity by making the 10-minute drive from Pantoll to the East Peak to watch the sun rise or set; to get there, take Pantoll Road, located directly across from the parking area. It takes about 15 minutes of hiking to reach the East Peak at 2,571 feet. I've seen mornings here where the sky looked like a scene from *The Ten Commandments,* with light beams boring through clouds glowing pink and orange, where every passing minute brings with it a new color, a new look, like the changing inflections of the one you love.

There are several other trips close to Pantoll. The Dipsea Trail, which loops down to Muir Woods to the east, also runs right through Pantoll. There are also excellent trailheads at the nearby Bootjack and Rock Springs parking areas. In my book *California Hiking* (Foghorn Press), of the 1,000 hikes I detailed, I picked 25 trails on Mt. Tamalpais alone, the largest concentration of high-rated trails in any area in the state.

When camping at Pantoll, you are within minutes of most of them. Somehow, the traffic jams, parking problems, and endless meetings back in San Francisco don't seem so bad after all.

Facilities: There are 16 walk-in campsites for tents. Piped water and flush toilets are available. Fire grills and picnic tables are provided.

Reservations, fee: No reservation; $14 fee per night ($12 in the off-season). Pets are allowed in your camp for $1, but are not permitted on trails.

Who to contact: Phone Mt. Tamalpais State Park at (415) 388-2070, or Marin District Headquarters at (415) 456-1286, or write to 801 Panoramic Highway, Mill Valley, CA 94941. A map/brochure of Mt. Tamalpais State Park is available for $1 at the Pantoll Ranger Station, or by mail from the address above. To obtain a topographic map of the area, send $3.50 to Maps-Western Distribution Center, U.S. Geologic Survey, Box 25286-Federal Center, Denver, CO 80225 and ask for San Rafael.

Directions: Take U.S. 101 in Marin County to the Stinson Beach/Highway 1 exit. Take this exit, heading west, and continue to the lighted T intersection (Highway 1). Turn left and drive about four miles uphill to the Panoramic Highway. Veer to the right on Panoramic Highway and continue for 5.5 miles (past the turnoff to Muir Woods) and turn left at the Pantoll parking area. A ranger station is located nearby. Reaching the camp requires a 100-yard walk.

59. ANGEL ISLAND ENVIRONMENTAL SITES
Angel Island State Park
Off U.S. 101 near Tiburon

At 4:30 P.M. each day, Angel Island can be transformed into your own private heaven. Because that is when the last ferry boat of the day departs the island to take visitors back to the mainland, along with most park workers and concession employees. Remaining are just a handful of campers and rangers, and suddenly, if you are among them, you can have a beautiful island just about all to yourself. Imagine that.

I'll never forget the first night I spent here. From the opening of my tent, right from my sleeping bag, I could see the lights of San Francisco and the Golden Gate Bridge, smell the cool salt breeze, and hear the wind rustling through the trees. Earlier that night, we'd made the steep trip up 781-foot Mt. Livermore, and it seemed that the entire Bay Area surrounded us in an incandescent glow. Like I said, I'll never forget it.

This experience is available only to those who stay overnight at one of the environmental campsites. There are nine such camps, each with a picnic table, food locker, running water, pit toilet, and barbecue unit. This kind of camping is not for everybody because reaching the sites requires a two-mile walk, and the nights can be cold, windy, and foggy. I had one stay here where the wind was howling, then in the middle of the

View of San Francisco skyline from Angel Island

night, an unexpected pounding rain slammed my tent for hours. I slept about zero.

But I rate camping at Angel Island as one of the most special outdoor adventures in California that doesn't require a long drive. The trip starts with the ferry boat ride, departing from Pier 43 1/2 in San Francisco ($9), Tiburon ($5), or Vallejo ($10). The price includes the state park entrance fee. The boat lands at Ayala Cove and deposits you at recreation headquarters for the park.

Here you will discover the trailhead for the Perimeter Trail, which will take you around the island, as well as shops for bicycle rentals, tram tours, kayak rentals, and the Cove Café.

The hiking and views at Angel Island have long been the feature attractions, topped by the 360-degree lookout at Mt. Livermore. Many of the trails provide easy walks with great views of the Bay along much of their routes. Visitors should be warned, however, that the hike to the Mt. Livermore summit is short but steep, a climb of 550 feet in a half-mile, and from Ayala Cove it's a round-trip of six miles.

A great option is to bring your bicycle or rent one for a ride around the island. There are eight miles of roadways and paths for bikes, including the Perimeter Road, which is partially paved. The Perimeter Road is wide enough to provide enough room for low-speed bikers as well as for people out enjoying a walk.

There is also plenty of room for a tram, another new feature at Angel Island. The tram consists of little open-air cars pulled at low speed on the Perimeter Road, past historical sites and lookout points. The ride takes about an hour, including several stops to allow participants to take photographs. The tram solves the perennial problem for people not physically able to hike, yet who desire a quality outdoor adventure, without diminishing the experience for other users.

But while all this is fun, you will enter a new dimension when the day-users depart for the night, the concessions close down, and you are left at your hike-in camp. Suddenly, it seems there is nobody here, nobody at all, and you will have the trails, the lookouts—hey, the whole darn island—all to yourself.

Facilities: There are nine walk-in environmental camps, each with a picnic table, food locker, running water, pit toilet, and barbecue unit. You need to bring all camping gear. A backpacking stove is essential.

Reservations, fee: Camping reservations are required; $14 fee per night, plus $6.75 reservation fee. Ferry boat rides are $9 from San Francisco, $5 from Tiburon, $10 from Vallejo. Ferry discounts are available for children, seniors, and groups. Bicycles are permitted for free on the ferries from San Francisco and Vallejo, and for $1 from Tiburon.

Insider's note: Tram rides are $4 per person, and you can get out as often as you wish. Bike rentals are available for $12 to $25 per day. Single kayak rentals are available for two hours for $20, and double kayak rentals are available for two hours for $35; experience and reservations are required.

Ferry information: Phone Red & White Fleet, San Francisco, (415) 546-2628; Tiburon-Angel Island Ferry, Tiburon, (415) 435-2131; Blue & Gold Fleet, Vallejo, (415) 705-5444.

Who to contact: To make a campsite reservation, phone Destinet at (800) 444-PARK. To make a kayak reservation, phone Sea Trek at (415) 488-1000. For recorded information at Angel Island State Park Headquarters, phone (415) 435-1915. To contact Ayala Cove, phone (415) 435-5390. To contact State Park District Headquarters, phone (415) 456-1286.

Directions to San Francisco Red & White Fleet ferry: From U.S. 101 on the Peninsula, drive north to San Francisco. At the Y for U.S. 101 and Interstate 80, take Interstate 80 to the right and continue toward the Bay Bridge. Take the Fourth Street exit and drive straight ahead (it turns into Bryant Street) until it dead-ends at The Embarcadero. Turn left and drive along the water-front for two miles to Fisherman's Wharf, then park at one of the pay lots.

Directions to Tiburon ferry: From U.S. 101 in Marin, take the Tiburon exit and drive east to downtown Tiburon. Park at one of the pay lots and walk a short distance to the terminal.

Directions to Vallejo Blue & Gold Fleet ferry: From Interstate 80 in Vallejo, take the Interstate 780 exit. From Interstate 780, head west on Curtola Park-way, which eventually becomes Mare Island Way. Continue on Mare Island Way to the terminal at 495 Mare Island Way.

60. CHABOT WALK-IN SITES
Anthony Chabot Regional Park
Off Interstate 580 near Oakland

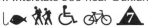

When I took my first steps on the John Muir Trail, the distance ahead from Mt. Whitney to Yosemite Valley seemed endless, and I thought about the thousands and thousands of times my boots would stretch forward and land, over and over again. Would we even make it? I remembered that apprehension at Chabot Regional Park as I took the first of a couple of hundred steps from the parking area to the walk-in campsites, then practically started laughing.

Do you think we can make it? Or will nature defeat the backpackers? Well, it turns out that we did complete the John Muir Trail, taking 20 days to do it, and we also made it all the way to the Chabot walk-in campsites, although it took only about five minutes.

Hiker in Anthony Chabot Regional Park

Right there is the magic of Chabot, where a backpack-style experience is available with everything but the long butt-kicker of a hike. Campsites are set in a grove of tall eucalyptus; an excellent spot for shore-fishing at Lake Chabot is only a half-mile walk away; and there's a bicycle trail and loop hike from the campground to the lake.

Because the walk-in sites are so close to the parking area, you can bring just about anything, as long as you don't mind carrying it for the short walk. Yet at the same time, you get a sense of hiding away from the car campers and motor homes at the 65 drive-in sites, situated up to a half-mile away.

When you first drive into the Chabot campground, pass the motor homes in the first 12 sites, then park, you might think you're in for a nightmare. That's what we thought. The park did not appear to come even close to matching our vision of what a hiking/camping destination would look like. But then we arrived at our campsite set on a wooded bluff from which you could see Lake Chabot a half-mile to the south—blue, calm, and inviting. Thus started our attitude adjustment.

That adjustment continues for most visitors on Huck's Trail, a half-mile walk from the trailhead near site 20 down to the shore of Lake Chabot. At the shoreline, the Huck Trail junctions with the Honker Bay Trail, which provides access to one of the better fishing areas at the lake. In the winter and spring, trout fishing is often good here, and in the summer, the same is true for crappie.

From the Honker Bay Trail, you can follow along the shore of the lake in a clockwise direction to cross a bridge and walk all the way to the marina, a one-way distance of 2.8 miles from the campground. Another possibility is a great bicycle loop, which allows you to cruise down from the campground to Lake Chabot on the Live Oak Trail, then link up with a route that circles the entire lake, a 12.4-mile ride. The route surface is mostly smooth, but does have one rough area.

While you won't mistake the walk-in campground for the high Sierra, there are pretty grass sites set amid tall eucalyptus. Each has a flat tent site, picnic table, and fire pit with grill, and piped water is available near sites 14 and 17. A rest room with showers is also located nearby, closest to site 13 and farthest from site 20.

Sunsets are often very pretty here, with the hills cast in changing hues of orange. At dusk, Lake Chabot below can appear almost cobalt blue. A light breeze may rustle the leaves of the eucalyptus, deer often emerge to browse on the neighboring grasslands, and quiet falls over everything.

What a deal, eh? For people who want an introduction to backpack-style camping without the investment of a long drive followed by a long and grueling walk, the Chabot walk-in camps provide an answer.

Facilities: There are 10 walk-in sites. Fire grills and picnic tables are provided. Piped water, toilets, and showers are available nearby. Pets are permitted. You will need to provide all gear as if this was a backpacking trip, although far more gear can be added because it is only a few minutes' walk from the parking area to the campsites.

Reservations, fee: Reservations are required; $13 fee per night.

Insider's note: Nearby there are 53 drive-in sites for tents or motor homes and 12 sites for motor homes with hookups, available for $13 to $19 per night, plus a $5 reservation fee. Additional vehicles per site are $5.

Who to contact: To make a campsite reservation, phone (510) 562-2267. To contact Chabot Regional Park Campground, phone (510) 635-0135, extension 2570. For a brochure or park information, phone (510) 635-0135, extension 2200.

Directions: From Interstate 580 in the Oakland hills, take the 35th Avenue exit. Turn east and drive up the hill and straight across Skyline, where 35th Avenue becomes Redwood Road. Continue on Redwood Road for six miles to the park entrance on the right.

61. SUNOL BACKPACK CAMP
Sunol Regional Wilderness
Off Interstate 680 in Sunol

The "off-season" for backpacking is actually the "on season" in the Sunol Regional Wilderness.

Summer can be extremely short and winters extremely long in the mountains, but Bay Area backpackers have a winter option here in the Sunol Regional Wilderness. A three-plus-mile section of the Ohlone Wilderness Trail is routed out to a quiet trail camp with spacious sites—some with views, some with shade—and best of all, piped springwater is available on site.

Your payment comes in the form of a 3.4-mile hike from park head-quarters at Sunol with a 1,000-foot climb—plus lots of up and down—then a 300-foot drop to the camp. In the process, you cross a pretty bridged stream, get great views of miles of untouched foothill country, and end up at a camping area with well-secluded sites. This is a popular trip between October and May, when the weather is coolest and Alameda Creek is at its prettiest, and can be spectacular with wildflower blooms in late March and early April.

Sunol Regional Wilderness is located in southern Alameda County, not far from Niles Canyon east of Fremont. It covers 6,400 acres, enough so you can find many spots to call your own. Highlights include Little Yosemite with its rocky gorge, Alameda Creek and its small pool-and-drop waterfalls, and a trailhead for the 28-mile Ohlone Wilderness Trail (another trailhead is in Del Valle Regional Park, south of Livermore).

The latter is your calling for this adventure. This backpack trip uses the Ohlone Wilderness Trail to offer the wilderness experience in a week-end installment. En route to the camp, the trail varies from a single-track dirt path to a former ranch road. The detailed trail map provided at the entrance station, along with the trail markers at each junction, will always keep you on track.

After starting at the sign-in panel, the trail crosses a bridge over Alameda Creek (elevation 390 feet), which is quite pretty after being recharged by rains. In the first quarter-mile, the trail is routed along the right bank of the stream.

Then you rise east out of the river canyon, crossing through bay and oak woodlands, and in the course of the next half-mile, find yourself transported to grassy hillsides. It's a small climb, just enough to start reminding the out-of-shape that they are now going up and that there is more up to come.

Having reached the foothills, you continue to climb. If you start puffing, you can stop occasionally, turn around, and enjoy the views. To the west is a panorama of the Sunol Wilderness, showcasing a deep valley and Flag Hill, along with miles of rolling foothills to the north.

After catching your breath, you march upward, rising to an elevation of 1,430 feet. Here you junction with Cerro Este Road, the highest point on this section of the Ohlone Wilderness Trail. The two trails overlap for one-third of a mile, and then you reach signpost marker 18. Turn right at this marker, following the sign for the Ohlone Wilderness Trail, and walk the final 1.3 miles to the camp. On this last part of the trip, you will descend 1.3 miles as the trail contours along the grassy hills.

You will find some of the campsites are shaded and some are more open with very pretty views. For instance, Sycamore Camp is shaded, while Sky Camp has a great view of the rolling hills. Most of the sites are secluded and out of view of the others. In addition, three springs have been developed and linked to a faucet, so water is available for drinking and cooking.

For those who like wildflowers: this trip can be spectacular in the spring, best when a wet winter is followed by a week of warm weather in March, then a few days of rain, then more warm weather. When that happens, you can't miss. The most abundant blooms are golden poppies, lupine (blue), and blue-eyed grass (purple), but there can be 15 or 20 other varieties. Of the 53 parks in the East Bay Regional Park District, Sunol is considered right at the top for wildflowers, and is renowned across Northern California as among the best places to see wildflowers.

Facilities: Sunol Backpack Camp has seven flat tent sites with picnic tables, each sized for 5 to 10 people. Three developed springs with faucets for piped water are located within the backpack area. No trash containers are available, so pack out everything. No pets or horses are permitted.

Reservations, fee: Reservations are required; phone (510) 562-CAMP; $5 fee per person per night, plus a $5 reservation fee.

Insider's note: For an optional return hike from the camp to the parking area, walk along Little Yosemite, which traces above the gorge and provides views of Alameda Creek.

Who to contact: Phone Sunol Regional Wilderness at (510) 862-2244, or East Bay Regional Park District at (510) 635-0135, extension 2200, or write to 2950 Peralta Oaks Court, P.O. Box 5381, Oakland, CA 94605.

Directions: From Interstate 680 in the East Bay, take the Calaveras Road exit in Sunol. Turn south on Calaveras and drive five miles to Geary Road. Turn left on Geary Road and drive two miles to the park entrance. From the kiosk, continue down the hill for a short distance, then turn left and park adjacent to park headquarters. Walk a short distance down Geary Road and look for the hiker's sign-in panel next to the trailhead.

62. BUTANO STATE PARK BACKPACK SITES
Butano State Park
Off Highway 1 near Pescadero

Where can you get sunny ridgelines and glimpses of the ocean, combined with a luxuriant redwood forest in a canyon? An 11-mile loop trail on the Butano Rim provides all of this, as well as a trail camp located exactly in the middle of the route, 5.5 miles out.

All of it is scenic, with the trails routed through redwood forest and on fire roads set on the Butano Ridge affording great lookouts of the Pacific Ocean and the canyon below. It is a great place to visit, and if you go, remember that Butano is pronounced "*Bute*-uh-no" and not "Bew-*tah*-no." Of the 150 parks in the Bay Area, Butano is the favorite for the few who know it well, and you can spot them immediately by how they pronounce it. In fact, Butano is the number one hiking destination for Don Murphy, the director of the California State Parks Department.

When you first drive up, you may wonder what could possibly create such devotion. The Pescadero area is pretty, primarily coastal foothills and grasslands, but hey, the number one favorite of the parks chief? Then you turn left on the park access road and find out why, entering a canyon that is a universe apart from the rest of the Bay Area.

The Butano Canyon is filled with redwoods, creating a classic forest habitat, complete with a stream, giant ferns, sorrel, trillium, wild iris, and even a few wild orchids. The hiking trails weave a network among this dense vegetation, a quiet setting, with the Butano Rim Loop rising to a viewpoint above it.

You start the trip at the Mill Ox Trailhead, which is located about a half-mile past the park entrance on the left side of the road, where there is a pullout parking area. The Mill Ox Trail (no bicycles permitted) starts by crossing a small creek in a dense redwood forest, then heads up a short but steep grade on switchbacks, emerging at the top of the canyon on the Butano Fire Road (bikes okay here).

Here you turn right, and get a more gradual climb as you head toward the park's interior. The fire road gets plenty of sun, and plenty of shirts are removed on the climb. Along the way, if you turn and look back to the west from time to time, you will discover views of the Pacific Ocean. The trail climbs steadily to 1,713 feet, providing more views of the ocean and Butano Canyon, then descends about 200 feet to the trail camp. An old abandoned airstrip is located nearby, one of the trail's oddities. This is all you need for a perfect first day, requiring just enough of a push to give you that good tired feeling at camp.

The second day is a dream, mostly downhill, taking the Olmo Fire Trail, then the Doe Ridge/Goat Hill Trail, a beautiful, soft dirt trail through the redwoods, back to the starting point. In the process you will have surveyed most of the park's 2,700 acres.

The backpacker's campground has one major drawback: no piped water. That means you have to pack in all the water you will need, at least two quarts per person. Two people require a quart of drinking water per person on the hike in, another quart for cooking dinner, and a fourth quart for the second day on the downhill hike back home.

Facilities: Butano State Park has eight individual campsites at a primitive backpacker's campground. Pit toilets are provided. There is no piped water. At the park's main drive-in campground, there are also 18 walk-in tent sites and 21 sites for tents or motor homes.

Reservations, fee: Reservations are required through park headquarters for backpack campsites; $7 fee per night. To reserve a campsite at the park's main campground, call Destinet at (800) 444-PARK; $14 fee per night plus a $6.75 reservation fee.

Insider's note: Bikes are permitted on 10 miles of fire roads but not on hiking trails. Mountain bikers can access the backpacker's camp on the Butano Rim Trail, but must start the trip off Cloverdale Road at a gated fire road, located a short distance north of the turnoff to the park entrance station. Confirm with rangers while checking in.

Who to contact: Call Butano State Park at (415) 879-2040, or write to P.O. Box 9, Pescadero, CA 94060. If there is no answer at the park, phone the Bay Area State Parks District (based in Half Moon Bay) at (415) 726-8800.

Directions: From the intersection of highways 1 and 92 in Half Moon Bay, drive 18 miles south on Highway 1 to the Pescadero Road junction. Turn east on Pescadero Road and drive past the town of Pescadero to Cloverdale Road. Turn right (south) on Cloverdale Road and drive a few miles until you see the signed park entrance turnoff on the left side of the road.

---

63. SUNSET BACKPACK CAMP
Big Basin Redwoods State Park
Off Highway 236 near Boulder Creek

One of my favorite places is Berry Creek Falls. Every year, sometime around my birthday, I try to give myself a present by hiking here at Big Basin Redwoods State Park. It's like an annual rite of passage, a time to take stock of affairs and try to form a vision for the future. Each year, no matter what I have gotten right or wrong, that waterfall is always waiting for me just the same.

To make the most of the trip, overnight it at nearby Sunset Trail Camp, a primitive backpacker's campground. This not only gives you two days to hike, but it allows you to spend as much time as you wish enjoying Berry Creek Falls, as well as nearby Silver and Golden falls, two other pretty cascades set upstream of Berry Creek Falls. That counts for a lot. Many people, starting late, have to rush back in order to complete the trip by darkness, adding a pressure edge that can diminish the pleasure.

In addition, by spring in the Bay Area, I start to long for the mountain experience, and with the high country still buried in snow, a trip like this is the best alternative. What you find is a primitive camp set near a shaded, wooded ridge, with 10 level campsites and a pit toilet and garbage facilities. While there is no piped water here and rangers suggest carrying in bottled water for cooking and drinking, it is possible to hike five minutes to Berry Creek, then head upstream a bit to find an untouched water source and filter-pump what you need, just as you would in the Sierra wilderness.

What everybody wants to know is this: "How long does it take to hike to Berry Creek Falls?" I get that question. Ann Marie Brown, author of *Easy Hiking in Northern California*, gets that question. The rangers get that question. Many people just returning from the trip are stopped in the parking lot and asked that question.

The answer is about two hours one-way (4.7 miles), five hours round-trip (10.1 miles), and six hours for the complete loop (12 miles). Cover that terrain over a weekend and you have yourself a great backpacking and camping trip. Before starting, go to park headquarters to get your Trail Camp permit (reservations are available by phone), which secures your campsite.

The trailhead is at the park's main day-use and overnight parking lot, putting you on the Skyline-to-the-Sea Trail. It starts by crossing Opal Creek, then passes through old-growth redwoods, including some monsters, before climbing up to the Big Basin Rim, elevation 1,200 feet, about a 20-minute trek. The trail then descends about 900 feet over a four-mile span to Berry Creek Falls, most of it quite beautiful. You will enter a canyon with plenty of sword ferns, sorrel, trillium, and the occasional banana slug and newt. You then cross the stream to the right, round a bend, and suddenly Berry Creek Falls comes into view, a 70-foot cascade framed like a painting by the canyon walls and redwood canopy.

Take your time and enjoy the place. There is a bench situated perfectly for a picnic and views (or if you're lucky, a kiss), as well as a viewing deck near the base of the falls.

From here, it is a one-mile climb to Sunset Camp, with the route passing Silver Falls and Golden Falls. On hot days at Silver Falls, some people take a quick dunk to cool off; the adjacent trail is staircased up and over the top. When you reach the ridge, turn right, then expect just a five-minute walk to Sunset Camp on the left.

On day two, you can sleep in and maybe venture back to the falls before breaking camp for the trip home. To avoid the crowds hiking in the opposite direction to see the falls, take the Sunset Trail, which loops back into the park's most remote sections over the course of 5.5 miles before being routed back to headquarters. Even though the trip to Berry Creek Falls is popular, this back loop get very little traffic, feels remote, and is the perfect way to complete this two-day backpack trip.

It's enough to make me wish I had more than one birthday a year.

Facilities: Sunset Trail Camp has 10 primitive campsites. A pit toilet and garbage facilities are available. There is no piped water or food lockers.

Reservations, fee: Reservations are advised; call park headquarters at (408) 338-6132 from Monday through Friday. The fee is $7 per night.

Insider's note: A stocked camper store is available at park headquarters. Leashed pets are permitted in the campground, but not on trails.

Who to contact: Phone Big Basin Redwoods State Park at (408) 338-6132. A park map is sold for $1 at the ranger station. To obtain a hiker's map, send $1.50 to Mountain Parks Foundation, 525 North Big Trees Park Road, Felton, CA 95018, and ask for Big Basin Trail Map.

Directions: From Santa Cruz, turn north on Highway 9 and drive approximately 12 miles to Boulder Creek. At Boulder Creek, turn left on Highway 236 and drive about 10 miles to the entrance sign for Big Basin Redwoods State Park. Continue past the sign for about two miles to park headquarters, then turn left at the kiosk for day-use and overnight parking.

64. BIG BASIN TENT CABINS
Big Basin Redwoods State Park
Off Highway 236 near Boulder Creek

If I get cooped up too long, there are nights when I can feel like a doggy on a short rope, bayin' at the moon, yearning to roam where a soft breeze blows through the redwoods. Sometimes it gets so bad that I'll walk up and down the stairs a few times to pretend I'm hiking, let the shower run to remind me of a waterfall, then get my sleeping bag out and sleep on the floor.

But it turns out there's another solution, one that is a lot more fun. You see, there's a beautiful state park in the Santa Cruz Mountains, Big Basin Redwoods, that has tent cabins available, which means that you can just pick up and go without elaborate planning. Just like that, you can cut that old chain to the television at home, head off, and discover a life of leisure, freedom, and fun in a beautiful redwood park.

The key is staying at a tent cabin. They are set on a loop road at Huckleberry Camp, well spaced in a towering redwood forest. The tent cabins are made out of wood and canvas, measure 12 by 14 feet and feature two full-size beds, a table, and a wood stove. If you visit during cold weather, it is vital to bring a stack of firewood with you to keep warm. Duraflames, Presto Logs, and other artificial logs are not permitted, and the $6 bundles of firewood (five or six small logs) sold at the park's General Store will provide warmth for only a few hours.

Staying at a tent cabin simplifies your adventure, and if you don't want to cook dinner, you can make life even easier by visiting one of the restaurants in Boulder Creek, about a 15-minute drive away.

Big Basin, of course, is best known for its giant redwoods near park headquarters, Berry Creek Falls (a 70-foot waterfall), and excellent hiking trails. There are 90 miles of hiking routes across a largely untouched landscape, highlighted by the 4.7-mile trip (one-way) to Berry Creek Falls, a beautiful silver cascade falling under a redwood canopy.

Though a warning sign on the trail says the round-trip takes six hours via the Skyline-to-the-Sea Trail, most people make it to the falls and back in less. My partner and I hiked it in four hours, which included a half-hour snack at the falls lookout, and we were in no great rush, walking in the rain and taking the time to watch water droplets bead up and trickle off on sorrel, ferns, and each other's noses. When the trail was near the stream, we also had to stay on the lookout for newts to keep from stepping on them; the little guys seemed to be everywhere, crossing the trail with that peculiar walk of theirs, where all four legs operate without regard for the others, as if driven by separate minds. I have some friends like that.

The trip to Berry Creek Falls and back is long enough to give you that good tired feeling at the end of the day, and you'll like the idea that awaiting you is a tent cabin with a bed on which to lay down both your sleeping bag and your body. The forest is very quiet out here and sound really carries, so a "quiet time" at the campground is enforced between 10 P.M. and 8 A.M.; otherwise campers are requested to keep their sounds from reaching their neighbor.

For the most part, everyone complies, and in turn, you get just what you came for: a getaway set in a redwood forest with great hiking, where you can camp in a tent cabin without having to organize all the detailed preparations required for most camping adventures.

Big Basin tent cabins, nestled in the redwoods

Facilities: There are 35 tent cabins. Two full-size beds with mattress pads, a table, bench, and wood stove are provided, and a picnic table, food locker, and fire pit with grill are located outside each cabin. There are two rest rooms, one with a coin-operated shower and with a coin-operated washer and dryer nearby. A stocked camper store is located at park headquarters. Leashed pets are permitted in the campground, but not on trails. There are also 107 drive-in campsites and 38 walk-in campsites, available for $14 to $16 per night, plus a $6.75 reservation fee. Reserve through Destinet by phoning (800) 444-PARK. Restaurants are available in Boulder Creek.

Reservations, fee: Reservations for cabins are required; $38 fee per night. Phone (800) 874-8368.

Insider's note: What you need to bring: A sleeping bag, lantern, cooking gear, cooler, and firewood. Lanterns can be rented for $6 per night, small bundles of firewood are available for $6 each at the Big Basin Store, and bedding is available for $10 per stay.

Who to contact: To reserve a tent cabin, phone the California Parks Company Reservation System at (800) 874-8368. To contact Big Basin Redwoods State Park, phone (408) 338-6132.

Directions: From Santa Cruz, turn north on Highway 9 and drive approximately 12 miles to Boulder Creek. At Boulder Creek, turn left on Highway 236 and drive about 10 miles to the entrance sign for Big Basin Redwoods State Park. Continue for 1.5 miles, then turn right at the sign for Huckleberry Campground, drive a quarter of a mile, then turn right again at the access road for campsites 6 to 41. The camp host is at site 7 in a small trailer.

65. TRAIL CAMP
Castle Rock State Park
Off Highway 35 near Saratoga

Where can you walk for just a few hours and see a beautiful waterfall, divine coastal views, strange rock formations, wildflowers along the trail, and hawks riding thermals, and end it all by camping at a secluded little backpack camp?

The answer is at Castle Rock State Park, where a 2.8-mile one-way hike to Trail Camp provides a mini-expedition, with everything scaled down but the natural diversity and beauty of the area. Where else can you get all this? The answer is nowhere else. This is one of the most stellar walks around, and when crowned with a stay at Trail Camp, one of the best overnight adventures available.

The park is just far enough away to make a trip there special. It is located on Skyline Ridge (Highway 35) on the south peninsula, perched at 3,000 feet, just south of the junction of highways 9 and 35. At first the park appears to be nothing more than a nondescript dirt parking lot with an outhouse and a self-pay register ($3). What's the big deal, huh? If you start walking, taking the trailhead for the Saratoga Trail, you will make the discovery.

The Saratoga Trail starts by dropping into a dense, wooded canyon, then follows along a small stream and suddenly arrives at a perfect lookout for a high and beautiful waterfall. The lookout has a railing and is set just above and alongside the falls, and after the Santa Cruz Mountains get a heavy dose of precipitation, this waterfall is transformed into a beautiful cascade, full and silvery.

The route then passes a series of huge honeycombed sandstone formations, giant gray rocks that look something like blocks of Swiss cheese. They are filled with miniature caves, where children can play hide-and-seek. As you hike on, you emerge along a rock facing where fantastic views suddenly loom to the southwest, where you can see from the Butano Rim past Big Basin to Monterey Bay. It is fronted by miles and miles of forest, and by now you will start to have the feeling that you really have discovered a new world.

It gets even better. When you reach a trail junction with the Ridge Trail, turn left and hike for another 10 or 15 minutes to Trail Camp. This is your calling.

Because so few people know about Trail Camp, no reservations are required and you actually self-register right at the campground, paying $7 per night. You then select the campsite of your choice. All come with a fire ring, food locker, and flat tent site, and piped water and a vault toilet are provided. Gathering firewood is illegal, but small bundles of firewood are available at the campground for $5 apiece. This is just enough wood to provide an evening glow; for cooking, bring a backpack camping stove.

Be sure you know the license plate number of the vehicle you are leaving at the parking area. That number is recorded with your campground registration. Otherwise, with no license number record, rangers will leave a ticket on your car for the $3 day-use fee charged other visitors, but not campers.

Trail Camp is the first camp on the 38-mile Skyline-to-the-Sea Trail, but almost no long-distance hikers stay here, choosing instead to walk much farther (9.6 miles) to the backpack camp at Waterman Gap.

If you take the Ridge Trail on your hike back to the parking area, you will come across a spectacular lookout. This route passes Goat Rock, an incredible perch for a view of Monterey Bay. But use caution, because while you can easily gain the top of Goat Rock from the back side, if you look over the front side you will discover it is a cliff with about a 50-foot drop, straight down. Regardless, this is one of the most perfect picnic sites at any of the Bay Area's 250 parks.

The hike then loops back, passing a lookout for a raptor breeding area, and is routed up the canyon with a 300-foot climb to return.

Later, you may wonder, That was so good, did it really happen? Yes, yes, yes.

Facilities: Each backpacking campsite has a fire ring, food locker, and flat tent site, with piped water and a vault toilet nearby. No pets are permitted.

Reservations, fee: No reservations are available. The campsite fee is $7 per night, with up to six people per site, and is paid at the campground on a self-registration basis, not at the parking area. Additional vehicles are charged $5 apiece; also pay at the campground.

Insider's note: Gathering firewood is prohibited, but small bundles of firewood are available at the campground for $5 apiece. Smoking, dogs, bicycles, and glass containers are not permitted. Trail use is not allowed after sunset.

Who to contact: For information on Castle Rock State Park, phone the park at (408) 867-2952, or district headquarters at (408) 429-2850, or write to

Castle Rock State Park, 15000 Skyline Boulevard, Los Gatos, CA 95030. They can also provide you with a park map. To obtain a topographic map of the area, send $3.50 to Maps-Western Distribution Center, U.S. Geologic Survey, Box 25286-Federal Center, Denver, CO 80225 and ask for Castle Rock Ridge.

Directions: From Highway 280 near Santa Clara, turn west on Saratoga Avenue and drive up the hill (the road becomes Highway 9) to the junction with Highway 35. Turn south (left) on Highway 35 and drive 2.5 miles to the parking area for Castle Rock State Park on the right side of the road.

If you are coming from San Francisco, drive south on Highway 280 to Woodside. Take the Highway 84 exit and drive up the mountain to Skylonda and the junction with Highway 35. Turn south (left) on Highway 35 and drive about 10 miles to the junction with Highway 9. Continue straight for 2.5 miles to the parking area for Castle Rock State Park on the right side of the road.

---

66. HENRY COE BACKPACK SITES
Henry Coe State Park
Off U.S. 101 near Morgan Hill

I've seen hikers so thirsty at Henry Coe State Park that they resembled iguanas. But there is a solution to that problem: short backpack trips of just two or three miles to isolated camps, including my favorite shorty to Frog Lake.

What happens is that people arrive at the park full of excitement over the prospects of great hike-in bass fishing, then head off without a reality check. The reality, you see, is that the best lakes require 25-mile round-trips from park headquarters, sometimes longer, including several butt-kicker climbs, often in hot, dry weather. Since nobody is out here selling canteens of cold water, most hikers really do start feeling like some form of reptile.

The best counsel is to try a practice trip, backpacking in to one of the 15 trail camps set within two miles of park headquarters. That will give you just the right taste of what this park is about before you take a bigger bite. And one of the best tastes is the 1.6-mile hike out to Frog Lake.

It is an ideal first-time backpack trip at Henry Coe State Park for many reasons. The trail departs from park headquarters, where you can obtain your backpacker permit, maps, and any information desired about the park and the backcountry. From here, the trail climbs a ridge, including a steep, 15-minute huff-and-puff, a mountain in miniature compared to some of the 3,000-foot ridges in the park. After topping the climb, the trail glides downhill through an oak and madrone woodland to a shaded, unimproved campsite on a flat, just above little Frog Lake.

From the camp, it takes just a minute or two to make the walk down to the pond, which is set in a sheltered valley and is green and calm with a few old snags poking out of it. Because the little lake is so close to headquarters compared to the rest of the ponds in the park, it gets fished often, and most of the bass and bluegill are small. But it's still a good taste, and your chance of seeing hawks, deer, and other wildlife is quite high.

After hiking to Frog Lake, believe me, you will know whether you will want to buy in for more on a future trip. And more is what this park has. Coe covers 80,000 acres of wild parkland, 120 lakes and ponds, 210 miles of abandoned ranch roads, and 35 additional miles of trails for hiking, biking, and horseback riding. But unfortunately, just about every trail to heaven goes via hell.

The best lakes for fishing are Coit Lake, Kelly Lake, and Mississippi Lake, and farther out in the Orestimba drainage at remote Jackrabbit Lake and Mustang Pond. On a good day in early summer, you might catch and release 20 or 30 bass. The farther you go, the better the fishing, but be prepared to undergo a long, grueling physical test in the process. Stay for several days, and your burden will be greatly eased, of course.

If you fall in love with the place, over time you will discover many

Mississippi Lake, Henry Coe State Park

attractions beyond the fishing. In the most distant Coe wildlands, for instance, is the Rooster Comb, a giant rock formation that looks like the back of a stegosaurus. Another favorite area is Los Cruzeros, which you pass on the route out to Kelly Lake, a pretty junction of two streams at the bottom of a canyon. Swimming in the ponds can just plain be a lot of fun.

Because of hot temperatures from mid-June through early September, timing is critical at this park. It is best visited in spring or fall, with winter passable and summer often a nightmare. At any time, though, it is vital that you have a water purifier and keep your canteen topped off. A backpacker permit is required, and prior to venturing out for the first time, review your trip plans with Coe Park rangers Kay Robinson or Barry Breckling.

You also might ask them if they'd mind if you set up a little concession stand in the wilderness, maybe sell a little water. You could make a fortune out there.

Facilities: There are 15 primitive backpack sites within two miles of park headquarters, including one at Frog Lake. You need to bring all camping gear required for a backpacking trip. A water filter and camp stove are essential. Come prepared to rely completely on yourself. Do not bring dogs into the backcountry.

Reservations, fee: Reservations are advised; $3 fee per night at backpack sites plus $5 day-use fee, $7 fee per night at drive-in sites, $12 fee per night at horse camps.

Insider's note: An additional 40 backpack camps are available in the park's backcountry. There are also 20 drive-in sites at park headquarters with good views of the hills; fire pits and picnic table are provided. Piped water, toilets, and showers are available nearby. Pets are permitted.

Who to contact: Call Henry Coe State Park Sector Office at (408) 848-4006, park headquarters at (408) 779-2728, or district headquarters at (209) 826-1196. For a trail and camping map, send $2 to Henry Coe State Park, P.O. Box 846, Morgan Hill, CA 95038.

Directions: From U.S. 101 in San Jose, drive south to Morgan Hill. Take the Dunne Avenue exit and head east past Morgan Hill and Lake Anderson and continue for 10 miles to the park entrance. The final section of road is very twisty.

Tahoe-Carson Pass

** For locations of camps, see map on page 9. **

67. COTTONWOOD LODGE LOG CABINS
North Tahoe
Off Highway 28 near Tahoe Vista

The sign for Cottonwood Lodge along Highway 28 just doesn't do the place justice.

Here is this retreat of 17 log cabins, that's right, real log cabins, set around a lily pond on the shore of Lake Tahoe, where only the lake's azure waters can match the blueness of the sky. Somebody had a vision for this place and you can see how that vision has been realized.

But the sign? It's this pedestrian-level lettering on orange neon, something you'd expect at a hayseed motel out in Winnemucca, which juts out from the parking lot along the lake side of Highway 28. See that, and your expectations can drop like an egg from a long-legged chicken.

Turns out, however, that the place works just fine. Those log cabins get high marks for cuteness. Several are set in a line on each side of the lily pond, a short distance from the lake frontage, a small beach, and a pier. The resort provides sunchairs and picnic tables with sunshades, and also has a small swimming pool. While many visitors might be apt to hang out and catch the rays here, eventually you will want more. And more you can get.

The best thing going for recreation is a bicycle path that starts about a mile south of the lodge. This is one of the more scenic bike routes available anywhere. It is paved, separated from car traffic, and follows along the northwest shore of Lake Tahoe, one of the most beautiful lakes on earth. The route peaks in and out of pines and firs, but is largely flat, making it a perfect bike trip for families. In addition, bike rental shops operate along Highway 28 so you don't even have to haul your bike along to get in on the fun.

If you prefer more aggressive mountain biking, Northstar-at-Tahoe converts its ski area to a mountain bike course every summer, complete with lifts in operation. Northstar is located along Highway 267 about midway between Truckee and Kings Beach, with a large, well-signed turnoff. Northstar also has a rock-climbing course in the summer months.

If you want to go fishing, note that it is typically a very early morning affair—being on the lake by 5:30 A.M., then finished by 9 or 10 A.M. That is because the water is very clear at Tahoe, which causes the trout to become extremely light shy. As the sun gets high in the sky, light penetration is increased, and the fish go down to Davy Jones's locker and hide

Mountain biking at Northstar-at-Tahoe near Cottonwood Lodge

until nightfall. Guided fishing trips are available out of North Tahoe Marina in Tahoe Vista. To the nearby south on Highway 28 at Tahoe City, there is a full marina, a boat launch, and fishing trip operators.

To the northeast on Highway 28, just past Crystal Bay, is Incline Village, with the largest collection of casinos at North Tahoe. Surveys show that although gambling is rated only fifth in attractions at Tahoe, some 87 percent of visitors still make the trip to a casino as if the venture was somehow destined. The only destiny most people find, however, is that they were fated to contribute a good chunk of cash to the Tahoe tourist economy.

But soon enough you will be back in safer confines, snuggling up at your little log cabin, knowing that giant Tahoe is sitting just yonder, and all is peaceful again. When your visit is complete and you head for home, your eye will catch that Cottonwood Lodge sign, and you might grin. It perfectly disguises the attraction of staying in a log cabin and adventuring in North Tahoe.

Facilities: Cottonwood Lodge has 17 cabins in a variety of sizes, each with a bath and kitchen or kitchenette. Picnic tables, sunchairs, and a pier are provided, and a beach and lily pond are nearby. A marina with fishing boats is available in Tahoe City. No pets are permitted.

Reservations, fee: Reservations are advised. The fees for cabin rentals range from $74 to $120 per night, based on the number of people and size of cabin. In the winter, the rates range from $59 to $84 per night.

Insider's note: Northstar-at-Tahoe, which offers a mountain bike circuit in the summer, complete with chairlifts, can be reached at (916) 562-2248. Bike rentals are available at Mountain Cyclery, (916) 581-5861, and Olympic Bike Shop, (916) 581-2500, both in Tahoe City. Fishing charters are available in Tahoe Vista through Mac-A-Tac Charters, (916) 546-2500, and at Carnelian Bay with Mickey's, (916) 583-4602.

Who to contact: Phone Cottonwood Lodge at (916) 546-2220, or write to P.O. Box 86, Tahoe Vista, CA 95732.

Directions: From San Francisco, take Interstate 80 east through Sacramento and continue to Truckee. At Truckee, take the Kings Beach/Highway 267 exit and drive 14 miles to the town of Tahoe Vista where the road intersects with Highway 28. Turn right on Highway 28 and drive a half-mile. Look for the Cottonwood Lodge sign on the lake side of the road.

68. LAKESIDE CHALETS
Carnelian Bay, North Tahoe
Off Highway 28 near Tahoe Vista

According to legend, the shiny pebbles on Lake Tahoe's shore at Carnelian Bay have magical properties for healthy living, and in the 1870s, a doctor actually got rich on that belief.

What people are discovering nowadays is what the doctor probably knew all along, that the real secret is just being here at Carnelian Bay, enjoying the divine views of Lake Tahoe and the surrounding mountain country. There is no better place to receive this treatment than at Lakeside Chalets.

Here you will find six cabins set right alongside Lake Tahoe. Even though there is a tremendous amount of outdoor recreation available nearby, you will find yourself in no great rush to do much of anything except sit there and soak in that lake view. The property has 225 feet of pebble beach, and when some visitors notice how much better they feel after a day or two here, they often sneak one of those pebbles to carry in their pocket in hopes of continued rejuvenation.

The cabins are in good shape and are well furnished, with excellent kitchens, and bed linen service is provided. Home? Home. At least for as long as possible, that is.

Mornings are typically calm here, and afternoons are windy. That makes the morning prime time for a bike ride on the great bicycle trail that is routed south out of Tahoe City along the lake. It also makes the afternoon perfect for trying windsurfing, which can be so much fun that Lakeside Chalets now offers a windsurfing school. There is no prettier place to try it.

Facilities: Lakeside Chalets has six lakeside cabins. Bathrooms, kitchens with cookware and utensils, bed linens, and stone fireplaces are provided. No pets are permitted. A 225-foot pebble beach, pier, and deck are available nearby. The chalet also features a windsurfing school. There's a boat hoist nearby at Sierra Boat Works, and a marina with a boat ramp and fishing boats at Tahoe City.

Reservations, fee: Reservations are advised. Cabin rates are $95 per night during the week and $125 per night on Fridays and Saturdays.

Insider's note: It's about a 10-minute drive to the nearest gambling action in Nevada.

Who to contact: Phone Lakeside Chalets at (916) 546-5857 or (800) 2-WINDSURF, or write to P.O. Box 270, Carnelian Bay, CA 96140.

Directions: From San Francisco, take Interstate 80 east through Sacramento and continue to Truckee. At Truckee, take the Kings Beach/Highway 267 exit and drive 14 miles to the town of Tahoe Vista where the road intersects with Highway 28. Turn right and drive four miles on Highway 28. Look for Lakeside Chalets on the lake side (left) of the road.

69. MEEKS BAY RESORT
Lake Tahoe's West Shore
Off Highway 89 near Tahoma

Meeks Bay Resort has developed into a micro-universe all its own at Lake Tahoe. It has a little bit of everything, and the best of some things, but at the heart of the resort are eight cabins, 12 condo-style units, a campground, and the awesome Kehlet Mansion. Most of the cabins have lake views, and the mansion actually has a deck that extends out over the water.

As you likely guessed, the cabins can be on the pricey side, and with a one-week minimum stay, the pretty two-story jobs will set you back better than a grand. The cheapest you can get still costs $550.

But what the heck, life ain't no dress rehearsal, right? You're better off spending it on yourself and your family than at the casinos, and here you get vacation grounds set on the threshold of outstanding boating, swimming, biking, and hiking. While the resort does not rent boats, it does have a concrete boat ramp that provides powerboats with access to nearby Emerald Bay to the south, the prettiest spot on the prettiest lake in California. There is also a great beach and a roped-off swimming area within short walking distance of the cabins.

A trailhead for access to Eldorado National Forest and the Desolation Wilderness (a wilderness permit is required for overnight use) is located virtually across the highway from the resort, and the famed West Shore Bicycle Path is set nearby to the north.

Facilities: Meeks Bay Resort has eight cabins in a variety of sizes, each with a bath and kitchen. Cookware, utensils, and bed linens are provided. Bring your own towels. There are 12 other condo-style units and the seven-bedroom Kehlet Mansion. A small general store, campground, beach, roped-off swimming area, boat ramp, small marina, and boat dock are on the property. Bicycle rentals and a marina with fishing boat rentals are available in Tahoe City.

Reservations, fee: Reservations are advised. Fees for cabin rentals range from $550 to $1,050 per week, with one-week minimum occupancy, based on the size of cabin and number of people. The Kehlet Mansion rents for $2,750 per week.

Insider's note: Bike rentals are available at Mountain Cyclery, (916) 581-5861, and Olympic Bike Shop, (916) 581-2500, both in Tahoe City. Fishing charters are available in Tahoe Vista through Mac-A-Tac Charters, (916) 546-2500, and at Carnelian Bay with Mickey's, (916) 583-4602.

Who to contact: Phone Meeks Bay Resort at (916) 525-7242, or write to P.O. Box 411, Tahoma, CA 96142.

Directions: From San Francisco, take Interstate 80 east through Sacramento and continue to Truckee. At Truckee, take the Highway 89 exit and drive to Tahoe City. Continue south on Highway 89 for 10 miles to Meeks Bay Resort at 7901 West Highway 89 (on the lake side of the road).

70. RICHARDSON'S RESORT CABINS
South Lake Tahoe
Off Highway 89 near South Lake Tahoe

Richardson's Resort is literally minutes from world-class bike riding in the summer, skiing in the winter, and gambling year-round, yet it's like being 100 years away in terms of mood and ambience.

That is because it is set on the southwest shore of Lake Tahoe, a perfect location for all kinds of outdoor recreation. Add some 46 cabins in the forest, many with great lake views, and you have one of the best places you can stay on a vacation at Lake Tahoe. The cabins are rustic, complete with knotty-pine ceilings, most have wood stoves, and with the resort completely self-contained, you don't have to drive anywhere once you get here.

A great bike route runs right through the resort. The bike trail runs three miles, then loops around by the lake for another three miles, with almost all of it perfectly flat for easy biking. Depending on your level of fitness and ambition, you can extend mountain bike trips for miles and miles into the adjoining Eldorado National Forest.

In the winter, the same routes make for some of the best cross-country skiing available anywhere, crowned by awesome lake views. The experience is absolutely wondrous at night under a full moon.

Top it off with a dinner at South Shore's only lakeside restaurant and a night in your cabin, and you've got the entire package. No extra pushing needed.

Facilities: Richardson's Resort has 46 cabins, each with bathrooms, kitchens, and wood stoves with gas heaters for backup. Bed linens and towels are provided, with maid service available at an extra charge. A boat ramp, boat rentals, and marina are within walking distance. Bike rentals are also available. A grocery store is on the property and there's a lakefront restaurant (lunch and dinner). In the winter, sleigh rides and cross-country skiing take place at the resort.

Reservations, fee: Reservations are required. In the summer, cabin fees range from $465 to $1,080 per week. Discount rates are provided in the winter, along with a reduced two-night minimum stay on weekends.

Insider's note: A special ski package is offered in the winter starting at $49 per person and includes lift ticket, lodging, light breakfast, skier gift package, and discount coupons for dinner.

Who to contact: Phone Richardson's Resort at (916) 541-1801 or (800) 544-1801, or write to P.O. Box 9028, South Lake Tahoe, CA 96158.

Directions: From San Francisco, take Interstate 80 east to Sacramento. In Sacramento, take Highway 50 to South Lake Tahoe. At the junction of Highway 50 and Highway 89, turn north on Highway 89 and drive 2.5 miles. Look for Richardson's Resort on the right side of the road.

71. ANGORA LAKES RESORT CABINS
Upper Angora Lake, South Tahoe
Off Highway 89 near Fallen Leaf Lake

For many people, a vacation at Angora Lakes is perfection. Unfortunately, perfection has its price.

It can take years on a waiting list to finally get a chance to stay at the cabins here. There are just eight of them, relatively primitive at that, but they are remote and situated on a pristine lake surrounded by Eldorado National Forest, so remote that a shuttle ride is provided for cabin guests.

The place is absolutely beautiful. The water often seems to be almost as blue as Lake Tahoe, circled by both beach and boulders and backed by forest. The boulders are perfect for making flying leaps into the lake, if

Hikers on the trail around Angora Lake

you can stand the cold water, for swimming. Little rowboats are available for oaring around; the trout fishing is decent, although the fish are often small; and the hiking in the area is excellent.

But trying to get a reservation will turn even the most die-hard Tahoe lover into a prisoner of hope. First off, there is a carryover list of guests who stay here for a week each year; that locks up most of the cabins for the summer. What is left is snapped up by those on a waiting list compiled over the winter, or when there is a rare cancellation. Your best bet is to make contact with the staff at Angora Lakes Resort in January, get the required waiting list form which requests your desired dates, fill it out, send it in, and start hoping.

Rarely do you come across something worth waiting for. Angora Lakes is one of those things.

Facilities: Angora Lakes Resort has eight cabins of varying design and size. Each has a kitchen, electricity, hot shower, and chemical toilet. No bed linens, towels or laundry facilities are provided. A snack stand is nearby. Rowboats are available for rent.

Reservations, fee: Reservations are required. Cabin rates range from $700 to $800 per week, depending on the size of cabin.

Who to contact: Phone Angora Lakes Resort at (916) 541-2092 in summer, (916) 577-3593 in winter, or write to P.O. Box 8897, South Lake Tahoe, CA 96158. For a map of Eldorado National Forest, send $3 to Office of Information, U.S. Forest Service, 630 Sansome Street, San Francisco, CA 94111.

Directions: From San Francisco, take Interstate 80 east to Sacramento. In Sacramento, take Highway 50 east to the Highway 50/89 split in South Lake Tahoe. Turn north on Highway 89 to Fallen Leaf Lake Road. Turn left on Fallen Leaf Lake Road and drive up the hill about three miles. When the road forks, bear left for one-quarter mile, then bear right on a dirt road

(Forest Service Road 12N14) and drive about six miles, past the Angora Fire Lookout, and park in the lot there. A half-mile shuttle ride to the cabins is available for guests and their gear, otherwise you must hike uphill.

72. ECHO CHALET CABINS
Echo Lake, South Tahoe
Off Highway 50 near Echo Summit

Echo Lake is an exquisite place, a high, blue, beautiful alpine lake set in granite and surrounded by forest. Here you will find 10 old cabins in only fair shape but with decks, great views, and such a beautiful setting that you may feel as if you have been deposited in heaven.

That's how I felt when Echo Lake was the destination of one of my hikes with my pal Michael Furniss—a hike that started at Yosemite National Park! Two weeks and 160 miles later on the Pacific Crest Trail, we arrived at Echo Lake, and believe me, it really did feel like heaven.

It is set at an elevation of 7,500 feet in a canyon near the Desolation Wilderness, not far from Echo Summit off Highway 50. The lake is shaped like an hourglass, with the lower portion best for waterskiing; everybody runs their boats in a clockwise direction around the lake. The upper portion is quiet, sprinkled with a few little islands, and is the choice for fishing and low-speed boating, like a canoe paddle during an awesome evening sunset. The one problem at the lake is the wind in the early summer; it can absolutely howl out of the west in the afternoon.

A great easy hike here is a three-miler that is routed along the eastern side of the lake, providing great views, seclusion, and a good trail that is relatively flat.

Facilities: Echo Chalet has 10 cabins with bathrooms. All but one have kitchenettes, cookware, and utensils. Bed linens and towels are provided. A boat ramp, dock, and rental boats are nearby, as well as a small store.

Reservations, fee: Reservations are required. Cabin rates range from $75 per night to $95 per night, depending on the size of cabin, and from $450 per week to $570 per week.

Who to contact: Phone Echo Chalet at (916) 659-7207, or write to 9900 Echo Lakes Road, Echo Lake, CA 95721. For a map of Eldorado National Forest, send $3 to Office of Information, U.S. Forest Service, 630 Sansome Street, San Francisco, CA 94111.

Directions: From San Francisco, take Interstate 80 east to Sacramento. In Sacramento, take Highway 50 east to Sierra-at-Tahoe Ski Area. Continue two miles past Sierra-at-Tahoe, then turn left on Johnson Pass Road and drive less than a mile. Turn left on Echo Lakes Road and drive to its end.

73. ZEPHYR COVE RESORT CABINS
South Tahoe, Nevada
Off Highway 50 near Stateline

A heavenly force casts a spell over many visitors at Lake Tahoe. If you're one of them, you'll know it. It opens your heart to a place that can seem sacred from its immense scope and cobalt-blue waters set in high mountains.

Add in a cabin with a view of the lake, a mile of sandy beach, a one-minute walk to a marina with boat rentals, paddleboats, and headquarters for the Tahoe cruise ship *M.S. Dixie II,* and you can figure out why Zephyr Cove Resort has become one of the most popular spots in South Tahoe.

But at Tahoe, while all these attractions add up to greatness, they also equal great numbers of people. Some can handle it, some can't. If you are one of the former, no problem. If not, but you still desire a hit of the Tahoe charm, an option here is renting a cabin, then parking your car and hiding the key for as long as you stay. Then, instead of driving around and getting jammed out by the traffic, you can be marooned at your cabin at the lake. And what a great place to be marooned.

Zephyr Cove Resort is located on the Nevada side of South Shore, just over four miles from Stateline. It has 24 cabins of different sizes, each with a bath and kitchenette, but all are within short walking distance of the lakeshore and beach, just a minute's stroll or so. Some of the cabins have gorgeous lake views, some have lake frontage, and of course, some are closer to the water than others.

The resort has a mile of beach frontage. Got that? A mile of beach frontage! At Tahoe? At Tahoe! This is where sand is as about valuable as gold. Like I said, it takes only about a minute to walk from the cabins to the beach. Now remember: What did I tell you to do with your car keys?

If you want to do more than lay around like King Tut and Cleopatra at the beach, the adjacent marina provides a huge variety of water sport activities, including the lake's famous tour on the giant paddleboat *M.S. Dixie II.* At the marina, also within very short walking distance, you can rent paddleboats or boats with motors, or arrange a fishing trip.

Only a few people know this, but the best fishing spot for big Mackinaw trout is at the southern end of the lake, just offshore of the casinos at a place called "The Nub." Even though the lake bottom is about 750 feet deep in this area, The Nub rises up like a giant dome to 160 feet deep, with its 50-yard crown covered with weeds and grass. This is where the big Mackinaw hide out, and right at dawn, if you troll a minnow or J-Plug over the top of the grass, you have the chance of catching some huge trout. In fact, this is exactly how Dan Hannum and I caught 12- and 10-pounders to win a Tahoe fishing tournament. Tahoe is huge, you know, but 95 percent of the fish are caught at five percent of the spots.

If you can't stand the idea of throwing away your car keys for a while, well, you can finally surrender and make the inevitable trip to Stateline for the obligatory gambling run. It won't take long, however, and you will discover the best bets at Tahoe have nothing to do with the casinos.

Facilities: Zephyr Cove Resort has 24 cabins of different sizes, each with a bath and kitchenette, and seven rooms in a lodge. Barbecues and a picnic area are provided nearby. A small general store, restaurant, bar, and a marina with boat rentals, paddleboat, and Lake Tahoe tours on the *M.S. Dixie II* are available. There's a campground with both RV and tent sites.

Reservations, fee: Reservations are often required. Fees range from a low of $55 to a high of $185 per night for cabins, depending on the number of people and size of cabin. Rooms at the lodge range from $50 to $75 per night. Off-season discounts are available after October 1.

Insider's note: Tahoe gets the least amount of visitors in the fall (after summer and before the ski season) and in late spring (after the ski season and before summer).

Who to contact: Phone Zephyr Cove Resort at (702) 588-6644, or write to P.O. Box 830, Zephyr Cove, NV 89448.

Directions: From San Francisco, take Interstate 80 east to Sacramento. In Sacramento, take Highway 50 east and continue for 100 miles to Stateline. Continue on Highway 50 past Stateline for four miles and look for the sign for Zephyr Cove Lodge on the left side of the street. Turn left (before the traffic signal) and park at an area just off the highway. Walk a short distance on a sidewalk to the resort office for check-in.

---

74. STRAWBERRY CABINS
Eldorado National Forest
Off Highway 50 near Twin Bridges

There are two towns in the Sierra Nevada called Strawberry, and they are similar enough to confuse thousands of visitors every year.

This is about the one located along the South Fork American River on Highway 50 near Echo Summit, a few miles from the Sierra-at-Tahoe Ski Area, just 15 miles from South Lake Tahoe and in the middle of

---

Hiking to Horsetail Falls on the border of Eldorado National Forest near Strawberry Lodge Cabins

Eldorado National Forest, blessed with many lakes, great hiking trails, and bike routes.

The "other" Strawberry is on Highway 108, set in Stanislaus Forest near Dodge Ridge Ski Area and Beardsley Lake. If you know the difference, you can win a lot of bets.

You can also end up spending the night in a Tahoe-style alpine chalet or vacation cabin. There are 11 available for rent, with no minimum stay. Just make sure you take Highway 50, not Highway 108, and since bed linens are not provided, make sure you bring sleeping bags and towels. That will get you off to a good start.

The peak season here is winter, not summer, with outstanding cross-country skiing in the immediate region, a snow-play area at Echo Summit, and downhill skiing at Sierra-at-Tahoe. Yet in the summer, the area is still like a recreation fortune hunt. The South Fork American River runs right through town, providing fair trout fishing, and the area is surrounded by Eldorado National Forest, which encompasses many lakes, including Wrights Lake and Dark Lake, the closest ones.

There is even a spot for rock climbing on Lover's Leap, a giant granite boulder located on the east side of Strawberry Lodge.

The place is easy to find. That is, as long as you are in the right town.

Facilities: Strawberry Cabins has 11 cabins and mountain vacation homes in the Strawberry area, each with a bathroom, kitchen with cookware and utensils, and wood stove or fireplace with a gas heater backup. Bed linens and towels are not provided. Bring your own sheets or sleeping bags and pillows. A grocery store and restaurant are located in Strawberry.

Reservations, fee: Reservations are required. In the summer, rates range from $125 to $175 per night, with discounts provided both in the off-season and for extended stays. Pets are permitted in some cabins.

Insider's note: In the winter, a day-use permit is required to park at the snow-play area at Echo Summit. Phone (916) 653-8569.

Who to contact: Phone Smothers Realty Service at (916) 659-7112 or (800) 409-6767, or write to P.O. Box 988, Twin Bridges, CA 95735.

Directions: From San Francisco, take Interstate 80 east to Sacramento. In Sacramento, take Highway 50 for 82 miles (42 miles past Placerville) to Strawberry. Continue through Strawberry for one mile and look for Smothers Realty on the right side of the road at 16202 Strawberry Lane. (All cabin tenants must check in at Smothers Realty to receive directions to a specific cabin.)

75. SORENSON'S RESORT CABINS
Toiyabe National Forest
Off Highway 88 near Hope Valley

It might seem like a pipe dream to imagine a place in the high Sierra where there are log cabins set amid pines and firs, with a pretty stream within walking distance and several lakes nearby for first-rate fishing.

In Hope Valley, this pipe dream is reality, at a place called Sorensen's Resort, although it is really more of a cabin village than a resort. Here you can make your base camp, using one of the cabins as your retreat, then spend as much time as you wish exploring the area, hiking or fishing, or venturing out to explore great recreation destinations such as the West Fork Carson River, Caples Lake, or the Pacific Crest Trail, among many.

Hope Valley is located along Highway 88, the winding two-laner that rises out of the Central Valley at Stockton. This is the little highway that passes Lower Bear River Reservoir, Silver Lake, and Caples Lake before finally rising over Carson Pass and being routed down into Hope Valley. Here at 7,000 feet in elevation is Sorensen's, and once you set up shop in one of their cabins, you probably won't feel like going home for a long time.

There are 29 cabins, including 10 log cabins. All but three have kitchens, but none have telephones or televisions to disrupt your stay. Like I said, the place looks like a cabin village, but the walls are thick and it is usually quiet, so you don't lose the sense of mountain solitude. A small but outstanding restaurant is located at lodge headquarters, and in the summer, an outside deck is available for dining.

Because of the high elevation, there is often snow here from late November or early December through May. That makes it appealing in the winter for cross-country skiers, and in addition, Kirkwood Ski Area is located about 15 miles to the west off Highway 88. It also means you need to be ready for anything when it comes to weather in the spring and fall. Summer is the prime time, of course, when the Sierra ice box defrosts and great high-country trails and lakes are unveiled.

My favorite hike here starts at Carson Pass, elevation 8,540 feet, at the trailhead for the Pacific Crest Trail. Heading north, the trail is routed up over a mountain rim for about two miles, with a great view of Caples Lake. After topping the rim, the Upper Truckee River Canyon comes into view to the north along with the headwaters for the Truckee River, and if you look to the far north, you can make out giant Lake Tahoe, an unforgettable scene.

Of course, you don't have to go far for a good walk, or fishing either. Just across the road from Sorensen's is a meadow and the West Fork Carson River, which provides an easy hike and also fair fishing for rainbow trout. The river is stocked by the Department of Fish and Game, usually near the Forest Service campgrounds along Highway 88.

There are also a number of quality lakes in the area. The best for fishing is Caples Lake, located 12 miles to the west, and Blue Lakes, located off Blue Lakes Road 12 miles to the east. Other nearby lakes include Woods Lake, Red Lake, Kirkwood Lake, Burnside Lake and Tamarack Lake. All provide opportunities for boating with cartop boats, fishing for trout, and hiking.

In addition, one of the best easy backpack trips in the Sierra Nevada is available at Winnemucca Lake (see the story on page 178), and it also makes a good day trip. The best trailheads are at Woods Lake, located off a spur road two miles west of Carson Pass, as well as at Carson Pass.

You know, I have spent hundreds of days backpacking in the wilderness, and only recently have I realized that many of the same qualities of a wilderness trip can be obtained in other ways. Staying in one of the cabins in Hope Valley, then venturing out on day trips, is one of the ways to accomplish that.

Facilities: Sorensen's Resort has 29 cabins of various sizes. All but three have kitchens. All provide electricity, but there are no electronic devices in the rooms; no telephones or televisions.

Reservations, fee: Reservations are advised; cabin fees are $55 to $300 per night.

Insider's note: This is a year-round resort. In the winter there is excellent downhill skiing at Kirkwood, a snow-play area at Carson Pass, and good cross-country skiing in the national forest.

Who to contact: Phone Sorensen's Resort at (800) 423-9949, or write to 14255 Highway 88, Hope Valley, CA 96120.

Directions: From San Francisco, take Interstate 80 to Sacramento. Continue east on U.S. 50 and drive about 90 miles to the U.S. 50 junction with Highway 89. Turn south (right) on Highway 89 and drive over Luther Pass to Highway 88. Turn left (east) on Highway 88 and drive one mile to Sorensen's Resort on the right side of the road.

If you're coming from Stockton: Drive east on Highway 88 for about 110 miles, passing through Jackson and Kirkwood and over Carson Pass. When you reach the Highway 88-Highway 89 junction, continue straight on Highway 88 for one mile to Sorensen's Resort.

76. KIT CARSON LODGE CABINS
Eldorado National Forest
Off Highway 88 near Silver Lake

The cabins at Silver Lake look so perfect that upon first sight, you might think they are private retreats for a few lucky rich folks. Guess again: they are private retreats all right, but for anybody who wants to rent them.

There are a lot of Silver Lakes in California and all of them are beautiful, but this one might just be the most special. This Silver Lake is set at 7,200 feet on the western slopes of the Sierra Nevada along Highway 88, pretty and blue, surrounded by granite and national forest, and is well stocked with trout. It is one of several lakes in the immediate region, along with Caples Lake, Woods Lake, Red Lake, and Kirkwood Lake, all located within a few miles. With relatively short drives, you can also reach Frog Lake, Blue Lakes, Burnside Lake, and Lost Lakes to the east.

It makes for a great trip—hiking, fishing, cartop boating, or just exploring and venturing out to find new places with new secrets.

And like I said, the cabins look perfect, sprinkled about the forest along the lake's northern shore. Several have lake frontage, including Beaver, Eastern Brook, Black Bear, and Wolf, and most of the others have lake views. While they are well equipped, it is critical that you remember to bring your own towels and dish soap, since they are not provided.

This is the high country and it can get extraordinary amounts of snow and ice in rough winters. In typical years, Silver and the nearby lakes will start melting off their ice between May and early June, with enough snowmelt in the adjacent forest for the lakes to become accessible by Memorial Day weekend. But not always, my friends, not always. In bad years, it can take until July. No foolin'.

While Kit Carson Lodge does provide boat rentals, they are quite expensive and this country is really better suited for visitors to bring their own cartop boat, such as a canoe. With a canoe, you can lake-hop for days, hitting them all, fishing, paddling, and playing. The fishing is often good at Silver Lake, with the top spot from Treasure Island on toward the inlet stream. Caples Lake is also exceptional for fishing, and the others nearby are decent for stocked rainbow trout.

This is also an excellent area for hiking, with several great trails available, including the short wilderness hike to Winnemucca Lake (see the story on page 178). One of the truly great day hikes in California is nearby, starting at the trailhead for the Pacific Crest Trail on the north side of Highway 88 near Carson Pass. The trail rises up a small mountain, providing a great view below of Caples Lake, then tops a ridge from which you can get a spectacular long-distance lookout to the north of Lake Tahoe, huge and blue, a dramatic sight.

Of course, you don't need to hike to get great views. The view from Eastern Brook cabin, for instance, is very beautiful, with Silver Lake lapping at its shore a short distance from your front porch, little islands in the foreground, and a sky painted that magic deep blue you only get in the high country.

Facilities: Kit Carson Lodge has 19 cabins with a wide variety of size and accommodations. Bathrooms, full kitchens with cooking utensils, bed linens, fireplaces, and gas stoves are provided, with barbecues on outside decks. Kitchen towels, bath towels, dish soap, and toiletries are not provided. Boat rentals, a boat dock, a small beach, and a swimming area are available. A store, post office, and Laundromat are nearby.

Reservations, fee: Reservations are available and required for discounted rates. Rates range from $120 per night for a cabin that sleeps three or four to $170 per night for a cabin that sleeps six. From June 17 through September 3, minimum stays are one week, with rates ranging from $500 to $990 per week. Daily rates are available from May 26 to June 16 and from September 4 to October 9, with a two-day minimum.

Insider's note: Mountain bikes are not permitted, either in designated wilderness or anywhere on the Pacific Crest Trail.

Who to contact: From May 15 through October 31, phone Kit Carson Lodge at (209) 258-8500, or write to Kit Carson, CA 95644. From November 1 through May 14, phone (209) 245-4760, or write to 5855 Carbondale Road, Plymouth, CA 95669. For a map of Eldorado National Forest, send $3 to Office of Information, U.S. Forest Service, 630 Sansome Street, San Francisco, CA 94111.

Directions: From San Francisco, take Interstate 80 over the Bay Bridge. At the 80/580 split, take Interstate 580 east and continue past Livermore to Highway 205. Take Highway 205 and drive north to Interstate 5 and continue north to Stockton and Highway 4. In Stockton, turn east on Highway 4 and drive three miles to Highway 99. Turn north on Highway 99 and drive about three miles to Highway 88. Turn east on Highway 88 and continue 52 miles past Jackson to Silver Lake. Turn at the signed entrance road for Kit Carson Lodge.

77. CAPLES LAKE RESORT CABINS
Eldorado National Forest
Off Highway 88 near Kirkwood

Some people complain to me that they have "No place to go, nothing to do." Then I ask them, "Have you been to Caples Lake?" They usually respond with a look that resembles a deer staring into headlights.

Caples Lake is not only pretty, its blue-green waters surrounded by forest at 7,800 feet with a backdrop of high wilderness peaks, but the cabin rentals and huge array of outdoor recreation possibilities can make any vacation seem far too short. The cabins are open year-round, offering boat and bike rentals and horseback riding in the summer and snowshoes in the winter. Kirkwood Ski Area is only a few miles away.

Of the half-dozen lakes in the immediate area, Caples provides not only the most consistent trout fishing, but typically the biggest fish as well. There are several trails from the resort for biking or horseback riding. There are also several wilderness trailheads (no bikes allowed) in the nearby region. The best two short hikes are from Woods Lake to Round Top Lake, or from Carson Pass to Winnemucca Lake, both about four-mile round-trips.

Facilities: Caples Lake Resort has eight cabins that vary in size. There are also eight guest rooms in the lodge. Bathrooms, full kitchens with cookware, utensils, bed linens, towels, and gas stoves are provided, and a boat dock, ramp, and small marina are available nearby. You can rent boats, bikes, and horses, and in the winter, snowshoes. A small store is located nearby.

Reservations, fee: Reservations are advised. Cottage rates in summer vary from $75 per night for two during the week up to $140 per night for six during the weekend, depending on the size of cabin and number of people. Rates are slightly higher in the winter.

Insider's note: Mountain bikes are not permitted in designated wilderness areas or anywhere on the Pacific Crest Trail.

Who to contact: Phone Caples Lake Resort (209) 258-8888, or write to

P.O. Box 88, Kirkwood, CA 95646. For a map of Eldorado National Forest, send $3 to Office of Information, U.S. Forest Service, 630 Sansome Street, San Francisco, CA 94111.

Directions: From San Francisco, take Interstate 80 over the Bay Bridge. At the 80/580 split, take Interstate 580 east and continue past Livermore to Highway 205. Take Highway 205 and drive north to Interstate 5 and continue north to Stockton and Highway 4. In Stockton, turn east on Highway 4 and drive three miles to Highway 99. Turn north on Highway 99 and drive about three miles to Highway 88 at Jackson. Turn east on Highway 88 and continue 63 miles to Caples Lake, about 1.5 miles past the turnoff for Kirkwood. Turn right at the sign for Caples Lake Lodge.

78. WINNEMUCCA LAKE BACKPACK SITES
Eldorado National Forest
Off Highway 88 near Carson Pass

A lot of people yearn for a place like Winnemucca Lake, but very few ever find such a spot.

Every year at various book signings, I always get asked, "Where is a lake in the wilderness that isn't too hard to reach? You know, a place where my wife and young kids can go, even though they've never done anything like this before."

Winnemucca Lake, as well as nearby Round Top Lake and Fourth of July Lake, provide the perfect answer for such a trip. They are beautiful high-mountain lakes, set just southwest of Carson Pass in Eldorado National Forest, yet are close enough to the trailhead that young families, seniors, and people who aren't in perfect shape can reach them without the adventure becoming an endurance test. Winnemucca Lake is two miles from the trailhead at Carson Pass, Round Top Lake is another mile, and Fourth of July Lake is another two miles in from Round Top Lake.

When introducing children to wilderness camping, it is critical to avoid grueling hikes. This backpack trip is short enough so that just as children start to tire, they will reach their destination. They will understand the payoff that comes with hiking, and as they grow older and stronger, become better prepared for more demanding trips.

The trailhead is at Carson Pass, elevation 8,580 feet, on Highway 88, where there is a parking area and trailhead on the south side of the road, as well as signs for Winnemucca Lake and the Pacific Crest Trail. For the first half-mile, you get to walk on the PCT, with the trail climbing gradually through a lodgepole pine forest. On my most recent trip through here, while hiking from Yosemite to Tahoe on the PCT, we came across both a young family and a group of seniors, all making the trip to Winnemucca Lake. The family was having their first backpacking experience, the seniors were on a day-hike.

After a mile, the trail breaks clear of trees, in the process furnishing great views of the surrounding landscape. You will notice this big mountain coming into view, straight ahead. That is Round Top Peak, 10,380 feet, the highest point in the Mokelumne Wilderness. The trail heads straight toward the north flank of Round Top but within a mile, feeds you right to the north shore of Winnemucca Lake, round and pretty.

There are several campsites at obvious places around the lake, so poke around, explore, and pick the one you like the best. This is wilderness camping, and that means you must bring everything you'll need; no form of mechanization is allowed, including bicycles. What is most important, of course, is ensuring that everyone will be warm, dry, and comfortable, that you have plenty of food and a water purifier, and know how to rig a bear-proof food hang.

Even though children may complain plenty at hiking two miles, once they see the payoff—a campsite at a pretty lake—it won't be long before they're ready for more. And there is plenty more to be had nearby.

Another mile westward on the trail, climbing to 9,500 feet in elevation, will route you to Round Top Lake, about a quarter of the size of Winnemucca. It makes a great side trip. If you want to venture further, the ambitious can scramble off the trail up the slopes of Round Top for some great views of the Mokelumne Wilderness.

There are a few vital elements that can greatly improve this trip. The most important is timing. To avoid large numbers of people, go during the week if possible, rather than on a weekend, or worse, a three-day holiday weekend. Another tip is also about timing, as in time of year. After all, this is the high country, and Carson Pass gets walloped with huge snowpacks almost every winter. In most years, it is best visited in mid-July through early September.

If I wanted to get children excited about wilderness camping, this is where I would take them. To be honest, I've spent thousands of days camping, and I get pretty excited about the trip myself.

Facilities: There are several primitive campsites at Winnemucca Lake. As this is part of the Mokelumne Wilderness, no facilities are provided.

Reservations; fee: No reservation; no fee.

Permits: A wilderness permit is required from Eldorado National Forest. Permits are free and available from Forest Service district offices. For information, phone (916) 644-6048.

Who to contact: Phone Eldorado National Forest at (916) 644-6048, or write to 3070 Camino Heights Drive, Camino, CA 95709. For a map of

Eldorado National Forest, send $3 to Office of Information, U.S. Forest Service, 630 Sansome Street, San Francisco, CA 94111. To obtain a topographic map, send $6 to Maps-Western Distribution Center, U.S. Geologic Survey, Box 25286-Federal Center, Denver, CO 80225 and ask for Carson Pass and Caples Lake.

Directions from San Francisco: Take Interstate 80 to Sacramento. Continue east on U.S. 50 and drive about 90 miles to the U.S. 50 junction with Highway 89. Turn south (right) on Highway 89 and drive over Luther Pass to Highway 88. Turn right (west) on Highway 88 and drive about 10 miles to Carson Pass. A parking lot is available on the left side of the road, and the trailhead is located at the parking lot, adjacent to the visitor center.

If you are coming from Stockton, drive east on Highway 88 for about 100 miles, passing through Jackson and Kirkwood to Carson Pass. When you reach Carson Pass, turn right at the parking area. The trailhead is located adjacent to the visitor center.

OTHER CABIN RENTALS NEAR CARSON PASS
Kay's Silver Lake Resort, 48400 Kay's Road, Pioneer, CA 95666; (209) 258-8598.

OTHER CABIN RENTALS IN NORTH TAHOE AND WEST SHORE
Cottage Inn at Lake Tahoe, (1690 West Lake Boulevard, Sunnyside), P.O. Box 66, Tahoe City, CA 96145.

Dunes Resort, (6780 North Lake Boulevard), P.O. Box 34, Tahoe Vista, CA 96148.

Tahoma Lodge, (7018 West Lake Boulevard), P.O. Box 72, Tahoma, CA 96142.

Tahoma Meadows, (6821 West Lake Boulevard), P.O. Box 82, Homewood, CA 96141.

Note: A central reservation number is used for all lodging information and reservations in North Tahoe. Phone (800) 824-6348.

OTHER CABINS RENTALS IN SOUTH TAHOE
Doc's Cottages, P.O. Box 3626, Stateline, NV 89449; (702) 588-2264.

Emerald Pines Resort Cottages, 681 Emerald Bay Road, South Lake Tahoe, CA 96150; (916) 541-3091.

Lazy S Lodge, 609 Emerald Bay Road, South Lake Tahoe, CA 96150; (916) 541-0230.

Yosemite

** For locations of camps, see map on page 9. **

79. LAZY Z RESORT CABINS
Stanislaus Forest
Off Highway 108 near Twain Harte

Twain Harte and the Highway 108 corridor leading up into the Sierra Nevada has always had a special appeal for me, this area being the transition zone where the Central Valley foothills give way to alpine forest.

But that is nothing like the appeal of the "swimming pool" at Lazy Z Resort. It is one of the most dramatic homemade pools at any resort in California. It looks more like a lake, as if the surrounding stone was carved out of mountain granite, complete with waterfalls that pour forth freshwater. Like a lake, it is not heated, but since air temperatures in the 90s are common during the summer here, the water temperature is perfect. It's even warmer than a real lake would be because this "lake" is eight feet deep.

A bonus for pool-goers are two adjacent Jacuzzis. You can hop in and out, from pool to Jacuzzi to pool, and in short order start feeling really good.

The resort is designed for absolute minimal stress, and you notice it right away in the resort office, which has light classical music playing in the background. The six cabins follow that lead, all first-class accommodations, supplied with everything that you might need except for food and drinks.

Lazy Z is located just outside of Twain Harte, elevation 3,500 feet, right on the dividing line between oaks and pines in the summer, and rain and snow in the winter. In the summer, this means you are out of the hot foothill country, just high enough in altitude to be in the shade of giant sugar pines. In the winter, it can be snowing like crazy uphill at the Dodge Ridge Ski Area near Pinecrest, but here at Twain Harte it will only be raining. Often you don't have to chain up your tires during winter storms.

The nearby vicinity is best known for Stanislaus National Forest and the Stanislaus and Tuolumne rivers, both good for fishing, swimming, and panning for gold. The best way to explore around here is with a map of Stanislaus National Forest, which shows all backcountry roads and access points to the rivers. I really like fishing the South Fork Tuolumne River here for rainbow trout—sneak-fishing and making short casts at the heads of pools. This is the river where I received my first fly-fishing lesson from my mentor, Ed Dunckel, followed by a trout barbecue.

There are also many other adventure possibilities nearby. The resort itself has a horseshoe pit, Ping-Pong table, and walking trails. Within an hour's drive in the mountains is Beardsley Reservoir, Pinecrest Lake, Lyons Lake, and of course, the Dodge Ridge Ski Area.

But after taking a dunk in the resort's pool, maybe followed by a plunge into the Jacuzzi, few visitors will feel like going anywhere else any time soon.

Facilities: Lazy Z Resort has six cabins of various sizes with bathrooms and kitchens. Cookware, utensils, and bed linens are provided. Some cabins have fireplaces, decks, patios, or barbecues. A swimming pool with waterfall and Jacuzzi are available on the property. No pets are permitted.

Reservations, fee: Reservations are required. Cabin rates on weekends range from $95 to $175 per night per couple, with a two-night minimum stay required. Weekly and seasonal discounts are available.

Insider's note: Do not attempt to gain access to the Stanislaus or Tuolumne rivers without a Forest Service map. Private property checkerboards much of the forest country and river areas, and trespassing is not tolerated.

Who to contact: Phone Lazy Z Resort at (209) 586-1573 or (800) 585-1238, or write to P.O. Box 1055, Twain Harte, CA 95383. For a map of Stanislaus National Forest, send $3 to Office of Information, U.S. Forest Service, 630 Sansome Street, San Francisco, CA 94111.

Directions: From San Francisco, take Interstate 80 east over the Bay Bridge. At the 80/580 split, take Interstate 580 east past Livermore to the Interstate 205 cutoff. Take the Interstate 205 cutoff and drive 14 miles, then merge with Interstate 5 north and drive three miles to Highway 120/Manteca. Turn east on Highway 120 and drive to Oakdale. In Oakdale, turn left on Highway 108/120 and drive past Sonora to Twain Harte. At Twain Harte, turn left at Mono Vista and drive a short distance to a stop sign (Longeway Road). Turn right at Longeway and drive about three miles to where it dead-ends at Middle Camp Road. Turn right on Middle Camp Road and look for the resort on the right side of the road.

---

80. EVERGREEN LODGE CABINS
Hetch Hetchy, Yosemite National Park
Off Highway 120 near Mather

Hetch Hetchy is the Yosemite you hear little about, and that is why the cabins at Evergreen Lodge remain a pretty good secret. Hetch Hetchy is the giant lake set in the dammed Tuolumne River canyon in the remote northwest sector of Yosemite National Park. Evergreen Lodge is located just a mile outside the park entrance and eight miles from the lake, a surprise for newcomers, and the site of an excellent trailhead for hiking and horseback riding. The cabins are quite old but comfortable, complete with porches that make for a perfect summer evening sit.

Evergreen Lodge is located at an elevation of 4,600 feet and surrounded by Stanislaus Forest. What makes it work is the short hop to Hetch Hetchy and the great hikes here to see Wapama Falls and Tueala Falls. A bonus is that lodge guests are provided free access to Camp Mather and its swimming pool; horse rentals are also available there.

Every year, thousands of people at overloaded Yosemite end up stuck without a spot, spending the night in their cars. Many would pay a million dollars for one of these cabins, but they just don't know they exist.

Facilities: Evergreen Lodge has 19 one- and two-room cabins with bathrooms. Bed linens are provided with daily maid service. There are no kitchens in the cabins, but a lodge restaurant is available. A swimming pool and horseback riding outfitter are located one mile away at Camp Mather, with free access provided to lodge guests. No pets are permitted.

Reservations, fee: Reservations are recommended. Cabin rates on weekends range from $69 for two to $94 for four, with no minimum stay. Weekly and seasonal discounts are available. The season runs from late April through October.

Who to contact: Phone Evergreen Lodge at (209) 379-2606, or write to 33160 Evergreen Road, Groveland, CA 95321.

Directions: From San Francisco, take Interstate 80 east over the Bay Bridge. At the 80/580 split, take Interstate 580 east past Livermore to the Interstate 205 cutoff. Take the Interstate 205 cutoff and drive 14 miles, then merge with Interstate 5 north and drive three miles to Highway 120/Manteca. Turn east on Highway 120 and drive to Oakdale. In Oakdale, turn left on Highway 108/120 and drive east for 25 miles to the turnoff for Highway 49/120 and Chinese Camp. Turn right on Highway 49/120 and drive 12 miles to Moccasin. At Moccasin, turn left on Highway 120 and drive about five miles to Groveland and continue for 28 miles (six miles past Harden Flat) to Evergreen Road. Turn left and drive seven miles and look for Evergreen Lodge on the left side of the road.

81. YOSEMITE VALLEY CABINS
Yosemite National Park
Off Highway 140 near Yosemite Village

We were walking back from the base of Yosemite Falls when suddenly we came upon a series of small wooden cabins where a few happy folks were sitting outside, looking so relaxed it was as if their muscles had been converted to marmalade.

We were shocked. Can people actually relax in Yosemite Valley? Could there actually be cabins in Yosemite Valley? Could it actually be possible to rent one? The answers: yes, yes, and maybe.

It's true that wood-sided cabins, some in a duplex configuration, are available as an extension of nearby Yosemite Lodge. They are located away and hidden from the main access road in the valley, yet right alongside the valley's great biking trail and within close walking distance of the

Lower Yosemite Falls from the meadow behind Yosemite Valley Cabins

base of Yosemite Falls. Sound good? Is good. Sound like it beats the combat camping at the valley's campgrounds? You ain't foolin'.

But it can be just about impossible to get a reservation for one of these cabins during the summer, although the wise few will still finagle their way in. There are three options: 1. Book a trip here up to a year in advance; 2. Make persistent phone calls (the reservation line is often busy), hoping that somebody has canceled out; 3. Schedule your visit for the off-season, particularly in November and March, when you can usually just call, reserve a cabin, then go, and see Yosemite Valley during one of the rare times when few others are visiting.

That can get you in. Otherwise you will be just like us, walking back from a pretty stroll, wondering how people ever get lucky enough to stay in such a place.

Facilities: Yosemite Valley has 189 wood-sided cabins (not to be confused with the tent cabins that are also located in Yosemite Valley, near Curry Village); 100 come with private bathrooms, 89 do not. The cabins have no kitchen facilities, but bed linens and towels are provided.

Reservations, fee: Reservations are required and are available one year in advance. Cabin rates range from $71.25 with a bathroom to $53 without.

Insider's note: To get a free map/brochure of Yosemite National Park, phone (209) 372-0265.

Who to contact: Phone Yosemite Lodging Reservations at (209) 252-4848, or write to 5410 East Home, Fresno, CA 93727.

Directions: From San Francisco, drive east on Interstate 580 past Livermore into the Central Valley. At the 205/580 split, veer south on Interstate 580 and continue about eight miles to Highway 132. Turn east on Highway 132 and drive to Modesto and Highway 99. Turn south on Highway 99 and drive to Merced. At Merced, turn east on Highway 140 and drive into Yosemite ($5 entrance fee), continuing into Yosemite Valley. At the first stop sign in the valley, turn left, drive over Sentinel Bridge, and at another stop sign, turn left again. Drive a short distance, then turn left at the signed turn for Yosemite Lodge.

---

82. MAY LAKE HIGH SIERRA CAMP
Yosemite National Park
Off Highway 120 near Tenaya Lake

The May Lake High Sierra Camp provides everything for the person who wants a wilderness-style experience but without the hard stuff. That means no long hike, no butt-kicker climbs, and believe it or not, no tent. That is because the hike to May Lake is only 1.2 miles and includes just a short up and down, and you can arrange to have a tent cabin waiting for you. At the High Sierra Camp, breakfast and dinner are prepared by staff and served family-style in a dining tent; picnic lunches are also available.

May Lake is a round, blue lake set at 9,329 feet, right at the foot of spectacular Mt. Hoffman (10,850 feet). The hike is made easier by a 2.5-mile cutoff road off Highway 120 that leads to the trailhead at Snow Flat, which gets you within an hour's hike of your destination. From Snow Flat, the trail crosses through a lodgepole pine forest, then rises largely above treeline to granite plates, climbing about 300 feet to a short pass at 9,600 feet. The trail then drops down to the lake's southern shore, where the High Sierra Camp is established.

It is a very pretty setting, with forest and greenery filling the southern end of the lake along the outlet stream, and a backdrop of a line of glacier-carved granite sheets leading up to Mt. Hoffman. The water is very cold, often too cold to swim in, and the fishing is usually quite poor.

Reservations for the tent cabins are completed by a lottery conducted every mid-December. Applications for the lottery must be completed on a specific form, available at the Fresno address listed below, and must be received between October 15 and November 30 for dates during the following summer.

Facilities: May Lake High Sierra Camp has tent cabins and tent sites for backpackers. Each tent cabin is outfitted with steel-frame beds with linens, pillows, and blankets; a wood-burning stove; hooks for hanging backpacks; shelves; a table and chairs; and candles. Dinner and breakfast are prepared by staff and served in a dining tent, with picnic lunches available. Piped water is provided. A drive-in campground is also available nearby at Tuolumne Meadows, on a first-come, first-served basis.

Reservations, fee: Reservations are required through a lottery system. To obtain the required lottery form, write to Yosemite Reservations, 5410 East Home Avenue, Fresno, CA 93727 and ask for High Sierra Camp Reservation Form. Lottery applications are accepted between October 15 and November 30 each year for dates the following summer. The lottery takes place on December 15. The camp fee is $90 per night, including all meals. For dinner and breakfast alone, the fee is $26.28 per night. For a box lunch alone, the fee is $6.45.

Insider's note: A wilderness permit is required for overnight use and is included with your reservation at a High Sierra Camp. Otherwise, free Yosemite wilderness permits can be obtained on a first-come, first-served basis at wilderness kiosks near your chosen trailhead or in advance by mail or phone. Reservations are permitted as far as six months in advance of your trip. Determine the dates you plan to enter and exit the wilderness, the specific trailhead you will take, your destination, the number of people in your party, and if any stock animals will be used. Then send $3 per person, making out your check to Yosemite Association, and send your request to

Wilderness Permit, Yosemite National Park, P.O. Box 545, Yosemite, CA 95389. Or phone (209) 372-0740 and have the information and a credit card ready. To obtain the free publication "Keep It Wild," phone Yosemite National Park at (209) 372-0308.

Who to contact: For information about Yosemite National Park, phone (209) 372-0200 (touch-tone only). To reach the Yosemite Park Backcountry Ranger Office, phone (209) 372-0740. For an excellent map of the area, phone Tom Harrison Cartography at (415) 456-7940.

Directions: From San Francisco, drive east on Interstate 580 past Livermore into the Central Valley. At the 205/580 split, veer south on Interstate 580 and continue about eight miles to Highway 132. Turn east on Highway 132 and drive to Modesto and Highway 99. Turn south on Highway 99 and drive to Merced. At Merced, turn east on Highway 140 and drive into Yosemite ($5 entrance fee) and continue toward Yosemite Valley. Just before reaching the valley, turn north on Highway 120 and drive 43 miles, then turn left on the signed access road to the May Lake Trailhead.

---

83. GLEN AULIN HIGH SIERRA CAMP
Yosemite National Park
Off Highway 120 near Tuolumne Meadows

When you stand alone and gaze at Tuolumne Falls, it can be hard to believe that relatively few miles away in Yosemite Valley are 20,000 packed-in people.

But it is here at the headwaters of the Grand Canyon of the Tuolumne in Yosemite National Park's backcountry where visitors not only get spectacular waterfalls and canyons sculpted in glaciated beauty, but comparably few visitors. Why so few? Because first you have to drive out of Yosemite Valley and up to the trailhead at Tuolumne Meadows, then you have to walk for two hours. Frankly, your average cow in the Yosemite Valley herd isn't willing to do that.

What makes it easy is the Glen Aulin High Sierra Camp, which requires only a five-mile, mostly level walk on the Pacific Crest Trail out of Tuolumne Meadows. That makes it a perfect overnight trip, with a cakewalk of a backpack hike both in and out. Glen Aulin has tent cabins, backpack campsites, and a staffed dining tent where you are served breakfast and dinner, with picnic lunches available. But remember, this is wilderness, so not only is a wilderness permit required (it's free), but you should come prepared to completely fend for yourself, including pump-filtering all drinking water and bringing rope and garbage bags for a counterbalanced food hang.

The hike is simple and beautiful. After obtaining your wilderness permit at the Tuolumne Backcountry Ranger Station, start walking north on the Pacific Crest Trail. The trail starts at 8,600 foot in elevation, crossing a high meadow sprinkled with lodgepole pine. A panorama of mountain peaks is the backdrop for your first steps, with Unicorn Peak (10,190 feet), Cathedral Peak (10,940 feet), and Fairview Dome (9,731 feet) in nearby view.

Although much of Yosemite's backcountry requires steep climbs and descents in deep canyons, here the trail is nearly flat, poking through a sparse lodgepole forest, then picking up the Tuolumne River and following it downstream. The trail is often bordered by bright green corn lilies, blooming violet lupine, and wild grasses with monarch butterflies gliding about. On the morning hike out, the only sounds are the happy songs of meadowlarks and the rush of moving water.

The trail glides by, then after about four miles, you arrive at a spot along the river where a cascading sheet of water pours in three tiers into a foaming pool, then flattens into an emerald-green slick. The natural beauty is divine, and it is one of my favorite spots to stop and pump-filter a canteen's worth of water, then relish its cold sweetness, the best tasting drink in the world.

It's just a start. In the next mile, you will drop down to the river and reach a bridge that is routed to the Glen Aulin Campground. From here, turn and look back upstream and you will discover a postcardlike view of Tuolumne Falls. The river narrows and pours through a granite slot in a 100-foot waterfall, cascading into a foaming crater of blue-white water, full of bubbles and freshness.

After setting up your base camp at Glen Aulin, there are several great sidetrip hikes. The best is farther downstream, into the Grand Canyon of the Tuolumne, where you can see spectacular Waterwheel Falls, as well as a few other pretty cascades. If you want to get completely away from people, hike from Glen Aulin up Cold Canyon on the Pacific Crest Trail, where you will find a high meadow so pristine that I call it "Church Meadow," and farther up, great views of the canyon below.

This is high-country wilderness, and in high snow years, it does not become accessible until July, with spring often arriving right around the Fourth of July weekend. In low snow years, the trail can be snow-free as early as Memorial Day weekend, although even then, the area can still get a surprise snowfall. Late July and August are often perfect here, and by Labor Day weekend, cold nights will start making their return, although the area doesn't usually get its first serious snow until Halloween.

If you have shied away from Yosemite because of all the thousands of visitors, this trip offers natural beauty similar to the fabled valley, yet without all the people.

Facilities: Glen Aulin High Sierra Camp has tent cabins and tent sites for backpackers. Each tent cabin is outfitted with steel-frame beds with linens, pillows, and blankets; a wood-burning stove; hooks for hanging backpacks; shelves; a table and chairs; and candles. Dinner and breakfast are prepared by the staff and served in a dining tent, with picnic lunches available. Piped water is provided. A drive-in campground is also available at Tuolumne Meadows, on a first-come, first-served basis.

Reservations, fee: Reservations are required through a lottery system. To obtain the required lottery form, write to Yosemite Reservations, 5410 East Home Avenue, Fresno, CA 93727 and ask for High Sierra Camp Reservation Form. Lottery applications are accepted between October 15 and November 30 each year for dates the following summer. The lottery takes place on December 15. The camp fee is $90 per night, including all meals. For dinner and breakfast alone, the fee is $26.28 per night. For a box lunch alone, the fee is $6.45.

Insider's note: A wilderness permit is required for overnight use and is included with your reservation at a High Sierra Camp. Otherwise, free Yosemite wilderness permits can be obtained on a first-come, first-served basis at wilderness kiosks near your chosen trailhead or in advance by mail or phone. Reservations are permitted as far as six months in advance of your trip. Determine the dates you plan to enter and exit the wilderness, the specific trailhead you will take, your destination, the number of people in your party, and if any stock animals will be used. Then send $3 per person, making out your check to Yosemite Association, and send your request to Wilderness Permit, Yosemite National Park, P.O. Box 545, Yosemite, CA 95389. Or phone (209) 372-0740 and have the information and a credit card ready. To obtain the free publication "Keep It Wild," phone Yosemite National Park at (209) 372-0308.

Who to contact: For information about Yosemite National Park, phone (209) 372-0200 (touch-tone only). To reach the Yosemite Park Backcountry Ranger Office, phone (209) 372-0740. For an excellent map of the area, phone Tom Harrison Cartography at (415) 456-7940.

Directions: From San Francisco, drive east on Interstate 580 past Livermore into the Central Valley. At the 205/580 split, veer south on Interstate 580 and continue about eight miles to Highway 132. Turn east on Highway 132 and drive to Modesto and Highway 99. Turn south on Highway 99 and drive to Merced. At Merced, turn east on Highway 140 and drive into Yosemite ($5 entrance fee) and continue toward Yosemite Valley. Just before reaching the valley, turn north on Highway 120 and drive 49 miles to Tuolumne Meadows. The wilderness permit kiosk is located two miles farther, well signed on the right side of the road. The trailhead, signed Pacific Crest Trail, is located near the parking area for Lembert Dome, on the north side of Highway 120, at the end of a gated dirt road.

84. CATHEDRAL LAKE BACKPACK CAMP
Yosemite National Park
Off Highway 120 near Tuolumne Meadows

Many lakes in the Yosemite wilderness are like mountain shrines. Cathedral Lake is not only a place of divine beauty, but you can actually reach it without first requiring a heart transplant.

That is because it is a 3.7-mile hike from the trailhead at Tuolumne Meadows, a mostly level walk on a good trail, with views of several spectacular mountain peaks. Your destination is a campsite along a truly pristine lake. This is one of those extremely rare treks, a chance to reach a beautiful place on a short hike without a major climb.

Cathedral Lake is located at 9,288 feet in elevation in Yosemite's backcountry, about a half-mile on a spur trail from the John Muir Trail. It was the nearby proximity to the JMT that led me here almost by coincidence. We were hiking the entire JMT, from Mt. Whitney to Yosemite Valley, and with the end of the trip in sight, picked Cathedral Lake for a night's camp. It was so pretty and easy to reach, and after hiking 200 miles on that trip, it was quite surprising to all of us that you only have to hike for a couple of hours (instead of a couple of weeks) to reach such a great spot.

The lake is in a classic glacial cirque, sculpted round in granite and colored emerald green, set below Cathedral Peak (10,911 feet) to the east. The campsites are close to the lake, set in flat dirt spots between giant boulders, with the smell of pine duff in the air. The water is cold, but not too cold for swimming; trout fishing is usually poor; and an excellent side trip is available to nearby Upper Cathedral Lake.

You start the trip by obtaining the required wilderness permit at the Tuolumne Backcountry Ranger Station. Trailhead quotas are in effect here, so reservations are always advised. Remember that while most of Yosemite's four million annual visitors don't have a clue about the Cathedral Lake backpack camp, there are still plenty who do, and they love the place enough to make a yearly trip here for two or three days of camping. So if you show up on the fly, without a reservation, you can end up quite disappointed.

If you start your backpack trip from the Tuolumne Backcountry Ranger Station, it will add more than two miles of hiking. The best trailhead is located about a half-mile west of the visitor center, on the south side of Highway 120. From here, the trail is quickly routed away from people, climbing very gradually through a forest of lodgepole pine,

Cathedral Lake and Cathedral Peak

occasionally poking free to provide views of the area's classic granite landscaping. The most prominent peak is Cathedral Peak, with its spire-like top, which seems to cast an aura over the valley to the northwest.

It is a 3.1-mile hike on the John Muir Trail to the Cathedral Lake turnoff. Here you turn right, and hike another six-tenths of a mile to the shore of Cathedral Lake, the final stretch being nearly flat, crossing a meadow and paralleling the inlet stream on the way to the lake.

The campsites are sprinkled near the shore of the lake, the best ones on the eastern shore. It is a great spot for photographs, both of the lake and the peak looming nearby, and also for exotic shots of moonrises or sunsets. It is vital that you use only existing fire rings; if you create a new one, rangers will write you a ticket. Because of the easy walk in, rangers make daily trips here, checking for wilderness permits, illegal campfire sites, and litter. They will also help you bear-proof your food if you haven't done so already.

Because of the high elevation, the trail in is usually locked up by snow until the Fourth of July, and the water is fed by snowmelt well into summer, keeping the lake chilly for swimming. On overcast days, it feels frigid, while on hot afternoons, it is refreshing. The trout fishing, as mentioned, is poor because the lake has very little spawning habitat and gets a lot of fishing pressure. The Park Service has also discontinued trout stocks; hence, very few trout.

The side trip to Upper Cathedral Lake is a winner, best reached by hiking back to the John Muir Trail, turning right, then making the 400-foot climb to the lake at 9,585 feet, set just below Cathedral Pass (9,730 feet) and nearby Tresidder Peak.

Everything out here is pristine, with pretty lakes, meadows, streams, and high peaks in the background. For a hike of just 3.6 miles to get here, what more could you ask for?

Facilities: No facilities are provided. Primitive campsites are available at dispersed locations along the lake's northwest shore. Plan to rely completely on yourself. A backpack camping stove and water-purification pump are essential. A drive-in campground is also available nearby at Tuolumne Meadows, on a first-come, first-served basis.

Insider's note: A wilderness permit is required for overnight use. It can be obtained on a first-come, first-served basis at the wilderness kiosk near your chosen trailhead or in advance by mail or phone. Reservations are permitted as far as six months in advance of your trip. Determine the dates you plan to enter and exit the wilderness, the specific trailhead you will take, your destination, the number of people in your party, and if any stock animals will be used. Then send $3 per person, making out the check to Yosemite Association, and send your request to Wilderness Permit, Yosemite National Park, P.O. Box 545, Yosemite, CA 95389. Or phone (209) 372-0740 and have the information and a credit card ready. To obtain the free publication "Keep It Wild," phone Yosemite National Park at (209) 372-0308.

Who to contact: For information about Yosemite National Park, phone (209) 372-0200 (touch-tone only). To reach the Yosemite Park Backcountry Ranger Office, phone (209) 372-0740. For an excellent map of the area, phone Tom Harrison Cartography at (415) 456-7940.

Directions: From San Francisco, drive east on Interstate 580 past Livermore into the Central Valley. At the 205/580 split, veer south on Interstate 580 and continue about eight miles to Highway 132. Turn east on Highway 132 and drive to Modesto and Highway 99. Turn south on Highway 99 and drive to Merced. At Merced, turn east on Highway 140 and drive into Yosemite ($5 entrance fee) and continue toward Yosemite Valley. Just before reaching the valley, turn north on Highway 120 and drive 49 miles to Tuolumne Meadows. The trailhead, signed John Muir Trail, is on the south side of the road.

85. LYELL FORK BACKPACK CAMP
Yosemite National Park
Off Highway 120 near Tuolumne Meadows

Yosemite is well known for its dramatic, steep canyons that can turn what is supposed to be a fun hike into a butt-kicker, especially in the remote northern backcountry. The four-mile tromp out of Tuolumne Meadows up Lyell Fork is a good way to circumvent that problem with a nearly flat, wide, solid trail that is routed along a pretty trout stream into the wilderness. You start at the trailhead for the Pacific Crest Trail, near the Wilderness Permit Station, then just stroll as slowly as you want to your camp.

It is the perfect trip for seniors or families with children, being short enough and flat enough that instead of forcing you into a head-down march, it allows you to enjoy the spectacular scenery, including glacier-cut Mammoth Peak and Kuna Crest to the east and beautiful Lyell Fork running nearby. Lyell Fork is a meandering stream, pretzeling through a meadow at its headwaters below Donohue Pass, then running through Lyell Canyon until joining with the headwaters of the Tuolumne River.

A series of wilderness campgrounds are located about three to four miles in, sites that are pretty, flat, and spacious, set amid lodgepole pines. At nearby Lyell Fork, the fishing is good for brook trout. Though the fish are small, during the early evening plenty of them are biting on small lures such as the 1/16-ounce Panther Martin, gold blade, black body with yellow spots. My brother and I have had evenings catching and releasing fish like crazy, maybe 30 or 40 apiece.

Be certain to return any fish that will not be eaten immediately, and not just for the sake of conservation. You see, this canyon is loaded with bears, sneaky ones at that, and you can plan on having a few creep by your camp at night, hoping you've left your food (or your fish) within reach. No problem: the park has rigged special high wires for bear-proof food hangs, ideal when using the counterbalance system with two food bags and a rope. We've never had a problem with the bears here when we've rigged up good food hangs. In fact, we always try to stay awake so we can surprise them in the night with a "Hey Yogi!" and watch them run off in shock, but alas, we always go to sleep and miss out. Even with a good food hang, though, don't try to store fish. The scent attracts animals and the fish usually go to waste anyway.

One other concern, especially for seniors, is the high altitude, with the trailhead at 8,600 feet in elevation. Your heart and lungs have to work overtime in order to assimilate oxygen into your bloodstream, so it's a mistake to arrive from sea level and then charge out into the wilderness. We advise camping the first night at Tuolumne Meadows to help your body get acclimated, then obtaining your wilderness permit the next morning and enjoying a leisurely walk up the canyon.

Once your camp is set, there are a number of great side trips, although most involve climbs. A favorite among kids is the climb up the Pacific Crest Trail to Donohue Pass, elevation 11,056 feet, which includes hopping over giant boulders, then getting a great view of the floor of Lyell Canyon and many wilderness peaks, including Yosemite's highest Peak, Mt. Lyell at 13,114 feet. Another good side trip, also requiring a climb, is the tromp up to beautiful Ireland Lake at 10,735 feet, which is pure and pristine, set above the tree line in glacier-carved granite. To get there, it's a hike of 4.5 miles, one-way, from the cutoff on the Pacific Crest Trail.

All in all, camping at Lyell Fork makes for a great trip: a nearly flat walk on the way in, good fishing, pretty campsites, and excellent side trips nearby. We'll be back.

Facilities: Primitive campsites are available at dispersed locations along the trail in Lyell Canyon. High wires are provided for making bear-proof food hangs using the counterbalance system with two bags. Plan to rely completely on yourself. A backpack camping stove and water-purification pump are essential. A drive-in campground is also available nearby at Tuolumne Meadows, on a first-come, first-served basis.

Insider's note: A wilderness permit is required for overnight use. It can be obtained on a first-come, first-served basis at the wilderness kiosk near your chosen trailhead or in advance by mail or phone. Reservations are permitted as far as six months in advance of your trip. Determine the dates you plan to enter and exit the wilderness, the specific trailhead you will take, your destination, the number of people in your party, and if any stock animals will be used. Then send $3 per person, making out the check to Yosemite Association, and send your request to Wilderness Permit, Yosemite National Park, P.O. Box 545, Yosemite, CA 95389. Or phone (209) 372-0740 and have the information and a credit card ready. To obtain the free publication "Keep It Wild," phone Yosemite National Park at (209) 372-0308.

Who to contact: For information about Yosemite National Park, phone (209) 372-0200 (touch-tone only). To reach the Yosemite Park Backcountry Ranger Office, phone (209) 372-0740. For an excellent map of the area, phone Tom Harrison Cartography at (415) 456-7940.

Directions: From San Francisco, drive east on Interstate 580 past Livermore into the Central Valley. At the 205/580 split, veer south on Interstate 580 and continue about eight miles to Highway 132. Turn east on Highway 132 and drive to Modesto and Highway 99. Turn south on Highway 99 and drive to Merced. At Merced, turn east on Highway 140 and drive into

Yosemite ($5 entrance fee) and continue toward Yosemite Valley. Turn north on Highway 120 and drive about 50 miles, just past Tuolumne Meadows. The wilderness permit station is located on the right side of the road, near Lembert Dome. The trailhead (Pacific Crest Trail) is located near the wilderness permit station.

86. TIOGA PASS RESORT CABINS
Tioga Pass, near Yosemite
Off Highway 120 near Lee Vining

How would you like to enjoy all the elements of the high-country Yosemite wilderness, yet be able to stay in a cozy cabin each night? That combination is exactly what makes Tioga Pass Resort Cabins such winners.

Tioga Pass Resort is located just two miles from the eastern entrance station of Yosemite National Park. The surrounding landscape has all the recreational qualities of Yosemite, yet is actually part of Inyo National Forest, with several nearby lakes for cartop boating and much better fishing than in the park, and excellent hiking. And if you want to make the quick getaway into Yosemite, a five-minute drive puts you inside park borders, and another 15 minutes gets you to Tuolumne Meadows.

This is the high country, elevation 9,600 feet, a land of wilderness, granite peaks, mountain slopes peppered with lodgepole pine and pristine lakes. The heart of your adventure is this resort with its cabins, as well as a small grocery store, a restaurant, and plenty of free fishing advice. It seemed to us that the people who run the place are about as nice as they could be, too.

Within a mile or two is Ellery Lake to the east and Tioga Lake to the west, both beautiful alpine waters that run pure, cold, and pristine, and are stocked with trout. Just four miles away, via a bumpy Forest Service road, is Saddlebag Lake, at 10,087 feet the highest drive-to lake in California, providing more high alpine beauty, an excellent trailhead, and good boating and fishing. And then you have Yosemite, with outstanding hiking out of Tuolumne Meadows: up Lyell Fork, to Cathedral Lake, down to Glen Aulin along the Tuolumne River, or up Lembert Dome.

Sound good? You ain't lyin' it sounds good. In fact, it can seem perfect. But there's always a catch, right? Right. In this case, it's the snow and iced-over lakes early in the season. The plan here is to open each year by May 20 for the summer season, and that usually works out fine. But in big snow years, like '83, '86, '93, and '95, Highway 120 at Tioga Pass was barely opened by July, with the nearby lakes still partially frozen over on the Fourth of July weekend. That means a trip planned here too early in the season can be rendered near impossible because of snow covering roads and hiking trails, and ice locking up lakes.

That is why a winter season is also available at the resort. From November 30 through April 30, the resort is accessed only from the east via Lee Vining, rather than from Yosemite. Cross-country skiing and trying to stay warm are the primary activities.

When you first arrive, you will discover the cabins set on a hillside behind the general store, in a variety of sizes to handle couples, families, or small groups. All are rented by the week. For shorter stays of two nights or more, motel-type units without kitchen facilities are available. The grocery store is small but well stocked with groceries, milk, and bread, as well as beer, wine, film, camping equipment, and fishing tackle.

The prime nearby destinations are the lakes: Tioga, Ellery, and Saddlebag. Tioga Lake, located just south of the resort, is in a gorgeous spot at 9,700 feet, with good cartop boating and fishing for rainbow trout and more rarely, golden trout. Ellery Lake, located just east of the resort, is similarly beautiful with spectacular deep-blue waters in a granite mountain setting, elevation 9,500 feet.

Saddlebag, accessible by driving east about a quarter-mile from the resort on Highway 120, then turning left at the signed Forest Service road, is high, stark, and cold, high enough that the thin oxygen and altitude can make you dizzy. A primitive boat launch provides access to these pristine waters, which afford the best fishing of the three lakes. A bonus here is a trail that loops around the eastern side of the lake and then is routed to a series of wilderness lakes, the best trail being a 1.5-mile climb to Steelhead Lake at 10,270 feet. It's a great day-hike, providing you don't suck too much wind on the way up.

Because this entire area is set high near the Sierra crest, it is subject to cold nights and afternoon winds. No problem, though. After all, you have a cabin to stay in, right? Right.

Facilities: Tioga Pass Resort provides cabins in one- and two-bedroom configurations. Each includes a kitchen with utensils, cookware, a stove, and refrigerator. A propane heater is provided. Motel-style units are also available for those not requiring kitchen facilities.

Reservations, fee: Reservations are required, and there's a weeklong minimum stay. A two-day minimum stay is required in the motel-style units. Cabin prices range from $410 to $540 per week, depending on the size of the cabin. Motel units rent from $50 to $60 per day.

Insider's note: Saddlebag Lake, the highest drive-to lake in California at 10,087 feet in elevation, is a two-mile drive from Tioga Pass Resort.

Who to contact: Phone Tioga Pass Resort at (209) 372-4471, or write to P.O. Box 7, Lee Vining, CA 93541. For an excellent map of the area, phone Tom Harrison Cartography at (415) 456-7940. Or send $3 to the USDA-Forest Service, 630 Sansome Street, San Francisco, CA 94111 and ask for Inyo National Forest.

Directions: From Reno or Carson City, drive south on U.S. 395 to Lee Vining. One mile past Lee Vining, turn west on Highway 120 and drive 12 miles up the grade toward Yosemite National Park. After passing the Saddlebag Lake turnoff, drive about a quarter-mile and turn right at Tioga Pass Resort.

If you are coming from San Francisco, drive east on Interstate 580 past Livermore into the Central Valley. At the 205/580 split, veer south on Interstate 580 and continue about eight miles to Highway 132. Turn east on Highway 132 and drive to Modesto and Highway 99. Turn south on Highway 99 and drive to Merced. At Merced, turn east on Highway 140 and drive into Yosemite ($5 entrance fee) and continue toward Yosemite Valley. Turn north on Highway 120 and drive about 65 miles through the Tioga Pass entrance station. Continue two miles and turn left at Tioga Pass Resort.

87. YOSEMITE-MARIPOSA KOA CABINS
Mariposa, near Yosemite
Off Highway 140 in Midpines

Every KOA in America should be like the one in Mariposa. Imagine staying in a little log cabin set next to a pond with ducks paddling around, then after an evening barbecue and a good night's sleep, driving into Yosemite National Park in the morning for a tour of nature's greatest showplace. That is exactly what you get here, right down to the duckies.

Mariposa KOA is located in the town of Midpines, about five miles east of Mariposa on Highway 140, in the transition zone where the Central Valley foothills rise into the mountains covered with pine forests. When you turn left and drive into the place, slowing down to about one mile per hour for the speed bumps, you will pass a series of drive-in campsites for motor homes, a small grocery store, and a swimming pool, then arrive at a pond with six of the KOA camping cabins perched just up from the shore.

These are the little log-style jobs, with a bunk bed on one side and a queen bed on the other. Each cabin has electric heat to keep you warm and a swing, barbecue, and picnic table out front. You bring the rest, including your own sleeping bags. Although the cabins have an electrical outlet, great for recharging portable computers (guess how I know), there

Log cabins and ducks on the pond at Yosemite-Mariposa KOA

is no telephone (whew) or bathroom (well, what do you expect?). A pay telephone and a rest room with three showers are available within short walking distance. At the pond, pedalboats are available, although most visitors head for the swimming pool instead.

It's a quality setting because of the lack of asphalt, especially around the log cabins, a problem at some other KOAs, and there's the rare bonus of a pond, which adds a lot of ambience. It is also very quiet here at night, and any family who breaks the 10 P.M. "quiet time" gets told to pipe down. Most who stay in the cabins will have a barbecue, try out the swing, then hit the hay for an early get-up-and-go to Yosemite.

From Mariposa KOA, it takes about an hour's drive on Highway 140 to reach Yosemite Valley, cruising along the Merced River through the Arch Rock entrance station then down into the valley. It can be the perfect driving tour, but it is critical to get an early start. From 6 A.M. to 8 A.M., there are relatively few people making the loop drive in the valley, or even hiking the short walk to the base of Yosemite Falls or Bridalveil Falls. By 8:30 A.M., it starts to pick up, and by 10:30 A.M., it can become a zoo on parade. Another recreation option here is taking a rafting trip on the Merced River; brochures are available in the KOA general store.

Other great driving tours are possible in Yosemite, of course. The best is up to Glacier Point, one of the most dramatic viewpoints in the world. There are several excellent short hikes with trailheads near here, including those to Sentinel Dome and Taft Point (located about a mile from Glacier Point) and on the Panorama Trail (located at Glacier Point). They are among the greatest short hikes anywhere.

The other option is driving up to Tuolumne Meadows, which takes about an hour from Yosemite Valley, a little less than two hours from the Mariposa KOA. This is also a great place for short hikes, including the nearly flat walks up Lyell Fork or down the Tuolumne River, or the short climbs to Dog Lake and the top of Lembert Dome, which looks out over miles and miles of high-country grandeur. Many of these short hikes, both near Glacier Point and at Tuolumne Meadows, are detailed in the book *Easy Hiking in Northern California* (Foghorn Press).

After a day in Yosemite, you will be ready to cozy up back in your very own little log cabin. Food and supplies are available in nearby Mariposa, but alas, if you forget to bring your sleeping bags for the bed mattresses in the cabins, it can be impossible to find sheets or blankets, especially if you don't start looking until the evening.

Now, how could I know this? Yeah, we pretty much screwed up in our packing. We ended up buying a couple of towels and pretending they were sheets. Slept like babies.

Facilities: Yosemite-Mariposa KOA has six camping cabins, each with electricity, a bunk bed, a queen bed, a small table, and outside, a swing, a picnic table, and a barbecue. No bedding is available. A rest room with showers is nearby, along with a small store, pay telephone, and swimming pool. At a small pond adjacent to the cabins, pedalboats are available. There are also 30 spaces for motor homes with full hookups, 40 sites for tents, and 10 additional sites for tents or motor homes.

Reservations, fee: Reservations are advised. There's a $37.50 fee per night for the camping cabins, $20 to $30 fee per night for motor home hookups.

Insider's note: A key to enjoying the Yosemite experience is to get there early. Even the most popular trails in the valley, to Yosemite Falls and Bridalveil Falls, are relatively uncrowded between dawn and 8 A.M. The same is true with Glacier Point until about 9 A.M.

Who to contact: Phone Yosemite-Mariposa KOA at (209) 966-2201, or write to KOA Mariposa, Box 545, Highway 140, Midpines, CA 95345. For an excellent map of the area, phone Tom Harrison Cartography at (415) 456-7940. A free map/brochure of Yosemite National Park is provided at park entrance stations as part of the $5 entrance fee.

Directions: From San Francisco, drive east on Interstate 580 past Livermore into the Central Valley. At the 205/580 split, veer south on Interstate 580 and continue about eight miles to Highway 132. Turn east on Highway 132 and drive to Modesto and Highway 99. Turn south on Highway 99 and drive to Merced. At Merced, turn east on Highway 140 and drive to Mariposa. At Mariposa, continue east for 5.5 miles to Midpines, then turn left at the Yosemite-Mariposa KOA.

88. THE REDWOODS CABINS
Yosemite National Park
Off Highway 41 in Wawona

The biggest surprises at Yosemite National Park are not Half Dome, El Capitan, Yosemite Falls, Bridalveil Falls, or the spectacular glaciated, watercoursed beauty of the valley. You already knew about them, right? Been there, done that.

The biggest surprises at Yosemite are the huge array of cabins and mountain vacation homes available for rent near Wawona at the southern border of the park. For people who have never ventured to the park's southern reaches, it can be a shock to discover there is an entire little township set within park borders, complete with a grocery store.

The town is within short distance of the trailhead for the hike to Chilnualna Falls, the prettiest waterfall in Yosemite's southern region, as well as the Mariposa Grove, the ancient forest of giant sequoias. Badger Pass Ski Area is 17 miles away, and it is about a 45-minute drive to either Glacier Point or Yosemite Valley. If you have never been here, you will likely be astounded to discover there is also a golf course nearby—that's right, a golf course in Yosemite National Park. When we drove by, the vote was 2-0 to fill in the 18 holes and sand traps and convert the fairways to a meadow for deer and other wildlife.

The settlement of dwellings is called The Redwoods, and it is composed of 127 vacation cabins, cottages, and homes that vary from a one-bedroom rustic cabin to a six-bedroom mountain home. They are all privately owned but are listed with The Redwoods for vacation rentals. Since the owners occasionally use them, they are furnished with whatever they would need for their own vacation, and that includes darn near everything. A small grocery store is also close by.

Even with all that development in a national park, the nearby hikes will quickly remind you that this is still the greatest show on earth. The best here is the hike out to Chilnualna Falls, with the trailhead at road's end at The Redwoods in North Wawona. It's a strenuous eight-mile round-trip, climbing 2,000 feet to the base of the falls at 6,000 feet. For overnighters, the trail goes on another eight miles, totaling 12 miles one-way, to the Chilnualna Lakes set below Buena Vista Peak (9,709 feet).

From The Redwoods cabins, Glacier Point Road's stunning viewpoint and excellent trailheads are less than an hour away.

An easier and more traditional venture is to the Mariposa Grove, located just east of the southern park entrance. If you want to enjoy this walk, get up early and be on the trail by 7 or 7:30 A.M. That's your lone chance for a little solitude among a few mammoth trees such as the Grizzly Giant, because after 9 A.M., the parade of tourists shows up en masse. A shuttle train buses them on a paved service road up the climb to the back of the grove, and you swear it's like a herd of cows going to the barn.

That's all we had to see to make us say, "We're outta here!" An hour later we were on a pretty hike off Glacier Point Road and life was perfect. Despite all the people in the park, if you can find a cabin and a secluded walk, Yosemite still can come as close to perfection as may be possible on this planet.

Facilities: The Redwoods has 127 privately-owned cabins and mountain homes for rent. Each is completely furnished, including cookware, utensils, and bed linens. A bed linen exchange program is provided at the main office for The Redwoods. A small grocery store is located nearby.

Reservations, fee: Reservations are required. Cabin and home rentals range from $88 per night for a one-bedroom cabin to $345 per night for a six-bedroom mountain home.

Insider's note: A wilderness permit is required for hikers spending the night in the adjacent Yosemite wilderness. For information, phone Yosemite at (209) 372-0200 (touch-tone only).

Who to contact: Phone The Redwoods at (209) 375-6666, or write to P.O. Box 2085, Wawona, Yosemite, CA 95389. For an excellent map of the area, phone Tom Harrison Cartography at (415) 456-7940. A free map/brochure of Yosemite National Park is provided at park entrance stations as part of the $5 entrance fee.

Directions: From San Francisco, take Interstate 80 over the Bay Bridge to the 80/580 split. Take Interstate 580 east and drive past Livermore into the Central Valley. At the 205/580 split, veer south on Interstate 580 and continue about eight miles to Highway 132. Turn east on Highway 132 and drive to Modesto and Highway 99. Turn south on Highway 99 and drive to Merced. At Merced, turn east on Highway 140 and drive to Mariposa. In Mariposa, turn south on Highway 49 and drive 30 miles to Highway 41 at Oakhurst. Turn left on Highway 41 and drive into the southern entrance station for Yosemite National Park ($5 entrance fee). Continue on Highway 41 to Wawona. Turn east on Chilnualna Road and drive 1.3 miles to The Redwoods. (You will receive specific directions to your cabin at The Redwoods when your reservation is confirmed).

---

89. OWL'S NEST CABINS
Fish Camp, near Yosemite
Off Highway 41 in Fish Camp

We like quiet. We like peaceful. We like privacy. So when we pulled up to Owl's Nest and saw that the cabins were right along Highway 41, we proceeded with a fair amount of apprehension. After all, we were just a mile from the southern entrance to Yosemite National Park, and the idea of a noisy parade of vehicles wasn't making us happy.

Instead, come 10 P.M., just about when we showed up after a day of adventuring in Yosemite, a funny thing happened at Owl's Nest Cabins: It was quiet. It was peaceful. It was private. It seems that come nightfall, the road is suddenly abandoned, with almost nobody at all going up and down that highway to Yosemite.

That makes it work, with three little cabins here in the town of Fish Camp, set at a 5,000-foot elevation outside of Yosemite's Wawona entrance. Two of the cabins, Ponderosa and Christmas Tree, can sleep up to eight and are completely furnished, with Christmas Tree providing a fireplace. The other, Tamarack, is a little sleeper cabin for two with no kitchen.

Horseback rides are available out of Fish Camp. They include scenic rides of an hour or two along with a five-and-a-half-hour trail ride to the Mariposa Big Trees. The same destination takes about 10 minutes by car and is best visited by 7:30 A.M., before the crowds show up. We also did a lot of hiking from trailheads along the road to Glacier Point, on some of the best day-hike trails in Yosemite, and clocked the drive to Glacier Point at about 50 minutes from Fish Camp.

Facilities: Owl's Nest has three two-story cabins. All have bathrooms, bed linens, and a deck. Two have kitchens with cookware and utensils, and one has a fireplace. A small grocery store is located nearby.

Reservations, fee: Reservations are required. Cabin rates are $95 per night for two people, plus $15 for each additional person. The maximum number of people per cabin is eight. A two-night minimum stay is required on weekends in the summer. Credit cards are not accepted.

Insider's note: Horseback riding rentals are available at Yosemite Trails Pack Station, (209) 683-7611 or (209) 683-9122.

Who to contact: Phone Owl's Nest at (209) 683-3484, or write to 1235 Highway 41, P.O. Box 33, Fish Camp, CA 93623. For an excellent map of the area, phone Tom Harrison Cartography at (415) 456-7940. A free map/ brochure of Yosemite National Park is provided at park entrance stations as part of the $5 entrance fee.

Directions: From San Francisco take Interstate 80 over the Bay Bridge to the 80/580 split. Take Interstate 580 east and drive past Livermore into the Central Valley. At the 205/580 split, veer south on Interstate 580 and continue about eight miles to Highway 132. Turn east on Highway 132 and drive to Modesto and Highway 99. Turn south on Highway 99 and drive to Merced. At Merced, turn east on Highway 140 and drive to Mariposa. In Mariposa, turn south on Highway 49 and drive 30 miles to Highway 41 at Oakhurst. Turn left on Highway 41 and drive 13 miles to the town of Fish Camp and look for Owl's Nest on the left side of the road.

---

90. BASS LAKE CABINS
Sierra National Forest, near Yosemite
Off Highway 41 near Oakhurst

If you get walled out in your attempt to stay at Yosemite National Park, Bass Lake Cabins are the next best option. And instead of a wall, you are more likely to get the welcome mat at the cabins and vacation homes at Bass Lake.

Bass Lake is located about a 25-minute drive from the Highway 41 entrance to Yosemite at Wawona. That means you get a two-for-one offer, a chance not only to boat, waterski, and fish at Bass Lake, but the opportunity to make the easy venture into nearby Yosemite. You do it by staying in one of a series of privately-owned vacation cabins along pretty Bass Lake, a long, deep reservoir set in a canyon at an elevation of 3,400 feet in Sierra National Forest. Pine Marina, a full-service marina with a boat ramp and boat rentals is situated on the eastern side of the lake, and a visitor information center directed by the Bass Lake Chamber of Commerce is located at the northwest end of the lake near Recreation Point.

There are a few things you need to know about Bass Lake. One is that it gets smokin' hot here in the summer, which is why it is such a favorite destination for waterskiers. Another is that it is about a 90-minute drive into Yosemite and to Glacier Point, the closest spectacular spots for views and hikes.

It can get extremely frustrating trying to reserve lodging on the outskirts of Yosemite. Here's a place where you not only bypass the frustration, but can end up with a great cabin near a lake as well.

Most people from the Bay Area and Sacramento approach Yosemite from entrances at the northwest side of the park, where lodging can be very difficult to obtain in the summer. Many never consider the southern entrance at Highway 41, or staying just beyond there at Bass Lake. Trying this option is like taking out an insurance policy to guarantee the success of your Yosemite vacation.

Facilities: Bass Lake Cabins has 15 privately-owned cabins and mountain homes for rent. Each is completely furnished, including cookware, utensils, bed linens, and towels. Small grocery stores are available at Bass Lake.

Reservations, fee: Reservations are required. Cabin rates range from $120 to $195 per night for a one-bedroom cabin. Small studio units range from $80 to $105. Off-season discounts are available.

Insider's note: For recorded information about Yosemite, phone Yosemite at (209) 372-0200 (touch-tone only).

Who to contact: Phone Bass Lake Rentals at (209) 642-2211, or write to P.O. Box 507, Bass Lake, CA 93604.

Directions: From San Francisco take Interstate 80 over the Bay Bridge to the 80/580 split. Take Interstate 580 east and drive past Livermore into the Central Valley. At the 205/580 split, veer south on Interstate 580 and continue about eight miles to Highway 132. Turn east on Highway 132 and drive to Modesto and Highway 99. Turn south on Highway 99 and drive to Merced. At Merced, turn east on Highway 140 and drive to Mariposa. In Mariposa, turn south on Highway 49 and drive 30 miles to Highway 41 at Oakhurst. Continue three miles on Highway 41 to the Bass Lake turnoff. Turn right and drive 3.5 miles to Bass Lake. Specific directions to your rental are provided with a reservation confirmation.

OTHER CABIN RENTALS NEAR YOSEMITE

Bass Lake Vacation Rentals, P.O. Box 349, Bass Lake, CA 93604; (209) 642-3600.

The Forks Resort, 39150 Road 222, Bass Lake, CA 93604; (209) 642-3737.

The Homestead, 4110 Road 600, Ahwahnee, CA 93601; (209) 683-0495.

Pine Mountain Lake Accommodations, P.O. Box 848, Groveland, CA 95321; (209) 962-5252.

Yosemite West Cottages, P.O. Box 36, Yosemite National Park, CA 95389; (209) 642-2211.

OTHER CABIN RENTALS NEAR TWAIN HARTE

Gables Cedar Creek Inn, P.O. Box 1818, Twain Harte, CA 95383; (209) 586-3008.

Mammoth Lakes

** For locations of camps, see map on page 9. **

91. EASTERN SIERRA HORSE TRIP
Ansel Adams Wilderness,
Inyo National Forest
Off Highway 158 near Silver Lake

The last time I was hiking out of the Rush Creek Trailhead, I came across a cowboy leading a team of horses, each loaded heavily with gear. He looked down from his saddle at me, stared at my big Kelty expedition backpack, then shook his head.

"Man, you backpackers really pay a price," he said with a laugh. "I just don't understand it. You ought to try it my way."

The same advice could be applied to anybody who has resisted taking a wilderness trip because they just plain don't like the idea of hiking with a heavy pack, especially over steep climbs at high elevations. Why not just ride in on a horse, after hiring an outfitter to bring in all the gear and food, as well as set up camp and cook?

A horse-pack trip solves all kinds of problems, most importantly, those that arise when there are huge differences in physical abilities among family members, especially because of age or experience. With everyone in a saddle aboard a horse, all are bonded by having the same adventures at the same time. All differences can be transcended. By having a cowboy bring in your gear, set up your camp, and do the cooking and cleanup, it leaves you and yours all the time in the world to explore, swim, hike, fish, or just sit on a rock and enjoy the pure mountain air without a care in the world.

The cost is $120 per day per person for a trip into the Ansel Adams Wilderness, or $550 for five days, with an outfitter called Frontier Pack Train. There are several other wilderness trips available, both shorter and longer ones. The shortest is a three-day adventure to nearby Parker Lake, with a day trip to Walker Lake, for $295 per person. The longest are various weeklong expeditions into different parts of Yosemite National Park, which cost $675 to $795 per person.

A typical multi-day trip into the Ansel Adams Wilderness goes like this: You depart from the Rush Creek Trailhead, elevation 7,200 feet, adjacent to the northern end of Silver Lake in the June Lake Loop in the east Sierra. From here the trail is routed 2.4 miles to Agnew Lake, rising steadily across a mountain face over about 1,200 feet in all, providing divine views along the way of Silver Lake below. The scenery is very beautiful, with classic high Sierra granite and turquoise lakes, but this is just the start.

From here, the trail is routed along the north shore of Agnew Lake, then a mile later, it traces along the north shore of beautiful Gem Lake, set at 8,052 feet at the base of a 9,714-foot granite peak. It may be difficult to leave this place. Gem Lake is big for a wilderness lake, as big as Silver Lake, with nice campsites, good fishing in the evening for brook trout, and decent swimming in the afternoon, despite cold water.

But onward you go, with the trail routed along Rush Creek, climbing all the way to Waugh Lake at 9,424 feet, seven miles in from the trailhead. This is yet another beautiful spot. A great day hike from here

Parker Lake, one of the many destinations possible on an Eastern Sierra Horse Trip

is to walk upstream from Waugh Lake and see the headwaters of Rush Creek, one of the prettiest streams anywhere—small, emerald green, and untouched, leaving deep swirls as it crosses boulders and bends.

Many people never see such great natural beauty because the physical demands scare them off. With a horse under you that is trained for the trail—and other horses carrying your gear—you get to just hold on for the ride.

There are some natural limits, of course. People weighing over 240 pounds can be refused service. You should also be reasonable in what you bring; 30 pounds should be plenty.

To really make this trip fly, bring your own group—your own family or circle of friends. In order to make the outfitter's job manageable, occasionally several groups of two or three are lumped together, creating a scenario in which strangers are sharing what should be a personal experience. Another option is paying a bit more to ensure your privacy. A group of two, for instance, can be outfitted for $250 per day. More expensive, yes, but worth it? Definitely.

One other thing. If you are accustomed to suffering through freeze-dried dinners on backpack trips, you've got a surprise coming: the food is incredible!

Facilities: All gear is provided. An outfitter with a horse team will carry in tents, cooking gear, food, and other equipment, including camp privy, solar showers, and chairs. The outfitter also will set up camp, cook, and clean up. You arrive to the wilderness camp separately on horseback. You provide your own personal gear, including a sleeping bag, fishing gear, and water-purification pump.

Reservations, fee: Reservations are required with a 20 percent deposit. Trip costs range from $295 for a three-day beginners trip to $795 for a weeklong trip into Yosemite. Custom small-group trips can be arranged at a higher fee.

Who to contact: From June through September, phone Frontier Pack Train at (619) 648-7701, or write to Star Route 3, Box 18, June Lake, CA 93529. From October through May, phone (619) 873-7971, or write to 2095 Van Loon, Bishop, CA 93514. For a map of Inyo National Forest, send $3 to USDA-Forest Service, 630 Sansome Street, San Francisco, CA 94111.

Directions: From Reno (via Interstate 80) or Carson City (via U.S. 50), drive south on U.S. 395 past Mono Lake. Continue south and turn right at the first Highway 158/June Lake Loop turnoff. Drive west on Highway 158 past Grant Lake to Silver Lake. Just as you arrive at Silver Lake, turn right at the small store adjacent to the RV campground and park.

For a longer, more scenic route, drive through Yosemite National Park on Highway 120 over Tioga Pass to Lee Vining and U.S. 395, then south on U.S. 395 to the Highway 158/June Lake Loop.

92. SILVER LAKE RESORT CABINS
June Lake Loop, Inyo National Forest
Off Highway 158 at Silver Lake

No television. No telephone. Nice old cabin. Pretty high-mountain lake. Little general store. Boats. Trout. Hikes. Stream nearby. And more. That is the recipe for a vacation at Silver Lake.

For most vacationers, this is everything they could ask for. Silver Lake is less developed than June Lake, the feature lake in the June Lake Loop, but it is just as pretty, set at 7,600 feet with 10,909-foot Carson Peak looming in the background. It is one of four drive-to lakes on the Loop, just west of U.S. 395 in the eastern Sierra.

A large but exposed campground and RV park are located directly north of Silver Lake, but nearby, off the northwest shore, is Silver Lake Resort and its 16 cabins, each different from the other. It's not so much a resort as it is a camp. It's just that the best camping here is in cabins, not tents.

Silver Lake gets its name because of the way the sun and afternoon winds send reflected silver flashes off its surface. It is a pretty scene, especially when the lake's deep blue-green colors are contrasted with the stark, ashen granite of the high mountain walls backing the Sierra Nevada.

The cabins come in all sizes and prices. The cheapest is Cabin 14, just a little job to hang your hat in, big enough for two people at $50 per night. The most expensive is the Creek House at $160 a night, which is big enough to handle up to eight people. In between is everything you can think of, but most are sized for four people and are priced at about $70 per night. All cabins are furnished with kitchen utensils and a stove and refrigerator. While maid service is not provided, you can get fresh bed linens when needed, and fresh towels are provided daily. Each cabin also has a propane wall heater.

Most people come here for the trout, and there are usually plenty, particularly near the dam, boat ramp, and in Reverse Creek near the campground. The lake not only has rainbow trout—Fish and Game makes sure of that by stocking nearly 50,000 a year—but also the more rare cutthroat trout and some elusive and big brown trout.

Boat and motor rentals are available through the resort. If you boat here, the best advice is to set your alarm and be on the lake early. The trout not only bite best here after first light (a high sun and clear water

Looking out over Silver Lake in the June Lake Loop

can make them spooky at midday), but the lake is at its calmest, windless best between dawn and 9 A.M. It often blows in the afternoon, especially in early summer, making the lake choppy. When the wind comes up, most anglers get off the lake and fish nearby Reverse Creek instead, with the best access out of the campground.

What I like to do is get out on the lake early, do a little trolling near the inlet, far shore, and outlet, catch my fish, clean 'em, and get 'em on ice. After a sumptuous breakfast with my partner and a short rest to let the food settle, we then put on our hiking boots for a good hike in the nearby mountains.

A great wilderness trailhead (Rush Creek Trailhead) is located behind the adjacent RV park, with a trail that is routed 2.1 miles to Agnew Lake with a steady climb of about 1,200 feet on the way. The trail is literally cut into the granite slope, and with nothing blocking your view to the east, you get great vistas of Silver Lake. After topping the rim, you get a divine look at Agnew Lake, set in granite. The trail skirts the north shore of the lake, and in another mile, rises to the shore of Gem Lake, which can be astonishing in its natural beauty.

Note that the Rush Creek Trailhead can be very popular and trailhead quotas for overnight use are established in order to minimize human impact.

There is no such limitation on having fun anywhere else in this area.

Facilities: Silver Creek Resort has 16 cabins, each furnished with a stove and refrigerator and all kitchen utensils. Towels are provided daily, and fresh linens are provided when needed, depending on the length of your stay. The cabins have propane heat but no telephones or televisions.

Reservations, fee: Reservations are required with a deposit of 50 percent of the total fee. Prices are $50 per night for a small cabin for two people, $70 per night for a cabin for four people, and $160 per night for the Creek House, which can handle up to eight people.

Who to contact: Phone Silver Lake Resort at (619) 648-7525, or write to P.O. Box 17, Highway 158, June Lake, CA 93529. For a map of Inyo National Forest, send $3 to USDA-Forest Service, 630 Sansome Street, San Francisco, CA 94111.

Directions: From Reno (via Interstate 80) or Carson City (via U.S. 50), drive south on U.S. 395 past Mono Lake. Continue south and turn right at the first Highway 158/June Lake Loop turnoff. Drive west on Highway 158 past Grant Lake at Silver Lake. Just as you arrive at Silver Lake, turn right at the small store adjacent to the RV campground and park.

For a longer, more scenic route, drive through Yosemite National Park on Highway 120 over Tioga Pass to Lee Vining and U.S. 395, then south on U.S. 395 to the Highway 158/June Lake Loop.

93. THE FOUR SEASONS CABINS
June Lake Loop, Inyo National Forest
Off Highway 158 in June Lake Village

When a lot of people envision a cabin in the mountains they see an A-frame, one of those high-peaked, steeply sloped cabins with a large downstairs and a loft for sleeping.

That is exactly what makes The Four Seasons so appealing to vacationers, along with a location near June Lake that's ideal for fishing, boating, hiking, and in the winter, snow skiing. What you get here is a chance to stay in an A-frame mountain chalet, complete with a wood stove and a view of the nearby high Sierra, then take part in your favorite outdoor sports.

Where? These cabins are located less than a mile from the June Lake Ski Area, less than a mile from Reverse Creek, and only a few miles from Silver Lake to the west, and Gull and June lakes to the east. In other words, it is situated in the middle of some of the best year-round recreation opportunities in the June Lake Loop. It is one of the feature areas of the eastern Sierra, a short drive off U.S. 395 south of Lee Vining and Mono Lake.

The A-frame cabins operated by The Four Seasons are set right on the edge of the eastern desert and the high Sierra, where chaparral meets conifers. The setting is prettiest in the winter, when all is covered in snow with the high Sierra ridge in the background. While the cabins are set fairly close together, the wide-open spaces to the west and east give them a spacious feel.

The cabins are "all electric," which means you get complete kitchen facilities, television (hey, you can always unplug the thing), and electric blankets. They are designed to sleep up to seven people, with rates adjusted according to group size, ranging from $79 per day for two people up to $145 per day for seven people during a peak winter weekend.

Prime time here is mid-December through early March for skiing, July and August for fishing, boating, and hiking, and mid-September to mid-October for viewing the fall colors when the aspens turn.

With the ski area less than a mile away, winter is when the cabins are most heavily booked and when reservations are most likely to be required. June Mountain is a small hill compared to nearby Mammoth to the south, but it is plenty big enough for most beginner and intermediate skiers, with six lifts, one tram, and 2,500 vertical feet of skiing. It is a particularly favored destination for families, especially when they can stay in one of these A-frame cabins. After all, Mammoth turns into a major L.A. scene on most winter weekends.

In the summer, I'm always surprised at how few people visit the June Lake Loop, despite there being three great lakes nearby (June Lake, Gull Lake, and Silver Lake), a good trout stream (Reverse Creek), and nearly 10 demanding hikes on Forest Service land that climb to great lookouts of the basin. The only real dud in the Loop is Grant Lake, the biggest of the four lakes, which is surrounded by barren desert country, is vulnerable to winds, and generally has poor fishing.

Of the lakes, June Lake is the prettiest, but it has the most nearby development; Gull Lake is the smallest, but often has the best fishing; and Silver Lake is pretty *and* has good fishing, but is susceptible to west winds, common in the early summer. You can rent a boat at any of the lakes, and a bonus here is that large trophy-size rainbow trout are planted in the summer. It's always quite a shocker when someone catches a rainbow trout that weighs 10 pounds or so. The lakes also have wild brown trout that grow to similar sizes, but can be extremely elusive.

There are many hiking trails in this area, all detailed on a map of Inyo National Forest, but few are easy. The best is the 2.1-mile hike to Parker Lake, which requires a 400-foot climb but passes along a pretty stream and many wildflower blooms before it deposits you on the shore of an attractive lake in a rock bowl. On the way back, you get great views of Mono Lake.

Facilities: The Four Seasons has all-electric A-frame chalets with kitchen facilities, living rooms with wood stoves and televisions, beds with electric blankets, and bathrooms with tub/shower combinations. The cabins are designed to handle up to seven people. No pets are permitted.

Reservations, fee: Reservations are advised in summer and often required in winter. Rates range from $79 per day for two people up to $145 per day for seven people. A minimum stay of two nights is required, longer during holiday weekends.

Who to contact: Phone The Four Seasons at (619) 648-7476, or write to Star Route 3, Box 8-B, June Lake, CA 93529. For a map of Inyo National Forest, send $3 to USDA-Forest Service, 630 Sansome Street, San Francisco, CA 94111.

Directions: From Reno (via Interstate 80) or Carson City (via U.S. 50), drive south on U.S. 395 past Mono Lake. Continue past the first Highway 158/June Lake Loop turnoff to June Lake Junction (a gas station/store is on the right). At June Lake Junction, turn right on Highway 158 and drive past June Lake Village. Continue for two miles past June Lake Village (one mile past the ski park), and turn left at the signed driveway for The Four Seasons.

For a longer, more scenic route, drive through Yosemite National Park on Highway 120 over Tioga Pass to Lee Vining and U.S. 395, then south on U.S. 395 to the Highway 158/June Lake Loop.

94. RED'S MEADOWS PACK TRIPS
Ansel Adams Wilderness
Off Highway 203 near Mammoth Lakes

There is a continual dispute over who runs the best horseback pack trips in California, but Bob Tanner's Pack Station out of Red's Meadows always garners a lot of votes.

The reason why is because of its ideal location, set next to Devils Postpile National Monument on the edge of the Ansel Adams Wilderness. The John Muir Trail runs within a half-mile of the pack station headquarters, so there is excellent access to a wide number of lakes, streams, and high-mountain wilderness within a day's ride. In addition, there is an outstanding short ride to Rainbow Falls, a spectacular waterfall that produces rainbows from refracted sunlight in the morning, so you can take a "test ride" to get accustomed to riding a horse and see whether or not this adventure is for you.

Most find out quickly that it is. After all, you don't have to carry your gear or do much of anything except ride your horse into some stunning country. A cowboy will bring in all the food and cooking equipment, then cook and clean up for you. A wilderness expedition doesn't come much easier. Trips cost anywhere from $395 for three days to $795 for a full week, with many four-, five-, and six-day trips also available.

Within a day's ride, for instance, 11 miles one-way heading north, is Thousand Island Lake with magnificent Banner and Ritter peaks in the background, the highest points in the Minaret Range. Ritter is the highest of the two, elevation 13,157 feet, and makes this one of the prettiest scenes anywhere along the John Muir Trail. The lake is sprinkled with dozens of little islands, with the awesome Minarets in the background. It's the kind of place where anybody can be turned into Ansel Adams with the click of a camera shutter. Well, almost anybody. Not me, for instance. But it is so pretty that it would be difficult for even me to screw up a picture here.

On the way north, you pass (or stop at) beautiful Shadow Lake or Garnet Lake, the latter providing good fishing for brook trout. No camping is permitted at Shadow Lake, but hey, your cowboy outfitter will make sure you end up at a lovely spot, putting the horses relatively nearby where they will be fed and rested.

The best way to get an idea of whether or not this is for you is to take the test ride to Rainbow Falls. It is about two miles to the falls, and a round-trip takes just a few hours, including selecting your horse and getting the saddle and stirrups set up right. Even on a short trip like this, you will be surprised at the rapport you can develop with the horse you're riding. If you don't get it, you'll know it. If you do, well, it's on to bigger things.

Because Red's Meadows is situated on the John Muir Trail, it is an ideal jumping-off spot for an expedition. Trips heading south on the JMT are routed past Purple Lake, Virginia Lake, Tully Hole, and to the head-waters of Fish Creek on to 12,000-foot McGee Pass, with awesome views of McGee Canyon and a camp at McGee Lake. I've been through all of this country and found it remote and beautiful, with good trout fishing and unbelievable stargazing during new moons. A round-trip like this on horseback takes six days and costs $695.

By the time you arrive at the pack station, you likely will have figured out what you have forgotten. Everybody forgets something, right? Right. Guess what? A small grocery store at Red's Meadows is well stocked, typically with just the gear you forgot. In addition, your last chance at a cheeseburger, fries, and milkshake awaits at the adjacent café. There are many takers.

Me? No, of course not. I'd rather take photographs of the wild-flowers while others ravage the purity of the wilderness experience. Yeah, surrrrrre.

Facilities: An outfitter with a horse team will carry in cooking gear, food, and camp privy, and will cook and clean up. You provide your own personal gear, including a tent, sleeping bag, fishing gear, and water-purification pump.

Reservations, fee: Reservations are required with a $100 deposit. Costs range from $395 per person for a three-day introductory trip to $795 per person for weeklong trips into Yosemite.

Who to contact: Phone Red's Meadows Pack Station at (619) 934-2345 or (800) 292-7758, or write to P.O. Box 395, Mammoth Lakes, CA 93546. For a map of Inyo National Forest, send $3 to USDA-Forest Service, 630 Sansome Street, San Francisco, CA 94111.

Directions: From Reno or Carson City, drive south on U.S. 395 to Lee Vining and continue for 25 miles to the Highway 203/Mammoth Lakes turnoff. Turn west and drive through the town of Mammoth Lakes, turn right on Summit Road, then continue past the Mammoth Lakes Ski Area, over the summit, and down to the valley. Bear left past the turnoff for Devils Postpile National Monument and drive two miles to Red's Meadows Pack Station.

Note: Visitors arriving after 7:30 A.M. at the Mammoth Lakes Ski Area are required to take a shuttle bus ($7) to the valley floor, unless they can provide proof that they are camping in the valley.

95. CRYSTAL CRAG LODGE CABINS
Lake Mary
Off Highway 203 near Mammoth Lakes

The natural beauty of Lake Mary is astonishing, a deep-blue pool set in Sierra granite, with Crystal Crag, an awesome granite spire, in the background. It makes for a great vacation setting, with cabins set just upslope from the lake, a boat ramp and boat rentals available, decent fishing, excellent hiking trails, and many other adventures possible in the region.

But what will keep you coming back is the beauty. It is often love at first sight. The lake is located high in the eastern Sierra at 8,900 feet, on the edge of the tree line where forest gives way to a sculpted ridgeline. It is the largest lake in the Mammoth Lakes region.

The cabins are situated upslope of the lake, and the office is just across the road from the boat dock. The cabins have been given names such as Lone Indian, Garnet, and Crystal, primarily after nearby lakes and landmarks, and come in all sizes. Each one is a bit different.

Most people come here for the peace and beauty, but the hiking and fishing are often excellent and provide great adventure. A great short walk starts at the back of Coldwater Camp, located just south of Lake Mary, and is routed up to Emerald Lake, about a mile away. The last time we made this little trip, it was early in the season and the trail was largely covered with snow. No problem! We hopped across the hard-pack like snow hares, and after a snack lunch at little Emerald Lake, we then skidded, slipped, and slopped our way back downhill to the trailhead at the parking area. Luckily, my butt broke my falls.

A longer, more strenuous hike is accessed from the same trailhead. It is routed south along Mammoth Creek up to Arrowhead Lake, and then in turn, up to Skeleton Lake, Barney Lake, and finally up to Big Duck Lake. Duck Lake is even bigger than Lake Mary, always a surprise upon first sight, and is just a mile from the Pacific Crest Trail.

As for the fishing, Lake Mary receives more trout stocks than any other lake in the Mammoth region, and that includes special batches of trophy-size fish arranged by the lodge. Most people catch trout here by fishing with Power Bait from either on the shore or a boat, but some do well in the evenings trolling or fly-fishing from a float tube. A key factor here is wind. When it is down and the hatch is up, the surface bite and fly-fishing can be good.

Rainbow Falls in Devils Postpile National Monument near
Crystal Crag Lodge cabins

Newcomers to this area always want to see "Mammoth Lake." Guess
what? There is no such place. The town is called Mammoth Lakes, but
there is no Mammoth Lake. Instead there is Lake Mary, Lake George,
Lake Mamie, and Twin Lakes. All are within a 10-minute drive of each
other. Another nearby destination that makes for a great day trip is Devils
Postpile National Monument, with a two-hour round-trip hike to beautiful Rainbow Falls. To get there, take the Minaret Summit Road over
Mammoth Pass (past the Mammoth Ski Area); to avoid taking the shuttle

and paying a $7 fee, get there before 7:30 A.M. or after 5:30 P.M. on long summer days.

Then again, you can just do nothing, that is, nothing but stroll down to the lake from your cabin, lean against a tree, and enjoy the beauty. That might be all it takes to make you happy.

Facilities: There are 21 cabins with kitchens and bathrooms. There is also a small marina with 14 aluminum boats (with or without motors) available for rent by the day or week. A small launch ramp and laundromat are available. Dogs are permitted. A small grocery store, horseback riding facilities, and a Forest Service campground are nearby.

Reservations, fee: Cabin reservations are strongly advised; fees range from $50 per night for one person in a studio cabin to $92 per night for two people in a one-bedroom cabin to $185 per night for a cabin that sleeps eight.

Insider's note: Because this lake is located at elevation 8,900 feet, snow can prevent the opening of Crystal Crag Lodge until late May or early June. After a heavy winter, there can be snow near the lake into July.

Who to contact: For reservations or a free brochure, phone Crystal Crag Lodge at (619) 934-2436, or write to P.O. Box 88, Mammoth Lakes, CA 93546. For a map of Inyo National Forest, send $3 to USDA-Forest Service, 630 Sansome Street, San Francisco, CA 94111. To obtain a topographic map of the area, send $3.50 to Maps-Western Distribution Center, U.S. Geologic Survey, Box 25286-Federal Center, Denver, CO 80225 and ask for Crystal Crag.

Directions: From Reno or South Tahoe, drive south on U.S. 395 to Lee Vining at Mono Lake and continue for 25 miles to the Highway 203/ Mammoth Lakes turnoff. Turn right and drive four miles on Highway 203/ Minaret Summit Road to Lake Mary Road. Turn left on Lake Mary Road and drive three miles to Lake Mary. The road circles the lake.

96. CONVICT LAKE CABINS
Inyo National Forest
Off U.S. 395 near Mammoth Lakes

The stark landscape along U.S. 395 south of Mammoth doesn't conjure up visions of paradise to most people. But just a five-minute drive can transport you to one of the most beautiful drive-to settings in North America: Convict Lake in the high southeast Sierra.

For newcomers, it may seem hard to believe Convict Lake is even here. After all, as you cruise 395, there is little to see for miles but high desert, stark and lonely, with glimpses of mountains off to the west.

When you reach the little Mammoth Airport, you turn west at the sign for Convict Lake, then drive up the two-laner, passing through dry hills dotted with chaparral and a few scrubby pines. After just five minutes, you top a crest and Convict Lake comes into view. Suddenly, your scope of what is possible in this world will extend into new dimensions.

The lake is deep and blue-green, set below high, sheer mountain walls and granite peaks, the kind of mountain beauty that you never forget. At the head of the lake, a small forest grows along the feeder creek, and beyond you can see a canyon that leads up to the bordering John Muir Wilderness. The air is fresh and quiet. This is the high country, 7,583 feet in elevation, and it is pristine and stunning.

Here you will find a series of rustic little cabins that you can make your headquarters for a mountain vacation. It is an ideal destination for hiking, fishing, boating, horseback riding, and exploring nearby hot springs at Hot Creek. A small store, a marina, and a dinner restaurant are available at Convict Lake, so you get the best of both worlds: the beauty of high Sierra wilderness as well as full accommodations and facilities.

The cabins have names such as Loch Leven, Golden, and Steelhead and vary in the number of people they can accommodate. Most are small, with just a kitchen, bathroom, and living space. Instead of feeling cramped, though, it seems to work out just fine. It makes a great base camp for a fun-filled trip that lasts as long as you wish, and many adventures are waiting nearby.

The most popular is renting one of the aluminum boats and motors at the small marina, or bringing your own, then motoring around the lake, trolling for trout and enjoying the scenery. The lake is small enough, about a mile long and a half-mile wide, to keep the setting intimate, yet deep enough to provide excellent fishing. I like motoring around in my canoe here, but many other campers will fish from shore along the southeast bank and catch trout dinners. Although most of the trout are planters, 11- and 12-inch rainbow trout, the lake does have some huge brown trout in the 10-pound class. One summer evening, right at sunset, I saw one roll near my canoe that I estimated at 15 pounds. I named it Horgon, and one of these years, I'm finally gonna hook that sucker.

The hiking can also be spectacular. From a signed trailhead off the access road, one route follows along Convict Lake's north shore, providing very pretty views. It rises in long, graded switchbacks above the lake and is routed back through the Convict Creek canyon, still climbing, but with a steady grade. Hiking up to the creek and back is a great morning trip, and horseback rides are also offered here. Ambitious backpackers can continue up to a basin with a series of beautiful lakes, but it's a long climb, gaining 3,000 feet in about eight miles, and includes a tricky stream crossing that can be dangerous at high water.

If your muscles get sore from hiking or horseback riding, or you just want to play in hot springs, nearby Hot Creek has a great section of stream where cold streamwater is mixed with very hot springwater. It's about three miles off U.S. 395, turning east on the road just north of the airport. Floating in the hot spring is a remarkable sensation—it is

Trolling for trout on Convict Lake

possible to feel very hot water at your chest and shoulders, cold water at your thighs, and warm water at your feet, then move a step in the stream, and have the mix change completely. Maps of several hot springs are available at the Convict Lake Store. There's nothing quite like it.

Facilities: There are 23 cabins with kitchens and bathrooms. There is also a small marina with 32 boats with five-horsepower motors, a launch ramp, horseback riding rentals, a four-star restaurant, a general store, a fish-cleaning facility, and pay phones.

Reservations, fee: Cabin reservations are strongly advised; fees range from $61 to $175 per night.

Insider's note: A Forest Service campground located nearby along Convict Creek has 88 campsites for tents or motor homes up to 22 feet long, with fire grills and picnic tables provided and piped water and flush toilets available.

Who to contact: For reservations or a free brochure, phone Convict Lake Resort at (800) 992-2260, or write to Route 1, Box 204, Mammoth Lakes, CA 93546.

Directions: From Reno or South Tahoe, drive south on U.S. 395 to Mono Lake and continue for 31 miles (past the Mammoth Lakes turnoff) to Convict Lake Road, located adjacent to the Mammoth Lakes Airport. Turn right (west) and drive two miles to the Convict Lake Store on the right.

OTHER CABIN RENTALS IN THE MAMMOTH LAKES AREA

Mammoth Mountain Chalets, P.O. Box 513, Mammoth Lake, CA 93546; (800) 327-3681 or (619) 934-8518.

Pine Cliff Resort, P.O. Box 2, Mammoth Lakes, CA 93546; (619) 934-2447.

Edelweiss Lodge, P.O. Box 658, Mammoth Lakes, CA 93546; (619) 934-2445.

Tamarack Lodge, P.O. Box 69, Mammoth Lakes, CA 93546; (619) 934-2442.

Wildyrie Lodge, P.O. Box 108, Mammoth Lakes, CA 93546; (619) 934-2261.

Monterey-
Big Sur

** For locations of camps, see map on page 9. **

97. SANTA CRUZ/MONTEREY KOA CABINS
Manresa State Beach
Off Highway 1 near Aptos

We're not big fans of asphalt, but we do like security, cuteness and nearby recreation. In the case of the KOA set by the shore of Monterey Bay, what we like wins out over what we don't like.

When you first drive up, you see an entrance station and sometimes even a security officer. After entering and passing a swimming pool on the right, you see this adorable double-tiered line of cabins on a hillside to the left. Along the way you also see a line of bicycles, available for rent, and realize the location is ideal for a short ride to nearby Manresa State Beach, and maybe a walk or a game of tag with the waves. Then you will notice that to keep the dust down, there is a lot of asphalt leading to the 50 cabins and 230 tent and RV sites across 30 acres of campground. After a while, you might get used to it.

On the swing at the Santa Cruz/Monterey KOA

The security is a nice touch. Although it may never be needed—because the campground is set in a friendly area—the presence of someone looking out for you is usually enough to keep it that way. The cute factor is high here, too, with those little KOA log cabins lined up, each with a bunk bed and a queen bed (bring your sleeping bag), electric heat if needed, and a swing out front. A few two-room models are available here as well.

But the best deal is the proximity to Manresa State Beach. It's only a short bike ride to this beautiful state park set along the shore of

Monterey Bay, with good beachcombing and hiking. The ocean is often quite calm here. Fishing is poor to fair for perch, with better prospects on boats leaving out of Santa Cruz or Monterey. Sunsets can be spectacular.

Facilities: The Santa Cruz/Monterey KOA has 50 camping cabins and 230 sites for tents or motor homes, plus a convenience store and 24-hour security gate. Bicycle rentals, a pool, a hot tub, two kiddie pools, a water playground, a game room, horseshoes, volleyball, basketball, and a batting cage are available.

Reservations, fee: Reservations are advised from June through September. Rates are $36.95 for a one-room cabin, $42.95 for a two-room cabin, and $27.95 for a site for tents or RVs.

Insider's note: Excellent side trips include Santa Cruz to the north, with its Boardwalk amusement park, and Monterey to the south, with its aquarium.

Who to contact: Phone Santa Cruz-Monterey KOA at (408) 722-0551 or (408) 722-2377, or write to 1186 San Andreas Road, Watsonville, CA 95076.

Directions: From Santa Cruz, drive 12 miles south on Highway 1. Take the Larkin Valley/San Andreas Road exit, turn west on San Andreas Road and drive 3.5 miles and look for the well-signed entrance on the left side of the road at 1186 San Andreas Road.

98. ROBLES DEL RIO LODGE
Carmel Valley
Off Highway 1 near Carmel

You might find it difficult to believe that a small settlement of cabins is perched above Carmel Valley and its procession of golf courses, expensive cars, and upper-class people. But here it is, Robles del Rio, which means "oaks of the river," set on a hill overlooking the valley, up here where all is quiet and pretty.

The lodge covers nine acres of oak woodlands, the kind of Monterey foothill country that John Steinbeck called "pastures of heaven." Well, the wildlife probably agree, anyway, including all the wild turkeys you see in the meadow near the cabins. Like I said, considering how close you are to big developed golf courses, it's hard to believe.

The place straddles two worlds, one of wild country and outdoor recreation, the other of excellence in accommodations and dining.

Outdoor recreation possibilities in nearby Los Padres National Forest include biking, hiking, and horseback riding. Horse rentals are available at the Holdman Ranch, about five minutes from the lodge, with trail rides into the Ventana Wilderness that last one hour ($30), two hours ($50), or longer. At the lodge itself, there is an Olympic-size swimming pool, along with a hot tub and sauna.

The cottages are in premium condition, yet feature the original board-and-batten paneling they had when constructed in 1928. They also have fireplaces, which makes them feel cozy.

You see Robles del Rio and it's easy to know why this is a favored hideaway of many luminaries. That makes another bonus here—you never know who you're going to run into at the hot tub.

Facilities: Robles del Rio Lodge has five cottages, along with two two-room suites, five rooms in a lodge, and 21 rooms in other buildings across nine acres. Bathrooms, kitchenettes, some cookware, utensils, bed linens, towels, and daily maid service are provided. A buffet breakfast is included in the price. A large swimming pool, hot tub, and sauna are available. A restaurant is located on the property.

Reservations, fee: Reservations are required. Cottage rates range from $160 to $250 per night, depending on the size and accommodations, with a two-night minimum stay on weekends. Room rates range from $89 to $130 per night.

Insider's note: Horseback riding is available at the Holdman Ranch, and can be arranged through the lodge. Two golf courses, Rancho Canada, (408) 624-0111, and Quail Lodge, (408) 624-2770, are located nearby.

Who to contact: Phone Robles del Rio Lodge at (408) 659-3704 or (800) 833-0843, or write to 200 Punta del Monte, Carmel Valley, CA 93924.

Directions: From Santa Cruz, drive south on Highway 1 just past Carmel to Carmel Valley Road. Turn east (left) on Carmel Valley Road and drive 13 miles to Esquiline Road. At Esquiline Road, turn right and drive one mile (over two bridges and up a hill) to the lodge entrance.

99. DEETJEN'S CABINS
Big Sur
Off Highway 1 near Big Sur

You can spend a ton of dough in a vacation at Big Sur. Then again, you can go to Deetjen's.

At Ventana Inn just to the south, it's possible to spend about $500 a night without much effort. For that you get a private deck with a hot tub, a fireplace, and a spectacular room with kitchenette. At the adjoining restaurant, you can spend $20 for a Caesar salad, that's right, just a salad, and then wonder why they didn't even use a whole head of lettuce. It's an incredible place, though, and maybe once in your lifetime you should check it out.

Deetjen's, on the other hand, is at the opposite end of the spectrum. Not that the place is cheap, it's just not Ventana. In fact, it's the reverse. You'll find a ring of little, woodsy cabins set in a grove of redwoods, located just east of Highway 1 in the heart of Big Sur. That means you are within close driving range of the best hiking and adventure destinations.

The cabins at Deetjen's are what the hosts call "rustic." In the case of the cabin I stayed at, "rustic" meant the hinge for the door of the Franklin stove was broken off, and when somebody took a shower in the adjoining cabin, the water pipes sounded like the Titanic hitting a glacier. But otherwise, rustic pretty much meant rustic, a cozy setting on a foggy night with a fire, and no telephones or television. The cabins are small, and before showing up with children in tow, you should make sure you secure a unit that's large enough for all of you. There is also a restaurant on the property, which is quite good for breakfast.

Big Sur is one of the most spectacular stretches of coastline in the world and the best way to see it is by driving from Monterey south through Big Sur on Highway 1. A good first-day destination is Lucia, about a half-hour drive south of Big Sur, highlighted by a little seafood restaurant perched on stilts on a cliff overlooking the surf.

The scenery on the drive from Carmel through Big Sur to Lucia can be breathtaking. Along the way you get views of ocean bluffs, huge rocky coastal outcrops, grassy foothills, redwood groves, coastal mountains, and places where the highway crosses dramatic bridges built over deep canyons. Unless you get stuck behind an RV, it can be one of the most spectacular driving tours anywhere.

But when you do get stuck behind an RV, which is almost inevitable, you will want to park, get out, and hike in this beautiful country. There are many great hiking trails in the area.

A very short yet outstanding walk is to the Point Sur Lighthouse, a 10-minute jaunt on ocean bluffs after parking at Point Sur State Historic Park. The lighthouse is now automated, of course, but the place does provide a sense of history and sweeping ocean views. It is located about a 15-minute drive north of Deetjen's at Big Sur.

Just south of Point Sur is another great place to explore, Andrew Molera State Beach, with 20 miles of hiking trails. From the parking area, the Beach Trail wanders in and out along the Big Sur River, and is routed about a mile to the beach. On my visit, I saw a number of sea otters here, but there are many other places along the beach to see them. Park rangers can provide a sheet that lists the best viewing areas.

Another highlight, particularly in winter and spring, is Pfeiffer Falls, a 60-foot waterfall that pours in a narrow cascade over a rock face and onto the beach below. You can see it at Julia Pfeiffer Burns State Park, located about a 10-minute drive south of Big Sur. On my visit, we hiked well up McWay Canyon, a good hike heading east along a small stream, routed through redwoods until climbing and emerging in the coastal hills.

You can hide out at Deetjen's and spend several days exploring and hiking at these parks. If you want more civilization, you can make the 25-mile drive north to Carmel, or head even farther to Monterey and visit the aquarium and the wharf, and take the Cannery Row tour.

And if you suddenly get a penchant to spend a lot of money, well, no problem. I know this place called Ventana that you will never forget.

Facilities: Deetjen's has 20 cabins, all with showers, beds, wood stoves, and otherwise stark provisions. Telephones and televisions aren't available. A restaurant is located on the property.

Reservations, fee: Reservations are required. Cabin fees range from $70 to $150 per night.

Insider's note: For a free travel packet about Big Sur, send a self-addressed envelope with a 55-cent stamp to the Big Sur Chamber of Commerce, P.O. Box 87, Big Sur, CA 93920.

Who to contact: Phone Deetjen's Big Sur at (408) 667-2377, or write to Highway 1, Big Sur, CA 93920. For a map of Los Padres National Forest, send $3 to USDA-Office of Information, U.S. Forest Service, 630 Sansome Street, San Francisco, CA 94111.

Directions: From Carmel, drive 26 miles south on Highway 1. Look for Deetjen's Big Sur Inn on the east side of the road.

100. RIPPLEWOOD RESORT
Big Sur
Off Highway 1 near Big Sur

Everybody has a favorite chair. You know, the kind that makes you feel "just right," no matter what mood you're in, what you are going through, or how long you have been away from it.

Ripplewood Resort in Big Sur has cabins like this. In fact, they have 16 of them. Each one is different, enough so that after surveying the place, you have a good chance of finding one that fits just right. Just like your favorite chair.

Cabin 2 is the most secluded. Cabin 6 has a postcard view of the Big Sur River. Cabins 1, 14, and 15 have stone fireplaces. On the low end is a cabin that looks like a small motel room, Cabin 17. On the high end is a multiple-room chalet with a redwood beam ceiling and stone fireplace,

Cabin 15. Get the idea? Right. Take a look, survey a few, and you'll find one that's perfect for you.

A real bonus here is the small grocery store and the fact that most of the cabins have kitchens. That means if you don't feel like going to a restaurant, or just want to spare the expense, you can make a quick shopping trip and create a meal yourself without having to drive. There are very few cabin settings where this is possible.

Ripplewood is set along Highway 1 in the heart of Big Sur, an ideal location for a mini-vacation. The cabins are surrounded by redwoods, several of them along the Big Sur River.

There is excellent hiking in the area, best of all in Andrew Molera State Beach, Point Sur State Historic Park, Julia Pfeiffer Burns State Park, Los Padres National Forest, and Ventana Wilderness. Several nearby scenic hikes are featured in the story on page 226 on Deetjen's at Big Sur.

What you will remember about Ripplewood is how the cabins feel. It is one place where you can find just the right fit.

Facilities: There are 16 cabins in various sizes and settings. All have bathrooms, most have kitchens, and some have river views. There is also a café that serves breakfast and lunch, a small grocery store, and a gas station.

Reservations, fee: Reservations are required. The fee is $55 to $93 per night. On weekends, there is a two-night minimum stay. No pets are allowed. Personal checks are not accepted.

Insider's note: For a travel packet about Big Sur, send a self-addressed envelope with a 55-cent stamp to the Big Sur Chamber of Commerce, P.O. Box 87, Big Sur, CA 93920.

Who to contact: Phone Ripplewood Resort at (408) 667-2242, or write to Highway 1, Big Sur, CA 93920. For a map of Los Padres National Forest, send $3 to USDA-Office of Information, U.S. Forest Service, 630 Sansome Street, San Francisco, CA 94111.

Directions: From Carmel, drive 25 miles south on Highway 1. Look for Ripplewood Resort on the west side of the road. Ripplewood's small gas station and store are directional landmarks.

OTHER CABIN RENTALS NEAR BIG SUR

Bide-A-Wee Cottages, 221 Asilomar Boulevard, Pacific Grove, CA 93950; (408) 372-2330.

INDEX

About the Author

Tom Stienstra is the outdoors writer for the *San Francisco Examiner* and the author of nine books with Foghorn Press. In 1995, he was named National Outdoor Writer of the Year (Newspaper Division), and also won first place for best camping writing in America from the Outdoor Writers Association of America.

Leave No Trace

Leave No Trace, Inc., is a program dedicated to maintaining the integrity of outdoor recreation areas through education and public awareness. Foghorn Press is a proud supporter of this program and its ethics.

Here's how you can Leave No Trace:

Plan Ahead and Prepare
- Know the regulations and special concerns of the area you'll visit.
- Visit the backcountry in small groups.
- Avoid popular areas during peak-use periods.
- Choose equipment and clothing in subdued colors.
- Pack food in reusable containers.

Camp and Travel on Durable Surfaces
On the trail:
- Stay on designated trails. Walk single file in the middle of the path.
- Do not take shortcuts on switchbacks.
- When traveling cross-country, choose the most durable surfaces available, such as rock, gravel, dry grasses, or snow.
- Use a map and compass to eliminate the need for rock cairns, tree scars, and ribbons.
- If you encounter pack animals, step to the downhill side of the trail and speak softly to avoid startling them.

At camp:
- Choose an established, legal site that will not be damaged by your stay.
- Restrict activities to areas where vegetation is compacted or absent.
- Keep pollutants out of the water by camping at least 200 feet (about 70 adult steps) from lakes and streams.

Pack It In and Pack It Out
- Take everything you bring into the wild back out with you.
- Protect wildlife and your food by storing rations securely.
- Pick up all spilled foods.

Properly Dispose of What You Can't Pack Out
- Deposit human waste in six- to eight-inch-deep catholes at least 200 feet from water, camps, or trails. Cover and disguise the catholes when you're finished.
- Use toilet paper or wipes sparingly; pack them out.
- To wash yourself or your dishes, carry the water 200 feet from streams or lakes and use small amounts of biodegradable soap. Scatter the strained dishwater.
- Inspect your campsite for trash and evidence of your stay. Pack out all trash—both yours and others!

Leave What You Find
- Treat our natural heritage with respect. Leave plants, rocks, and historical artifacts as you found them.
- Good campsites are found, not made. Do not alter a campsite.
- Let nature's sounds prevail; keep loud voices and noises to a minimum.
- Control pets at all times. Remove dog feces.
- Do not build structures or furniture or dig trenches.

Minimize Use and Impact of Fires
- Campfires can have a lasting impact on the backcountry. Always carry a lightweight stove for cooking, and use a candle lantern instead of a fire whenever possible.
- Where fires are permitted, use established fire rings, fire pans, or mound fires only. Do not scar large rocks or overhangs.
- Gather sticks no larger than an adult's wrist.
- Do not snap branches off live, dead, or downed trees.
- Put out campfires completely.
- Remove all unburned trash from the fire ring and scatter the cold ashes over a large area well away from any camp.

For more information, call 1-800-332-4100.

FOGHORN PRESS

Founded in 1985, Foghorn Press has quickly become one of the country's premier publishers of outdoor recreation guidebooks. Through its unique Books Building Community program, Foghorn Press supports community environmental issues, such as park, trail, and water ecosystem preservation. Foghorn Press is also committed to printing its books on recycled paper.

Foghorn Press books are sold throughout the United States. Call 1-800-FOGHORN (8:30-5:30 PST) for the location of a bookstore near you that carries Foghorn Press titles. If you prefer, you may place an order directly with Foghorn Press using your Visa or MasterCard. All of the titles listed below are now available, unless otherwise noted.

The Complete Guide Series

The Complete Guides are the books that have given Foghorn Press its reputation for excellence. Each book is a comprehensive resource for its subject, from *every* golf course in California to *every* fishing spot in the state of Washington. With extensive cross references and detailed maps, the Complete Guides offer readers a quick and easy way to get the best information available.

California titles include:

The Bay Area Dog Lover's Companion: (349 pp) $13.95
California Beaches: (800 pp) $19.95, available 4/96
California Boating and Water Sports: (768 pp) $18.95, available 6/96
California Camping: (864 pp) $19.95, new edition available 3/96
The California Dog Lover's Companion: (864 pp) $19.95, available 3/96
California Fishing: (828 pp) $19.95
California Golf: (864 pp) $19.95
California Hiking: (851 pp) $18.95
California In-Line Skating: (500 pp) $18.95, available 6/96
Great Outdoor Getaways to the Bay Area & Beyond: (628 pp) $16.95
Northern California Kayaking: (200 pp) $14.95, available 5/96
Tahoe: (700 pp) $18.95

The Easy Series

The Easy books are perfect for families, seniors, or anyone looking for easy, fun weekend adventures. No special effort or advance planning is necessary—just get outside, relax, and enjoy. Look for Easy guides to Southern California and other favorite destinations in the fall of 1996.

Easy titles include:

Easy Biking in Northern California: (240 pp) $12.95, available 4/96
Easy Camping in Northern California: (240 pp) $12.95
Easy Hiking in Northern California: (240 pp) $12.95

A book's page length and availability are subject to change.

For more information, call 1-800-FOGHORN or write to:
Foghorn Press
555 De Haro Street, Suite 220
San Francisco, CA 94107